# THE ADIRONDACK 46 IN 18 HIKES

## The Complete Guide to Hiking the High Peaks

**JAMES APPLETON**

Foreword by Jonathan Zaharek

**BOOKS**

**NORTH COUNTRY BOOKS**

North Country Books
An imprint of The Globe Pequot Publishing Group, Inc.
64 South Main Street
Essex, CT 06426
www.globepequot.com

Distributed by NATIONAL BOOK NETWORK

British Library Cataloguing in Publication Information Available

**Library of Congress Cataloging-in-Publication Data**

Names: Appleton, James, 1986– author.
Title: The Adirondack 46 in 18 hikes : the complete guide to hiking the
  high peaks / James Appleton.
Description: Essex, Connecticut : North Country Books, An imprint of The
  Globe Pequot Publishing Group, Inc., 2025. | Summary: "The Adirondack 46
  in 18 Hikes takes readers through each of these towering giants mountain
  by mountain. Equal parts information, entertainment, and storytelling,
  it offers readers everything they need to know to climb each of these
  peaks safely and successfully"—Provided by publisher.
Identifiers: LCCN 2024042578 (print) | LCCN 2024042579 (ebook) | ISBN
  9781493086061 (paperback) | ISBN 9781493086078 (epub)
Subjects: LCSH: Hiking—New York (State)—Adirondack Mountains—Guidebooks.
  | Trails—New York (State)—Adirondack Mountains—Guidebooks. |
  Adirondack Mountains (N.Y.)—Guidebooks.
Classification: LCC GV199.42.N652 A3537 2025  (print) | LCC GV199.42.N652
  (ebook) | DDC 796.5109747/5—dc23/eng/20240916
LC record available at https://lccn.loc.gov/2024042578
LC ebook record available at https://lccn.loc.gov/2024042579

This book is dedicated to my daughters, June, Penny, and Rosemary.
Your dad went from being the guy who couldn't make it up the
mountain to the guy who wrote the book about them.
Life is a wild adventure, and you will achieve incredible things when
you believe in yourselves, embrace hard work, and never give up.
I pray that you believe in yourselves just as much as I believe in you.
Being your dad has been my greatest adventure.

And to the love of my life, Kinnon.
Thank you for always holding down the fort
when I'm running around in the mountains.
It's because of you that I'm able to have these adventures.

## DISCLAIMER

This book and this author do not guarantee that trail information is 100 percent correct and cannot guarantee your safety on the trails. Climbing mountains is an inherently risky activity. By using this book, you are accepting all risk that accompanies its use. The author and publisher are not liable for any property loss, damage, personal injury, or unfortunate death that may occur while hiking the trails outlined in this book. Hike at your own risk and always be overprepared.

# CONTENTS

# FOREWORD

The journey of a 46'er is a challenge that tests the mind, soul, and body. It requires much commitment and open-mindedness for growth and change. In the words of Paul Jamison, "It is easier to become a Forty-Sixer than to be one. The art of being is to keep one's sense of wonder after the excitement of the game is over. There are few experiences in life that do not need to be expressed in words. Becoming a Forty-Sixer is one. How to be one is up to the individual." There are plenty of things to learn and see along the way of this journey. You don't just find yourself in the midst of it, but you discover the hidden beauty of the Adirondack Mountains.

Just like a treasure chest waiting to be found, you will discover the secret beauties and hidden wonders that make these mountains so special. You will have an inexpressible feeling that can only be captured by climbing all of them. And this guidebook is designed to help you do just that. There is a plethora of confusing information regarding the trails in the High Peaks. This book is meant to eliminate the confusion so that you can have a safe, efficient, and memorable journey along the trails.

In the journey of becoming a 46'er, you discover a part of yourself that you never knew existed, a manifestation of adventure, passion, and thrill only to be understood by yourself. The Adirondacks will present to you some of the most beautiful things a human can experience. I urge you to use this book to educate yourself and formulate respect for these mountains. People have been exploring them for hundreds of years, each person in the pursuit of finding themselves and discovering the unknown. Remember that they cannot be tamed nor conquered. They bring value to us that cannot be purchased. Something that we must protect. A sacred place of refuge for the soul. So I urge you, the reader, to take this journey seriously and to receive all it has to offer.

Jonathan Zaharek #11,171W
9 × 46'er

# The 46 High Peaks of the Adirondacks

(Listed in order of elevation)

| | | |
|---|---|---|
| 1 | Marcy | 5,344' |
| 2 | Algonquin | 5,114' |
| 3 | Haystack | 4,960' |
| 4 | Skylight | 4,926' |
| 5 | Whiteface | 4,867' |
| 6 | Dix | 4,857' |
| 7 | Gray | 4,840' |
| 8 | Iroquois Peak | 4,840' |
| 9 | Basin | 4,827' |
| 10 | Gothics | 4,736' |
| 11 | Colden | 4,714' |
| 12 | Giant | 4,627' |
| 13 | Nippletop | 4,620' |
| 14 | Santanoni | 4,607' |
| 15 | Redfield | 4,606' |
| 16 | Wright Peak | 4,580' |
| 17 | Saddleback | 4,515' |
| 18 | Panther | 4,442' |
| 19 | Tabletop | 4,427' |
| 20 | Rocky Peak | 4,420' |
| 21 | Macomb | 4,405' |
| 22 | Armstrong | 4,400' |
| 23 | Hough | 4,400' |
| 24 | Seward | 4,361' |
| 25 | Marshall | 4,360' |
| 26 | Allen | 4,340' |
| 27 | Big Slide | 4,240' |
| 28 | Esther | 4,240' |
| 29 | Upper Wolfjaw | 4,185' |
| 30 | Lower Wolfjaw | 4,175' |
| 31 | Street | 4,166' |
| 32 | Phelps | 4,161' |
| 33 | Donaldson | 4,140' |
| 34 | Seymour | 4,120' |
| 35 | Sawteeth | 4,100' |
| 36 | Cascade | 4,098' |
| 37 | Carson (South Dix) | 4,060' |
| 38 | Porter | 4,059' |
| 39 | Colvin | 4,057' |
| 40 | Emmons | 4,040' |
| 41 | Dial | 4,020' |
| 42 | Grace Peak (East Dix) | 4,012' |
| 43 | Blake Peak | 3,960' |
| 44 | Cliff | 3,960' |
| 45 | Nye | 3,895' |
| 46 | Couchsachraga | 3,820' |

# PREFACE

On November 17, 2009, a Lake Placid kid in his early 20s reluctantly joined his friends for an Adirondack Mountain adventure. The plan for the day was to drive down to Keene Valley and climb a High Peak called Big Slide. Big Slide is one the shorter treks of the 46 High Peaks at roughly 7.5 miles round-trip. Despite not being a hiker, his friends begged him to go, so he tagged along. Time to hit the trail.

Growing up in the heart of the High Peaks region of the Adirondacks, he wasn't a stranger to hiking, but he also never took to it either because, frankly, climbing mountains is hard. Every time he agreed to go hiking, it always came with extra-heavy breathing, burning legs, and pounding feet. What was there to enjoy? Sure, the summit views are nice, but they required a lot of work for minimal payoff in his mind. They usually came with the feeling of death upon arrival.

They pulled into the Garden trailhead just after 10 a.m. The four of them quickly signed in and began hiking. The plan today was to hike Big Slide via the Brothers trail to the summit and back. This trail gains elevation quickly and consistently to the tune of 2,200' in the first 2.5 miles.

Less than 15 minutes into the hike, however, gasping for air from the immediate and relentless climb up Big Slide, he yelled ahead to his group, "Hey guys, I need a break." His friends obliged his request. After a quick pit stop and a snack, the hike continued.

His friends moved much faster up the trail than he did. With less heavy breathing as well. Every so often they stopped to let him catch up, but he would inevitably lag once they continued hiking.

"I need another break!" he yelled up to his friends. "This mountain is steep!" They indulged his request once again. The second break was a little longer than the first as he desperately tried to catch his breath from the seemingly endless and unrelenting climb.

Ten minutes later they continued hiking. Only his pace slowed down even more. Once again the distance between them grew as his friends moved up the trail. Out of breath, uncertain, and fed up, he knew there was no way he could hike an entire High Peak like this.

So, upon catching up with his friends, he boldly declared, "I'm turning around. This is too hard." His friends tried to convince him to stay, but to no avail. His mind was made up that hiking sucks, it's too hard, it's not enjoyable, and he was going back to the car.

Since they drove one vehicle, they coordinated a pickup time later. Embarrassed, he took his friend's car keys, said good-bye, and turned around. It was a long, lonely, disappointing walk back to the car—a walk that involved a pit in his stomach and frustration with himself. He couldn't even climb a small High Peak because he was too out of shape, physically and mentally.

Hours later he returned to pick them up and heard all the stories from the hike. They told him, "We were less than two minutes away from the first Brother when you turned around. You should have stayed. It was easy from that point on." Talk about a punch in the gut. The kid from Lake Placid quit too soon and didn't experience the stories, the camaraderie, the victories, or the views that come with hiking mountains. He chose to quit when things got hard instead of persevering. A life lesson was learned that day.

Weeks later a mutual friend innocently asked us, "Why is James in the picture of you guys at the trailhead but not at the summit?" We exchanged an awkward look. She quickly figured out why.

Now for the plot twist that you probably saw coming—I am the kid from Lake Placid.

On November 14, 2009, I turned around trying to hike Big Slide Mountain because it was too hard. Fast-forward 14 years, and I am now writing a book on how to hike these very mountains.

Life is wild. You never know where it will take you. Keep pushing forward, dream big, bet on yourself, and thanks for picking up this book.

My Adirondack 46 High Peaks journey changed the trajectory of my life. I am in awe of these peaks. Climbing their trails is a privilege, and each mountain is a character in my own High Peaks adventure story.

These mountains will teach you a lot about yourself and life if you let them. They will soon become characters in your unique adventure story too, and what an amazing adventure it's going to be!

Throughout this book I am going to remove the overwhelm and uncertainty of the Adirondack 46 High Peaks by giving you an actionable plan to hike all 46 in 18 hikes so you can climb with confidence. I will methodically teach you the who, what, where, when, why, and how of these beloved mountains. Additionally, you will come with me on my own journey to 46 and read my story as it unfolded, hike by hike, mountain by mountain, trail by trail.

It is an honor to be a small part of your High Peaks journey.

Let's begin your adventure . . .

Enjoying a perfect summer day from Mt. Colvin. *Photo by Jonathan Zaharek*

# ABOUT THIS BOOK

## What This Book Is

In this book I will break down and offer a simplified approach to climbing the 46 High Peaks of the Adirondacks. You will learn the "traditional" route through the High Peaks so you can have a successful, safe, and transformative High Peaks adventure. This book is equal parts information and entertainment. You will be given practical information to apply to your own ADK hiking trips, along with the complete story of my Adirondack 46'er journey start to finish. From the trails to the summits, to the mishaps, early mornings, summit sandwiches, my war with Cliff Mountain, and even some post-hike meals—you'll get the entire story.

Figuring out how to climb all 46 High Peaks can feel like a daunting task. Where do you start? Where are the trailheads? Do you hike them all individually, or do some group together? There's a lot of information to know before setting out on any backcountry adventure, let alone one that sometimes has you 15 miles from the nearest road with zero cell service. I wrote this book to ease your mind so you can formulate and execute a successful plan climbing all 46 High Peaks.

One thing to keep in mind as you read through this guide is that this does not replace studying the map; rather, it pairs well with the High Peaks map to give you a visual of what to expect on the trail. It is up to you to do your due diligence in planning and "pre-hike homework." Think of this guide as the CliffsNotes version of the book your teacher assigned you to read for homework. Sure, you will get the main gist of the "book" by reading the CliffsNotes, enough for you to talk about it in class and answer a question or two to fool the teacher into thinking you did last night's reading assignment. The CliffsNotes, however, may not be enough to write an essay about the book come test day. Only in this case, the "test" is hiking in mountains that could, quite literally, kill you if you're not prepared. Sounds fun, right? This is a good time to let you know that the mountains don't care about you. It is important to respect them by properly preparing for them.

As you get to know the map, you'll notice a seemingly endless trail system in the High Peaks. You'll see that some mountains have numerous trails up, down, and around them. That's because this outdoors paradise, known as the Adirondack Park, has a trail system unlike anywhere else in the world. Don't feel like you have to stick firmly to the itinerary I lay out in this book, either. Feel free to try different routes on different trails if you want to get creative. Getting creative with your outdoors adventure is what it's all about.

In this book I will, however, give you a traditional route to climb all 46 mountains. Some hikes will be easier than others. Some hikes will require you to push yourself mentally and physically and "dig a little deeper." It is my goal to have you trail-ready so that you're prepared when those times come.

This book aims to create educated and informed hikers. You'll learn about other topics, from Adirondack camping rules and regulations to winter hiking, proper outdoor etiquette, and more. My hope is that readers will build good habits from the start so they have a successful High Peaks adventure, ultimately creating more stewards of the Adirondacks and outdoors.

Your Adirondack adventure awaits, and it's going to be the adventure of a lifetime!

## What This Book Is Not

This book is not meant to be your only source of research before a hike. This book is an additional resource to utilize as you plan your hiking adventure. This book will familiarize you with what you need to know, what to expect on the trail, what you should have with you, and what to be aware of when hiking in the High Peaks.

## What This Book Will Accomplish

By the end of this book, you will have a firm grasp on hiking the 46 Adirondack High Peaks. You will know where the trailheads are, what gear to have, how to prepare for your hike, how to group the mountains, and much more. I am certain your High Peaks confidence will increase and your overwhelm will decrease. You'll soon realize that the number 46 isn't as daunting as it once seemed. In fact, the 46 High Peaks are often climbed in 17 to 20 hikes. Doesn't that feel a lot less than 46? See? This book is already easing your mind.

You will undoubtedly feel a burning desire to experience the transformative power of the Adirondack High Peaks for yourself. You will feel the call to write your own ADK adventure story.

I am a firm believer that people won't become stewards of the great outdoors until they have positive experiences in the outdoors. My goal is to create more stewards of the Adirondacks (and beyond) by helping you create those positive experiences.

Climbing the 46 High Peaks of the Adirondacks is a true journey. A life-changing experience for all who embark on it. Before it's over, I am certain the Adirondack Mountains will grab hold of your heart and teach you valuable lessons about life in the process.

## Who Am I?

My name is James Appleton, and I am an Adirondack guide, a 46'er, and most notably a podcaster. I grew up and live in the High Peaks region of the Adirondacks in the town of Lake Placid, New York. I'm always in the woods climbing mountains big and small and taking advantage of life in this outdoor paradise I am privileged to call home.

I am the host of *The 46 of 46 Podcast*, a show centered around the Adirondack Park, the mountains, and the people who passionately explore them. I turn my days on the trails into a docu-style audio experience designed to both entertain and educate. These episodes take the listener along for the ride from sign-in to summit. I aim to help people feel connected to the Adirondacks when they can't be in the Adirondacks. I make it a point to ensure that the Adirondack Park is the star of every episode, not me, my stories, or my guests. The park is the star of the show. *The 46 of 46 Podcast* is a celebration of the beautiful and rugged place we call the ADK.

I am someone who simply loves this park. I share my knowledge to help others enjoy the magic of the Adirondacks so they can have a safe, successful, responsible, and transformative experience in these woods. My desire is to help anyone who wants to go on this journey. I want your Adirondack adventure to be one you talk about for the rest of your life.

I wrote this book to help you successfully climb these mountains, but more than that I wrote this book so you can experience the same transformation I did because of these glorious mountains. Speaking of transformation . . .

A fall day on Mt. Jo with MacIntyre Range in the distance. *Photo by Jordan Craig*

# THE ADIRONDACK EFFECT

The "Adirondack Effect" is a notion of mine that these mountains, lakes, and rivers make people better versions of themselves. I believe every mountain is a character in a story, each with a different lesson to teach you. Like many before me, I went on my 46'er journey and came out the other side a transformed man thanks to the lessons they taught me. They will teach you too if you listen . . .

They will strengthen you.
They will heal you.
You'll forge grit climbing them.
You'll learn to persevere despite uncomfortable conditions.

The journey will be hard, wet, challenging, beautiful, and oh so muddy, but it's attainable for anyone who wants to experience the transformative powers these peaks possess.

I'm not going to sugarcoat it, though; climbing Adirondack mountains is hard, and it's not for everyone. If you quit easily and purposely avoid doing hard things, this may not be for you. It takes a lot of determination, perseverance, and good old-fashioned work to get to the summit. Every view is earned. Some days you'll climb in the rain and mud for zero views. Other days it will be sunny all the way up only to finish socked in a small cloud at the summit. Some days you'll climb in pouring rain but then ascend above the clouds and experience a beautiful cloud inversion. Other days will be warm and sunny with blue skies are far as the eye can see—we call them "bluebird Adirondack days." There will even be days you describe as "brutal." Every day, every hike, every mountain is another chapter in your unique High Peaks adventure story, though. Embrace them all because they all contribute to bringing out the best in you.

Every day you're in the mountains you are becoming better. Hard days and perfect days, they're all important. It's a journey filled with highs and lows—literally and figuratively. Sunny days climbing Marcy or Gothics are just as memorable as the tough days on Blake or Couch-sachraga, but for different reasons. Warm, sunny, bluebird days enrich your soul, while cold, rainy, wet days build grit. Your journey will be unique, and every mountain will tell a different story on a different day. I guarantee, at the end of your story you will be a stronger version of yourself.

The Adirondack Effect is real, and it's felt within your soul the moment you pass the iconic "Now Entering Adirondack Park" sign. Thousands can attest to being transformed by these mountains, and they will do the same for you. That is why I believe the Adirondack Effect exists. These mountains, lakes, and rivers know how to bring out the best in every one of us.

**Thank God for the Adirondack Park.**

An October morning at Marcy Dam with Mt. Colden peeking through the clouds.
*Photo by James Appleton*

# HIGH PEAKS HISTORY

The Adirondack Park dates back centuries; however, it wasn't until 1892 that it was constitutionally deemed a "forever wild forest preserve." The Adirondacks was the first of its kind thanks to the vision and work of people like Adirondack legend and mountain surveyor Verplanck Colvin. Soon you'll even be climbing a mountain named after him.

Upon its inception in 1892, the Adirondack Park totaled just over two million acres. Today it's comprised of over six million acres, making it the largest state park in the continental United States—a park so large it could fit Yellowstone, Glacier, Grand Canyon, Everglades, and Smoky Mountain National Parks inside of it. All of them. Combined. Yes, it's that big.

The 46 High Peaks (mountains over 4,000' elevation) are undeniably the main attraction in the Adirondacks, along with more than 3,000 lakes, rivers, streams, and hundreds of smaller peaks throughout this outdoors paradise. Whether you're looking to hike, camp, paddle, rock climb, mountain bike, ski, hunt, fish, or do anything outdoors, there's no better place than the Adirondack Park.

## The Adirondack Forty-Sixers Organization

Climbing all 46 High Peaks to become an Adirondack 46'er is no small task. It's a major accomplishment and a privilege to join the official Adirondack Forty-Sixers club. The Forty-Sixers organization is a non-profit dedicated to protecting and preserving the wilderness character of the High Peaks and sponsors a variety of programs to steward the land, maintain trails, and educate fellow Adirondack hikers.

The club dates to the 1920s, and at the time only 12 of the 46 High Peaks had official trails. Even those trails, however, looked quite different from what we're used to hiking today. They were sans trail markers with only a handful of signs along the way. At that time, the land also looked drastically different, as large expanses of forest were cut by the timber industry (they had to build New York City somehow, I guess), along with the aftermath of forest fires. Needless to say, hiking trails weren't high on the priority list back then.

The first recorded people to climb all 46 High Peaks were brothers Bob and George Marshall and their local guide, Herbert Clark. They began their journey through the rugged and untamed Adirondack wilderness with a climb of Whiteface Mountain on August 1, 1918, and completed their journey on the summit of Emmons on June 10, 1925. Since then, over 15,000 people have followed in their footsteps to officially become Adirondack 46'ers.

Now that you have a background on the mountains, me, and what to expect from this book, let's get you trail-ready.

The Great Range as seen from the summit of Dial Mountain. *Photo by James Appleton*

# HIKING PREPARATION

## What to Know before You Go

"You guys are idiots! . . . Look at all this ice! . . . I can't believe we're out here right now. . . . This is stupid, can we please turn around?" my poor wife yelled to her brother Josh and me as we attempted to climb up to Copperas Pond one February day wearing nothing but sneakers. It was the typical opening scene in what would make a classic search-and-rescue movie. There we were going for an innocently reckless snowy trek up to Copperas Pond just outside Lake Placid. No experience, no gear, in the dead of winter. Just some Adirondack locals doing what people do in the winter—go outside.

This trip to Copperas Pond took place long before I started hiking. None of us had the proper knowledge or gear to be hiking in the winter either. The trail up to Copperas Pond was like an ice-skating rink that day. "How are we going to get back down this ice?" my wife nervously asked us. Next, we did what most young, foolish, "invincible" men do; we shrugged and kept climbing. It wasn't long, however, before we began pondering that very question: "She's right . . . how *will* we get back down this ice?" Soon we all came to our senses and decided it was time to turn around. It was a disaster waiting to happen. My wife was right—we were "idiots" and it was "stupid." To this day my wife still mentions the day we almost made it to Copperas Pond. We had no business being out there that winter day with no experience, even less gear, and no understanding of the situation. We honestly just didn't know any better. Thankfully my wife's senses saved us all and we made it home, despite some slips and falls on the way down.

Hiking requires preparation because going in the mountains without the proper equipment and understanding can have tragic consequences. Arriving at a trailhead for an outdoors adventure can be nerve racking when you aren't sure what to expect or whether you even have the right gear. In this chapter I will help you "know before you go" so that you can hike with confidence, knowing you're properly prepared for the mountains, weather, and terrain. This information will help you develop good habits early on and set you up for success. Building good pre-hike habits early on will help you avoid uncomfortable situations in the backcountry. Being eight miles deep in the woods is the last place you want to have an "uh-oh" moment.

It's important to remember the mountains don't care about you or your feelings, and they're not to be taken lightly. They demand your respect. People die in these mountains every year for one reason or another. My mission with this book is to help you avoid those circumstances by becoming an informed, self-reliant, prepared Adirondack hiker.

In this chapter, I'll dive into all the information you needed to know before you got to the trailhead but no one had time to tell you. No more anxious pre-hike jitters. Instead, you will arrive prepared with clarity and confidence for your High Peaks adventure. Time to go over hiking etiquette, how to do your pre-hike homework, and what to have in your backpack, gear, footwear, food, and more.

Let's start with hiking etiquette and the unwritten rules of the trail so you can avoid being "that guy."

A winter sunset from the summit of Phelps.
*Photo by James Appleton*

# Hiking Etiquette and the Unwritten Rules of the Trail

Climbing mountains is more popular today than ever before. It's mentally and physically rewarding, and it's even a spiritual activity for many. No matter what a person's reason is for climbing mountains, we can all agree that it doesn't take long to fall in love with the feeling of walking on the trails, climbing up rocks, the aroma of those spruce and pines, the sound of the leaves on the hardwood trees, and of course the reward of magnificent summit views. The feeling is unmatched.

So often in life we set our sights on the destination and forget to enjoy the journey. I'm certainly just as guilty of this as the next person. When it comes to scaling mountains, however, the journey is just as enjoyable as the destination. The summit views are unbelievably satisfying, but so are the rivers, the animals, the sounds, the smells, the trees, and the entire natural world around us.

People are retreating to the great outdoors in record numbers as they seek to unplug from technology and recharge their batteries in nature. Personally, I think this is fantastic. I know how transformative an outdoors life has been for me, so I can only encourage others to experience those same joys. And sure, more people outdoors means more people on the trails, in the parks, on the lakes, and in the woods, but nature is big. If you're out there to avoid the crowds, there are always places to go and trails less traveled to experience, especially in the Adirondacks. Personally, when I come across people in the woods, I look at it as coming across like-minded people. There are always going to be some bad eggs out there who disrespect the mountains, of course, but for the most part the people you'll encounter are looking for the same adventure you are. You immediately have that in common. The outdoors is also the great equalizer. The mountains don't care about you; they don't care about your politics, beliefs, bank account, or anything else. You will either get to the top of the mountain or you won't. I love that.

Like anything, hiking is an activity with plenty of unwritten rules meant to be followed for the good of the land, the trails, the experience, the wildlife, and other hikers. Most of us learn these "rules" on our own through experience. I hope to shorten that learning curve for many new hikers and campers. I say it often, but unless people have a good experience in the outdoors, they won't become advocates for the outdoors. I want to create as many advocates for the outdoors and Adirondacks as possible.

Below I have listed some of those unwritten rules to learn before you hit the trail so you're not "that guy" in the woods. It's better to be overprepared than underprepared, right?

## The Quick Version

- Learn, memorize, and follow the 7 Leave No Trace Principles (this will solve a lot of hiking mishaps and etiquette woes in general; more on these principles later).
- BE PREPARED, Part 1: Study your map. Create a loose itinerary and know your route before you head out. Your life (and others') could literally be at stake.
- BE PREPARED, Part 2: Have the appropriate gear for the terrain and conditions you'll be hiking in. Once again, your life (and others') could literally be at stake.
- Check the mountain forecast for the day(s) you plan to hike. There are many websites, but for the sake of ease, mountain-forecast.com is a good resource. Remember, the weather can drastically change without warning in the backcountry—be prepared for everything.
- Do not build fires where fires are not permitted. Fires are prohibited in the Eastern and Central High Peaks Wilderness, and everywhere in the Adirondack Park above 4,000'. Don't be the guy that burns down the Adirondacks, because I'll lead the army to find you.
- Camping: Learn the regulations before you go. In the Adirondacks as it pertains to the High Peaks, camping is prohibited on summits, above 3,500' unless at a designated site, and where "No Camping" signs are seen. Unless at designated campsites, off-trail camping is permitted but must be 150' from any trail, roadway, or water source.
- Snowshoes are required when the snowdrift in the mountains is more than 8'. This is the case from basically December to May.

- No cotton clothing. Wet cotton does not dry easily. Pick up "moisture-wicking" clothes to stay dry. "Cotton kills," as the old saying goes.
- Leave the Bluetooth speaker in your car. Nobody wants to hear your music out there. If you want to listen to music, use one earbud so you can still hear your surroundings (e.g., other hikers, animals, Bigfoot, thunder).
- Hikers climbing *up* the trail have the right of way. Step to the side of the trail, smile, say hello, and wish them a good hike. And for the love of God, don't just blankly stare at the ground and pretend you're not humans passing each other in the woods. That's awkward and weird. Say hello.
- Don't tell hikers coming up the trail "you're almost there!" if they are, in fact, not almost there. You may have good intentions, but it's not always the right thing to say. Sometimes people really do need to turn around on a hike they're not ready for. Yes, this is partially a playful joke, but it's also truthful. It's better for someone to turn around early on their own accord than to keep pushing, eventually needing a ranger rescue further up the trail because they were told they were "almost there!" It's great to be positive and encouraging to other hikers; just be honest as well.
- If you carry it in, carry it out. Everything. Every time. Banana peels and all.
- No cotton clothing. A second time for good measure.
- You're not the only person on the trail, so be mindful of others. Remember the Golden Rule.
- Stay on the trail and go through the mud, not around the mud. Yes. Walk directly through the mud. Your boots will be fine. This is aimed to stop the widening of trails.
- The slowest hiker should lead the group so you all travel at his/her pace. If you do split up to hike at different paces, you should reconnect every 15 minutes; however, I recommend staying together and hiking at the same pace. Slower is still OK'er. That's a word, right?

- When camping, store all food and scented items in your bear canister and place the canister on the ground at least 100' away from your tent/lean-to. Don't forget to put your toothpaste in there too!
- If going number 1 or number 2, do so at least 150' off trail and away from any water sources.
- Dogs: New York State regulations always require leashes. Your dog may love everyone, but that doesn't mean other people, or other dogs, love your dog. Dogs are also prohibited on AMR property.
- Take nothing but pictures and leave nothing but footprints . . . unless you strike gold, in which case, please call me.

## The Leave No Trace Center for Outdoor Ethics

Since we're talking about proper etiquette, now is a great time to discuss the 7 Leave No Trace Principles. The Leave No Trace Center for Outdoor Ethics (www.lnt.org) is a Colorado-based organization whose

A bluebird Adirondack summer day surrounded by the High Peaks.
*Photo by James Appleton*

mission is to teach people how to enjoy the outdoors while minimizing their impact on the land, water, wildlife, and trails. After all, it's important for us to treat the outdoors with respect and remember that we are guests in the wilderness. These principles are worth learning and applying in all your outdoor pursuits.

The 7 Leave No Trace Principles are:

1. **Plan Ahead and Prepare:** Study the map, know your route, make a game plan for your hike, and have everything you need for a safe and successful day in the backcountry.

2. **Travel and Camp on Durable Surfaces:** Stay on the trails, avoid walking on fragile vegetation ("do the rock walk"), and camp in designated campsites.

3. **Dispose of Waste Properly:** Take all trash out of the park with you, including apple cores and banana peels. When going number 2, dig a 6' cat hole in the ground 200' off trail and 200' away from water sources. After you take care of your business, fill in the hole and cover it with leaves.

4. **Leave What You Find:** Don't pick that pretty flower you're eyeballing; take a photo instead. Leave it for the next person to enjoy just like you did.

5. **Minimize Campfire Impacts:** Only make campfires in designated preexisting campfire rings (where permitted). Fires are prohibited in the Eastern and Central Zones of the High Peaks Wilderness (see official zoning on High Peaks map).

6. **Respect Wildlife:** View animals from afar with your eyes and keep your voices low. Remember, you're a guest in their home.

7. **Be Considerate of Other Visitors:** Be respectful and don't take away from others' outdoors experience, the same way you don't want others to take away from yours.

## Let's Talk Gear: What to Have in Your Backpack

When you're on the trail, your backpack is the mother ship of the expedition. After all, you're not going to carry that delicious triple-decker peanut butter and jelly sandwich all the way to the summit in your pocket, right?

I climbed the entire 46 High Peaks (and more) with a simple book-bag-style backpack, and it worked just fine. I did eventually buy a "fancy" hiking backpack, and I will admit it was a total game changer. When a backpack fits your body properly, it feels better and decreases your shoulder/back fatigue that often develops over a long day in the woods. Investing in the correct-size pack for your torso is worth its weight in gold. In the end, though, what's inside the pack is more important than the pack itself. I would also like to remind you that whatever backpack you use, it's going to get beat up out there. Keep that in mind.

The "10 Essentials" are a good starting point for what to have in your pack. Over time you will develop your own workflow for what gear you like to have and what you don't need, but the 10 essentials are called "essentials" for a reason. I recommend always having these items.

### Pro Tip

Line the inside of your backpack with a garbage bag and put everything inside the garbage bag to keep your gear, food, and clothes dry inside your backpack if/when it rains. Rain covers on backpacks tend to be more cumbersome than helpful in my experience, and a small garbage bag weighs very little.

My signature red backpack on the summit of Mt. Jo in January. *Photo by James Appleton*

## The 10 Essentials List

1. **Navigation:** Map, compass, GPS device, personal locator beacon (PLB) or satellite messenger.
2. **Headlamp:** Don't forget extra batteries. An extra headlamp is even better since they're small, relatively inexpensive, and clutch when you need it. It's way easier to throw on your other headlamp than to switch batteries in the dark. And no, your cell-phone flashlight does not count.
3. **Sun protection:** Sunglasses, sunscreen, sun-protective clothing, hat, etc.
4. **First aid:** Including foot care, insect repellent, band-aids, ACE bandage.
5. **Knife:** For obvious reasons.
6. **Fire:** Matches, waterproof matches, lighter, flint rod, and tinder. Bic lighters are cheap and seem to be indestructible. Multiple fire starters are ideal.

7. **Shelter:** A light, emergency bivy sack and space blanket with paracord makes a good emergency shelter and takes up minimal space in your pack.

8. **Extra food:** More is better. Hiking burns a lot of calories, and you're out there to perform and keep your body fueled. Bring extra food because it's better to have it and not need it than need it and not have it. Climbing mountains, specifically High Peaks, isn't the time or place to try "losing weight." Save that for the gym, not when you're eight miles deep in the woods.

9. **Extra water:** Bring a water filtration device and double the water you think you'll need. Once again, it's better to have it and not need it than need it and not have it. Fortunately, the ADK has a lot of fast-flowing river streams, but when you need the water and there isn't a stream around, you'll be glad you have extra.

10. **Extra clothes:** Changing into a dry shirt and socks mid-hike is a game changer. It's also safer if you get wet and need new clothes. Being wet in the outdoors can quickly lead to hypothermia (even in the summer). I think you already know hypothermia is something we aim to avoid, right? Personally, I keep a heavy fleece, gloves, and a winter hat in my pack all year. If you get caught out there overnight, temperatures can drop dramatically, and they're great items to have in an emergency scenario.

## James's Honorable Mentions on the "10 Essentials List"

- **Zip-ties:** These weigh nothing and work well in a pinch to fix broken backpacks, tents, snowshoes, boots, zippers, etc.

- **Duct tape:** Wrap a few feet of duct tape around an old credit card to save a lot of space. You know how useful duct tape is.

- **Raincoat:** It should go without saying, especially in the green, lush, rainy ADK, that having a quality raincoat is a must. Rain pants are also recommended.

- **Extra set of shoelaces:** Have you ever been 10 miles deep in the High Peaks with a broken shoelace in the middle of January? I have. It's awful. I would have gladly paid $100 for a $.97 shoelace that day.
- **Water filter:** Bring one just in case.
- **Trekking poles:** These will save your muscles on ascents and save your joints on descents. They help with balance and even pole-vault you over rivers and mud pits. Crossing rivers and wet slabs is significantly easier with trekking poles. They may seem awkward at first, but after an hour you will see their magic. Another item worth their weight in gold.

My victory photo nearing completion of the Adirondacks' 138-mile Northville–Lake Placid Trail. *Photo by Sara King*

# Footwear

Another one of the most crucial elements when venturing into the backcountry is your footwear. Our feet take us to the summit and back to the trailhead, so they must be treated with great importance. I never recommend shoes or boots because footwear is not "one size fits all" in any capacity. Everybody's feet and preferences are different. Some prefer waterproof hiking boots, some prefer water-resistant hiking boots with more flex, while others hate boots and prefer trail runners. Some will spend $300 and others $65. Footwear is extremely personal, so it's important to find out what works for you and never settle in this category.

There's plenty of gear you can pinch your pennies on, but footwear should not be one of them. I'm not saying "the more expensive, the better." I'm saying get the right shoe regardless of the price because it's the right shoe for you. Sometimes it takes five or six different shoes to find the right one. Try on a lot of shoes and don't buy one solely off someone's recommendation. A shoe might fit their foot well, but that doesn't mean it will fit yours well.

If you're not comfortable and excited about your footwear, hiking will suck, plain and simple. If it isn't enjoyable, you'll never want to hike, right? I've had five pairs of the same hiking boot (Timberland Mt. Maddsen) because the second I first put my foot in them I knew, "Yes. A perfect fit." Call it the hiking equivalent to love at first sight. You will know immediately when it's the right shoe for you, Cinderella.

Make sure whatever shoe you choose can handle the wet and muddy Adirondack terrain. Walking six miles out of the woods with blisters on both feet is rough, and I do not recommend it. I'm looking at you, Dix Range!

## Map and Compass versus GPS . . . or Better Yet, Use Both!

### Map and Compass

Wherever you're hiking, it's important to have the area's official map in your backpack. Study the map before every hike to learn your route, bailout points, and notable landmarks. The night before new hikes, I often find myself going through the map all night long in my head: "Okay, go right at the first trail junction, then a mile later take a left at the second junction just after the river crossing, followed by an immediate right which will take me to the summit."

All night long I'm memorizing my route. I find it useful to even draw the route on a small flash card because it's easier to pull that card out of my pocket to reference compared to the big map. You'll figure out what tricks work for you and find your groove with planning and navigating.

If you're unfamiliar with how to use a compass, what the difference between true north and magnetic north is, what the word "declination" means, or how to take a bearing, you can head over to YouTube University to get an understanding of the process. Better yet, you can enroll in a map and compass workshop. I've taken one before, and I highly recommend it. The more equipped you are with practical knowledge in the outdoors, the better off you will be.

## GPS and Cell Phones

Let's talk about GPS. Navigation apps like All Trails, Gaia, OnX, and more have become oddly controversial in today's outdoors world. The argument is that these apps give people excuses to skip their pre-hike homework and rely solely on a cell phone to get them to the summit and back. It gives them a false sense of security. I do understand all those complaints, and they're valid. However, there is no stopping the addition of new technology in any part of life, including hiking. So embrace it and learn to use this new technology properly. I mean it's not like Verplanck Colvin was standing on the High Peaks in the 19th century wearing an ultralight down puffy jacket and trail runners, right? Technology advances, and we do too. GPS apps are a helpful *tool* and should be treated as such, another tool. A carpenter doesn't build a house with one tool; it requires many tools working together. GPS should be treated the same. We all know cell phones can die, break, or fail out in the woods, but they are still a useful tool, nonetheless. A map and compass, however, should forever remain your foundational tools. They are nonnegotiables in your backcountry pursuits.

I fully recommend utilizing these GPS apps *in addition to* your real map. Again, they do not replace having your map and studying it, but they're a great complement to it on the trail. These apps provide a great reference on a hike. It's easy to be unsure whether the trail split you're at is the junction you're looking for, but GPS can alleviate that uncertainty and offer reassurance that you're on the correct trail. Peace of mind in the woods is worth its weight in gold. I would argue that GPS apps have saved more people from being lost in the woods than it has caused search and rescues for "overconfident, underexperienced" hikers. That's just my humble opinion.

Real GPS devices, like a Garmin inReach, are a much better option for backcountry travel. They have SOS features, and they're rugged because they're built for the demands of the great outdoors. They're a hefty investment (key word: investment), but I always hike with my Garmin and highly recommend it for many reasons, from its durability to its battery life to its functionality. Think of it as a life insurance policy while you're hiking.

Being lost in the woods is a serious issue, and if a tool like a GPS app can help remedy that, I'm all for it. Of course, you all understand how cell phones work and how batteries die, how the GPS could stop working, or how you could drop it in the water at the floating logs on your way up Mt. Marcy. So much can go wrong, which is why your map and compass must be your foundation, but GPS apps are indeed a great additional tool in the toolbox to have a safe and successful day in the woods.

All this talk about technology, backpacks, shoes, and maps has made me hungry. Now let's talk about the most important item in your hiking backpack—your summit sandwich.

## Food, Water, and the Summit Sandwich

Earlier in the book I unapologetically declared that the Adirondack Mountains turn us into better people (the Adirondack Effect), but you know what makes hiking the Adirondack Mountains better? Enjoying a delicious summit sandwich while you take in those majestic mountain views. Nothing quite beats getting to the top of the peak, covered in sweat and mud, knowing you're about to dive into the most delicious and perfectly crafted summit sandwich the mountain has ever seen. Some of us hike for the views; some of us hike for the sandwiches. To my fellow Team Sandwich brothers and sisters, I salute you.

In all seriousness, though, having adequate food and water can easily become the deciding factor in whether you make it to the summit, turn around, or need to be rescued. It's essential to bring more food and water than you anticipate needing. After all, you're climbing mountains; you're going to burn an excessive number of calories and sweat a lot. Therefore, it's important to constantly refuel throughout the day so your body performs at its highest level. When you're hiking in the mountains, your focus must be on physical performance. So set your body up for success and bring the right amount of fuel for the journey.

Enjoying a meticulously crafted summit sandwich and colorful fall summit view on Big Slide. *Photo by James Appleton*

## The Summit Sandwich-ability Scale

It's believed the Summit Sandwich-ability (SSA) Scale was invented by the legendary Great Adirondack surveyor Verplanck Colvin in the late 19th century. Historians report that he and his crew recorded each mountain's elevation along with the likelihood of hikers enjoying a sandwich on the summit. The more wooded, the lower the SSA ranking. The more open, the higher the score. Sadly, historians believe Colvin's crew lost the official SSA Report deep in the Adirondack woods, so it was never recovered. Have no fear, though. I am here to bring the SSA Report back to life and will let you know how the mountains rank on the Summit Sandwich-ability Scale. It's always good to know where to stop and enjoy that sandwich, right?

Yes, Verplanck Colvin's SSA Report is a joke, but there is nothing to joke about when it comes to enjoying a well-earned sandwich on an Adirondack summit. I'm hungry just thinking about it.

## "How Much Should I Eat?"

Food is fuel, right? I recommend eating 50 to 100 calories every hour you're hiking to keep your body perpetually fueled. I have found it's better to avoid hunger rather than wait for it. You're eating for performance when you're hiking, so it's important to continually throw a log on the performance fire. Keep it burning hot all day long so you avoid dehydration, cramps, and fatigue. Once a person gets dehydrated, it's game over. Recovering from cramping muscles and dehydration in the backcountry is hard to do. I have been out there many times (especially in the winter) when I foolishly didn't eat/drink enough because I wanted to keep moving, and I paid the price. It's scary standing on a High Peak summit in the dead of winter when your body stops working properly, when your legs cramp up with every step. It's not good, but it's easily avoidable. Eat and drink more than you need to, even if you must remind yourself to do it.

It will take time for each hiker to dial in how much food they need and what food works for them, but always bring more rather than less. I have said it in this book already, and I'll say it again: Climbing mountains is not the time to try to "lose weight." Save weight loss for the gym. This is the time to fuel your body to reach the summit and get back to the trailhead without issue.

Below is an example of what I personally bring with me to keep me properly fed and hydrated for a typical day in the High Peaks. Some days I run out of food and water near the end and other days I have plenty left over, but this is a good example of what I pack for a full day of hiking. For reference, I am a 6'0", 220-pound male who likes to eat and lift heavy weights. So I may pack more food than you need, but this is what I've found to work well for me. This is also a good time to remind you that calories on the trail don't count. So eat up and bring plenty of those special treats!

## James's High Peaks Lunch Box

### Water

- **2 Nalgene bottles (1 liter each) with two electrolyte tablets in each bottle:** Remember, if you get dehydrated, water alone will not typically fix the problem. You need salt and electrolytes. It's also a good idea to keep a few salt packets in your backpack for this reason.

- **3-liter water bladder and hose:** The constant ease of sipping water throughout the day makes a water bladder a must-have for me. It's also an easy reminder to keep drinking water.

- Water is usually accessible thanks to the abundance of ADK rivers and backcountry lakes. Still, I'd rather be safe than sorry. If you plan on bringing less and refilling throughout the day, make sure you locate your water sources on the map ahead of time, especially the last water source.

### Food

- **1 sandwich per summit:** It may sound excessive (okay, it probably is), but it's the formula that works for me. Sometimes they're a nice turkey, cheese, lettuce, and tomato type of sandwich, and other times I'm eating peanut butter and jelly. I have found that eating real substance like a sandwich (protein, carbs, and fats ... and delicious) is the way to go compared to little snacks. Plus, did you even climb a mountain if you didn't enjoy a sandwich at the summit?

- **Chips:** A great item for the trail to get quick carbs and salt . . . nothing beats that salty crunch.
- **1 Blue Line Bakery gourmet cookie:** Not many things taste better on a High Peak than a cookie from the Adirondack Park's cookie lean-to, known as the Blue Line Bakery. Bonus points for eating a cookie on the mountain it's named after.
- **2 bags of peanut or peanut butter M&M's:** These are great to munch on while on the move to keep getting calories and quick carbs down the hatch. I snack on these throughout the day.
- **1 king-size Snickers and/or protein bar:** Hungry? Why wait? Grab a Snickers. You're not you when you're hungry. Snickers and protein bars fill your stomach and give you quick energy in a short amount of time. I usually eat one during the first swig-and-a-snack break on the way up the first mountain and then eat the other half before the final push back to the trailhead. Calories on the trail don't count, right?
- **Shot Bloks and/or Gu:** I also like to pick up Shot Bloks and Gu packets for that quick energy on the go, because sometimes you don't feel like eating more M&M's. You can pick these up at any outdoors store, bike shop, fitness store, or online. They're great items to keep in your pocket to eat as needed or before a big climb.

As you can see, I bring a lot of food and water out on the trail because I'd rather have it and not need it than need it and not have it. Some days I eat and drink it all, and other days I have an extra sandwich to eat in the car on the drive home. Whatever you do, don't cut corners when it comes to food and water. It's also nice to be able to give some food away to struggling hikers who didn't bring enough.

**Pro Tip**

After you finish your day in the High Peaks, nothing on planet Earth tastes better than a Stewart's Shops milkshake. So be sure to head directly to the closest Stewart's convenience store and treat yourself. Extra thick. Trust me.

### Your Pre-Hike Homework Assignment

1. Study your map and memorize your route, trails, and landmarks.
2. Check weather forecasts for the day(s) you're planning to hike. Call an audible if the weather will be dangerous—the mountains don't care about you.
3. Fill your pack with the proper gear, food, and water so you can have a successful Adirondack High Peaks adventure.

## Climb with Confidence

Showing up to climb a mountain can be nerve racking when you're unsure where you're going or if you have the proper equipment. It's even more intimidating when you're worried about getting lost in the woods. Arriving at the trailhead beaming with confidence because you did your pre-hike homework and have the proper understanding, gear, and food will make all the difference.

You are now equipped with the knowledge you need to hike with confidence so you can focus on enjoying the adventure. You have the right gear in your backpack and on your feet, you studied your map and checked the weather report, your trail etiquette is top notch, and your summit sandwich is packed. It's time to get you to the trail.

-+-

In the next chapter I'll talk all about the trailheads: where they're located, what to expect, how big they are, and when you'll use each one. Before we get into it, though, here's a hot tip regarding trailheads. Grab your highlighter or write this next sentence down.

You'll always get a parking spot if you start hiking at 5 a.m. Miles in the dark don't count!

### Let's Talk Trailheads

"Parking Lot Full." Crap.

It was a cool, colorful September morning and the culmination of a summer spent on the trails. It was the morning I'd been working toward for months, the day I would make my triumphant return to Big Slide Mountain and finish my Adirondack 46'er journey. Like a kid on Christmas Eve, excitement was in the air, and I barely slept the night before.

Per usual, my hiking partner, Josh, and I left nice and early from Lake Placid to drive down to Keene Valley to the Garden parking lot. I was sitting at 45 of 46 High Peaks as my quest to become an Adirondack 46'er in one summer was becoming a reality. It was also time to revisit Big Slide, a mountain that was "too hard" for me years ago, forcing me to embarrassingly quit and turn around, leaving my group to continue hiking without me. This day was going to be different. This was going to be the big finish on my High Peaks adventure!

We drove down Route 73, through the Cascades, past Keene, into Keene Valley, and turned right toward the Garden trailhead. Throughout the drive I was looking for places we could potentially park and walk to the trailhead if the parking lot was full. I was nervous we might not get a parking spot. A lot was riding on today—I took off work to become a 46'er, and my family was even coming to celebrate with pie at Noon Mark Diner after the hike. I was determined to climb Big Slide no matter what, but it was evident there wasn't anywhere else to park. My nerves grew.

As we hit the dirt road surrounded by local camps and houses, we came to a yellow sign with brown letters that read, "Parking Lot Full." My heart sank. This was the day I was working toward, and now we couldn't hike because of a parking space. Unbelievable. I quickly started mapping how far the walk from the Noonmark trailhead would be as Josh said, "Let's check it out anyways," and continued driving toward the trailhead. "Maybe someone left overnight."

We slowly drove up the road as the sound of Josh's truck tires rolled along the dirt, and we entered the trailhead. Low and behold, the most beautiful sight awaited us, a near empty parking lot. Hallelujah! There were only three or four cars in the entire place. A parking lot that holds dozens of cars. Yes! The hike was on.

A few hours later I became an Adirondack 46'er. If it wasn't for Josh's hiking experience and knowing that the sign isn't always accurate, I would have turned around. I wouldn't have become a 46'er that day. The more you know about what to expect at the trailheads, the better you can plan, and I don't want you to miss out on your adventure due to a lousy parking space.

One of the most impressive aspects of the Adirondack High Peaks is its extensive trail system offering hikers an abundance of routes. As the old saying goes, there's more than one way to skin a cat (but seriously, who needs to skin a cat, though?). Similarly, there's more than one way to climb most of these mountains. From utilizing different trailheads, to different trails, and pairing different mountains together, your adventure has unlimited options. Fortunately, there are only a handful of trailheads to hike from, which helps keep things simple.

Despite the endless choices for your High Peaks hiking journey, I am confident the majority of Adirondack 46'ers would agree that the route outlined in this book is a typical route through the High Peaks. In this chapter I'm going to dispel the overwhelm by giving you what you need to know regarding trailheads. You'll learn where they are, what mountains you'll hike from each one, pertinent parking information, and more.

So now that your backpack is loaded up, let's get you to the trailhead.

## Adirondack Loj/Adirondack Mountain Club

*Trailhead Coordinates: 44.182810, −73.963720*

The Adirondack Loj, located in Lake Placid, is a unique place filled with Adirondack history. Whenever someone visits the ADK to hike with me, I make sure we start from the Loj because it is a cool place. Hikers can book rooms at the historic mountain Loj, there are tent sites, and more. There's also an info center where you can buy and rent gear, including bear canisters, which are mandatory when camping in the High Peaks. In my opinion the Loj is the real gateway to the High Peaks.

The Adirondack Park is not a national park, but the Loj would be the closest thing to offering that national park feel. There is a fee to park here along with an abundance of parking, but the lots can fill up quickly in the summer, especially on weekends. Holiday weekends are always sure to fill up, so arrive early. You'll never have trouble parking when you start hiking at 5 a.m., though. You have a headlamp, right?

Mountains often hiked from the Adirondack Loj include Marcy, Skylight, Gray, Algonquin, Iroquois, Wright, Street, Nye, Colden, Phelps, Tabletop, Cliff, Redfield, and Marshall.

## Upper Works Trailhead
*Trailhead Coordinates: 44.089010, −74.056270*
Upper Works trailhead is another popular choice located on Upper Works Road in Newcomb. This trailhead is popular for hikers driving north up I-87. This trailhead offers a scenic approach through the area known as Flowed Lands. It's the Adirondacks, though—every direction is scenic. Most of the mountains accessed from the Upper Works trailhead are the same mountains one would access from the Adirondack Loj (the Lake Colden area), but from a different direction with different mileages. This is one of the bigger trailhead parking lots in the High Peaks, holding around 60 vehicles.

Popular mountains to hike from the Upper Works trailhead include Marshall, Cliff, Redfield, Marcy, Skylight, Gray, and Colden.

## The Ausable Club/AMR/St. Hubert's
*Trailhead Coordinates: 44.149570, −73.768150*
The Ausable Club, located in Keene Valley along Route 73, is another popular trailhead that accesses many High Peaks. As of writing this book, there is a parking reservation system in place at this trailhead from May 1 to October 31. Hikers will need to reserve their parking spots beforehand at hikeAMR.org. There is no cost for the reservation. For people traveling from afar, this relieves the uncertainty of whether

you'll have a parking space or not upon arrival for your day in the backcountry. This is the only trailhead in the Adirondack Park that has a parking permit system. The Ausable Club is a private business with an easement with New York State for access to the hiking trails through its property. Be respectful of the property. Dogs are prohibited on AMR property, so if you're hiking with your dog, you will have to use alternative routes for these mountains.

After parking your car, walk up the dirt road past the golf course and turn left between the tennis courts to the trailhead. Your trek will begin and end on the infamous "lake road." Loved by some, loathed by others, you will get to know the lake road well throughout your 46'er journey.

Popular mountains to hike from AMR include the Lower Great Range (Sawteeth, Gothics, Armstrong, Upper Wolfjaw, Lower Wolfjaw), Dial, Nippletop, Blake, and Colvin. This is also the typical access point for the very popular Indian Head lookout.

### Garden Trailhead
*Trailhead Coordinates: 44.188940, −73.815990*
The Garden trailhead, located in Keene Valley, is a small parking lot that typically fills up quickly, so the earlier you start hiking the better. There is a fee to park here. The Garden is a popular place to park for camping weekends along the Great Range as well as at the popular John's Brook Lodge. This is the main access for John's Brook Lodge.

Mountains often approached from the Garden include the Upper Great Range (Haystack, Basin, Saddleback), Big Slide, and the Lower Great Range (Sawteeth, Gothics, Armstrong, Upper Wolfjaw, Lower Wolfjaw).

### Cascade Trailhead
*Trailhead Coordinates: 44.218970, −73.887670*
The Cascade trailhead is in Lake Placid along Route 73. Cascade Mountain is the most hiked mountain in the High Peaks thanks to its smaller size, shorter trail, and accessibility. The parking here, however, fills up quickly and spots are along the road, so be careful of oncoming traffic. Please park in designated legal parking spots. Starting early is

highly recommended as parking fills fast on weekends, holidays, or most summer days. This trailhead is usually full by 8 a.m. There is a new Cascade trailhead and trail being cut from the Mt. Van Hoevenberg Olympic Sports Complex, but it is not complete as of writing this book.

Mountains hiked from the Cascade trailhead include Cascade and Porter.

### Giant Mountain Trailheads
Ridge Trailhead and Roaring Brook Trailhead
*Ridge Trailhead Coordinates: 44.138640, −73.743930/Roaring Brook Trailhead Coordinates: 44.150430, −73.767270*
These two trailheads will be listed together though they are separate trails, albeit not far apart, located along Route 73 in Keene Valley. The Roaring Brook Trailhead is directly across Route 73 from the Ausable Club/AMR trailhead, while the Ridge Trail is just up the road and has designated parking spots along the side of the road. Park in designated legal parking spots and be mindful that you are on a 55 mph road with oncoming traffic. Both trails for Giant Mountain offer terrific experiences. Both trails are a great choice for hiking Giant, but I give the edge to the Ridge trailhead.

Mountains hiked from the Ridge and Roaring Brook trailheads include Giant and Rocky Peak Ridge.

BONUS: If you have two cars, you can take on the Giant/Rocky Peak Ridge New Russia Traverse and park one car at the New Russia trailhead and the other at the Giant trailhead. This traverse offers an exceptionally scenic hiking experience.

### Corey's Road Trailhead
*Trailhead Coordinates: 44.191740, −74.263450*
The Corey's Road trailhead is located on Route 3 between Saranac Lake and Tupper Lake and is the westernmost High Peaks trailhead. Upon turning onto Corey's Road, you'll drive roughly seven miles back into the woods, mostly on a dirt road, until coming to the Sewards

trailhead. Again, this is another small trailhead with limited parking, so the earlier you arrive the better. If you arrive at 5 a.m., you will always get a spot. If you couldn't tell, I'm a big advocate of the early starts.

Mountains hiked from the Corey's Road/Sewards trailhead include the Seward Range (Seward, Donaldson, Emmons, and Seymour).

### Allen/Mt. Adams Trailhead
*Trailhead Coordinates: 44.081300, −74.055170*
The Allen Mountain trailhead is located on Upper Works Road in Newcomb, along with a couple of other High Peaks trailheads including the Upper Works and Santanoni trailheads. These trailheads are deep in the woods, so make sure you have gas in your tank before traveling out here (the closest gas station is under the I-87 overpass at exit 29). You likely will not have cell-phone service either.

After getting off exit 29 on I-87, there's a good 30 miles of driving deep in the Adirondack wilderness to the trailhead. The Allen trailhead is located along the Upper Works Road on the right-hand side, just past the old MacIntyre Iron Furnace (a giant stone structure—you can't miss it). If you arrive at the Upper Works trailhead, you went too far.

Mountains hiked from the Allen trailhead include Allen Mountain (and Mt. Adams, which is not a High Peak).

### Santanoni Trailhead
*Trailhead Coordinates: 44.069070, −74.061490*
The Santanoni trailhead is located on Upper Works Road just before the Macintyre Iron Furnace, on the left-hand side of the road. The Santanonis are often hiked later in one's trek through the High Peaks due to its remote and challenging nature, including the infamous Couchsachraga bog.

Mountains hiked from the Santanoni trailhead include the Santanoni Range (Santanoni, Couchsachraga, Panther).

### Marble Mountain Trailhead/Atmospheric Science Research Center

*Trailhead Coordinates: 44.394380, −73.857720*

The Marble Mountain trailhead is located just off the Whiteface Mountain toll road in Wilmington and is the northernmost High Peaks trailhead. This may also be the smallest trailhead in the High Peaks in terms of parking, so you will want to arrive early since Whiteface Mountain is one of the more popular mountains to hike.

Mountains hiked from the Marble Mountain trailhead include Whiteface and Esther.

### Elk Lake Trailhead

*Trailhead Coordinates: 44.020810, −73.827760*

The Elk Lake trailhead is in North Hudson and is a popular location to tackle the Dix Range. The overflow parking lot is three miles before the main Elk Lake parking lot, so get there early to avoid adding an additional six miles of dirt road walking to an already big day. This parking lot holds roughly 20 vehicles.

Mountains hiked from Elk Lake include the Dix Range (Dix, Hough Peak, South Dix, Grace Peak, Macomb).

Marcy Dam in the middle of the night while sunrising Marcy to begin the Great Range Traverse. *Photo by James Appleton*

# Miles in the Dark Don't Count

If you couldn't already tell, I am a big advocate of arriving at the trailhead as early as possible for logistical reasons and for the overall hiking experience. Logistically, the earlier you start, the higher likelihood you have of obtaining a parking spot. That's always a win. You also set yourself up to have more daylight later to complete your hike. Giving yourself more time rather than less is always preferred, in my opinion, because you never know what you might encounter in the backcountry. Limiting the chances of an unplanned overnight in the woods is always worth waking up a couple of hours earlier.

When it comes to the hiking experience, I always like to say, "Miles in the dark don't count." What do I mean by this? When you start in the dark with your headlamp on, by the time the sun rises you're already miles deep and your hike is well underway. Those miles you hiked in the dark become a distant memory, and suddenly it feels like you were given a couple-mile head start to the day. It's a great feeling.

Hiking in the dark might feel intimidating at first, but within five minutes you'll adjust to navigating via headlamp just fine. It truly becomes business as usual. Additionally, there's nothing that beats watching the sun rise from on top of a mountain or being miles back in the woods when the forest wakes up. The sounds of the birds, the chipmunks, and the trees first thing in the morning never get old. It's a privilege to experience.

When your plan for the day is to climb High Peaks, I believe that task should be given the utmost importance and become your primary focus. By starting early you're demonstrating how serious you're taking this task because, again, the mountains don't care about you. So it's important to show respect for the mountains by your actions. You do this by intentionally setting yourself up for a successful day in the woods. Sure, you can start hiking at 10 or 11 a.m. and still respect the mountains, but I believe that when you go out of your way to start earlier than your workday alarm, you approach the mountains with an entirely different mind-set, one that shows total dedication to the adventure at hand. You're starting your adventure with laser focus and respect for the woods.

So set that early alarm because you're not going to work; you're going to climb some mountains! What a privilege that is. Don't forget your headlamp, some spare batteries, and remember that miles in the dark don't count.

Say good morning to the Adirondack forest for me.

## Time to Hit the Trail

Well, your gear is prepped, your pack is loaded, and now you know where all the trailheads are located. Set that early alarm because it's time to hit the trail. Suddenly, climbing 46 High Peaks from only 11 different trailheads doesn't seem as daunting, right? Now you can confidently plan your hiking adventure knowing exactly what peaks you'll climb from what trailhead and where that trailhead is located. Adventure awaits you in the next chapter where you'll learn your 18-hike route through the 46 High Peaks. You're also going to come with me on my own 46'er journey from trailhead to summit and get the entire story from start to finish.

Time to throw a log on the fire and keep reading because you've got mountains to climb!

Sunset at Silver Lake on the Northville–Lake Placid Trail.
*Photo by James Appleton*

# 46 HIGH PEAKS IN 18 HIKES

This is the chapter you've all been waiting for—the 46 High Peaks in 18 hikes. Becoming an Adirondack 46'er is a transformative journey for anyone who has the courage and determination to climb all 46 peaks. You will not be the same person when you summit number 46 as you were when you summited your first peak. You will look at these mountains, the Adirondacks, and the great outdoors differently. Perhaps even more importantly, you will evolve into a different person. A better person. Someone who challenged themselves in the name of adventure and pushed their limits to experience more. Most people will never climb a single mountain in their life, let alone 46. They'll only see these majestic views in photos, but you're going to earn and experience them in all their glory. After all, pictures rarely do the mountains justice, and they only tell a small portion of the story. You are going to live the entire story. What an honor it is going to be. Even as I sit here typing these words, I get excited, emotional, and grateful for these mountains and everything they represent. It's going to be a transformative adventure.

## Trail Descriptions and My Trail Journal

In this chapter I am going to give you descriptions of each hike, tips, tricks, and what to expect so you have many successful days in the woods. Following each hike, I'll share the story of my own journey exactly as it unfolded. These stories came directly from my trail journal written during and directly following my 46'er journey years ago. You're going to get the whole adventure, all the trails, summits, sandwiches, and blisters.

# A Note about the Order of the Hikes

The numbering of the hikes from my trail journal refers to my own Adirondack 46'er journey. The numbering is not always in chronological order in the guided portion of the book. Based on my experience hiking these mountains multiple times throughout the years, I feel the route outlined in the guided portion is the optimal order for hikers, so don't be confused about some of the numbers. The mountains and hikes are still the same.

# Day Hikes Only—No Tents Necessary

I have broken down the 46 High Peaks into a list comprised solely of day hikes. Camping is fun; however, it adds additional logistics. So, for simplicity's sake, I'm keeping this guide to day hikes. Plus, how good is a hot meal and shower after a long day on the trail, right? Don't worry, though. I will also recommend some camping options throughout the book. If you want to camp, you should, because it's a great experience. There will be some big days, but challenging yourself in the High Peaks and building grit is all part of the 46'er journey.

Next, I will list the mountains and hikes in the order that I recommend climbing them—at least to start your journey. I believe every hike builds off the last, and if you follow my list in order, you will build your experience and hiking ability in a linear fashion. Each hike will prepare

A fall day on little Seymour Mountain looking at Scarface and Sawtooth mountains and the Seward Range. *Photo by James Appleton*

you for the next. However, I understand that weather happens, life happens, and this is your adventure. After completing the first four or five hikes in order, you will have a better understanding of the High Peaks, the trails, your gear, and what the terrain looks like. At that point feel free to go in whatever order you see fit.

# The Mountains

1. Cascade and Porter Mountains
2. Phelps and Tabletop Mountains
3. Whiteface and Esther Mountains
4. Street and Nye Mountains
5. Giant Mountain and Rocky Peak Ridge
6. Dial and Nippletop Mountains
7. Colvin and Blake Mountains
8. MacIntyre Range (Algonquin Peak, Iroquois Peak, Wright Peak)
9. Lower Great Range (Sawteeth, Gothics, Armstrong Mountain, Upper Wolfjaw Mountain, Lower Wolfjaw Mountain)
10. Dix Range (Dix Mountain, Hough Peak, South Dix, Grace Peak, Macomb Mountain)
11. Mt. Marcy, Mt. Skylight, and Gray Peak
12. Cliff Mountain and Mt. Redfield
13. Mt. Colden and Mt. Marshall
14. Upper Great Range (Mt. Haystack, Basin Mountain, Saddleback Mountain)
15. Santanoni Range (Santanoni Peak, Couchsachraga Peak, Panther Peak)
16. Allen Mountain
17. Seward Range (Seward Mountain, Donaldson Mountain, Emmons Mountain, Seymour Mountain)
18. Big Slide Mountain

A winter sunrise on Cascade Mountain overlooking the Great Range. *Photo by James Appleton*

Waiting for the sunrise on a subzero winter morning on the summit of Cascade Mountain. *Photo by James Appleton*

# 1 | Cascade and Porter Mountains

Cascade (4,098'), Porter (4,059')
**Mileage:** 5.6 miles
**Elevation Gain:** 2,286'

Starting at the Cascade trailhead, this is where new hikers (or new to hiking the ADK) often start. It's not surprising this is the most traveled High Peaks trail in the park thanks to its accessibility and short mileage. It's also an awesome hike. You will begin gaining elevation

## CASCADE AND PORTER MOUNTAINS

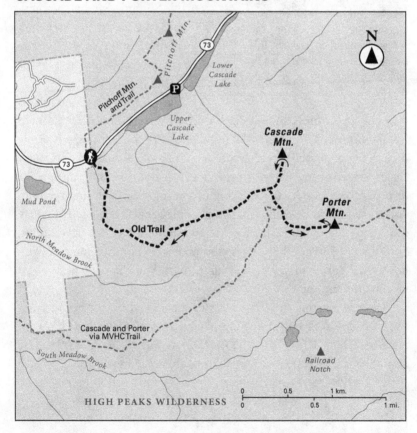

Experiencing another amazing subzero February sunrise on Cascade. This mountain never gets old. *Photo by James Appleton*

right from the start and climb at a consistent rate all the way to the top. Once arriving at the trail junction for Porter—0.8 miles to the right—you're just below the summit of Cascade. Most of the time I go over to Porter first then come back and spend more time on Cascade. Both mountains are great to hang out on with big summit views. Cascade is enormous, though, whereas Porter is smaller. They both score high on the Summit Sandwich-ability (SSA) Scale, though, so you can't go wrong either way. Cascade scores a perfect 5/5, while Porter sits at 4/5 on the SSA Scale.

The trail up these mountains is impossible to miss, so you don't need to worry about that. Cascade has an enormous exposed rocky summit, one of the best in the Adirondacks. Follow the yellow blazes on the rocks to the Cascade summit and back to the tree line on your way back. It is not surprising this hike is so popular because it's fantastic, high bang for your buck, and typically doesn't require your entire day to accomplish; but if it does, that's okay too: keep on climbing. Making it to the summit is what matters most, not how fast you got there. These mountains do not have summit signs; however, there are survey markers in the rock. You'll know when you've reached the summits.

After completing this hike, don't be afraid to drive further through the Cascade Lakes toward Keene and take a dip in the Cascade lakes. It's quite refreshing. If you have kids or don't swim well, however, please be aware the lake becomes extremely deep almost immediately.

# Cascade and Porter Mountains

*May 18, 2018. Day 1 on my quest to become an Adirondack 46'er. I started with the popular Cascade and Porter Mountains (as many tend to do). It was a cool crisp spring morning with blue skies. Great weather for hiking. There was still snow and ice at higher elevations, but it was melted everywhere else. I arrived at the trailhead parking lot on Route 73 at 5:45 a.m. I quickly gathered my gear, and I was ready to start my High Peaks adventure.*

*I packed lots of water, snacks, and peanut butter and jelly sandwiches for today's hike. When it comes to outdoor recreation, for better or for worse, I am a textbook "overpacker." I suited up, locked my car, took a swig of water, and walked to the trailhead as the excitement for beginning the journey to 46 was officially underway. Then it hit me like a ton of bricks. A feeling no one wants to experience away from home let alone in the woods. The feeling of that dreaded . . . number 2. Yup. At the time I had never gone "number 2" in the woods, but fortunately for me that day, there was a porta potty right at the trailhead parking lot. A godsend, really. Thankfully, it was also clean. So I took care of my business, boldly declared "Now I'm ready to hike," and then walked down from the road to the trail register and signed in at 6 a.m. on the dot, the first sign-in of the day. We're off to the races. The journey to summit all 46 High Peaks in one season begins now!*

*My plan for today on this 5.5-mile hike with 2,300' of elevation gain was to hike up to the Cascade and Porter trail split, head over to Porter first and then finish on Cascade. Growing up in Lake Placid I've actually hiked Cascade a few times in my life, but I never once hiked the 0.7 miles over to Porter on any of those hikes. Probably because every time I hiked Cascade (including once on a high school field trip), I was physically dying by the time I got to Cascade, and the idea of adding another mountain to the mix just wasn't happening. Ah, the good old days.*

*The trail begins with a gradual climb right from the start. One of the reasons this mountain is so popular is because, well, it's a High Peak for starters, but it's arguably the easiest and most accessible High Peak since there isn't a long approach from the trailhead. Another reason for its popularity is the fact that Cascade has an amazing, wide-open summit with 360-degree views for days. It has a lot of bang for its buck (but so do many* non–High Peak mountains in the Adirondacks). The trail is well traveled, and a lot of trail work has gone into keeping up with the foot traffic over the years, so while it's very worn, it's well marked and easy to navigate. The trail changes throughout the climb going from sections of rock hopping to some slab climbing, to gentle flat sections, followed by steeper climbs, before leveling off again. In general, it's a consistent gradual climb from the trailhead to the summit.

I'd say after the initial gentle climb this hike has three or four steep climbs. A steep climb up rocks, and boulders, followed by the trail leveling off allowing you to catch your breath, followed by another climb, then more leveling off, and so on. The trail does not run along a drainage like so many other High Peaks trails do, so make sure you bring all the water you'll need for the day. And a good rule of thumb in general is to bring double the water you think you'll need if you're unsure of water sources to refill.

I was making great time ascending this trail, and there was no sign of snow or ice yet, which is rare for May. I was pleasantly surprised that I was not breathing too heavily while going up the steeper sections. Amazing how much more enjoyable hiking is when you're in decent cardiovascular shape. No sign of other people yet, which was to be expected since I signed in first that day and which made it that much more surprising when I saw a hiker coming toward me about 100' before the Cascade and Porter trail split. I guess I wasn't the first to sign in after all. The lone hiker and I chatted for a minute, and it turns out he did a sunrise hike and started at 2 a.m. Wow! The idea of starting a hike at 2 a.m. was unfathomable at that point in time. Oh, how things would change throughout my journey through these mountains. In fact, today's 6 a.m. sign-in would end up being the latest start time on my entire High Peaks journey (I would eventually go on to start as early as 3:30 a.m. in the Santanonis). I asked the other hiker if there was any snow or ice above, and he told me, "Yeah, just a little ice on the way to Porter but that's it." Great. We wished each other well and went our separate ways. He was planning to go hike Giant and Rocky Peak Ridge today too, so he had a big day still ahead of him. Hiking four mountains in one day was yet another idea that seemed wild to me at that time. Ah, the innocence of a new High Peaks hiker, am I right?

Seconds after we parted ways, I arrived at the trail junction for Porter, 0.7 miles away, which is marked by a wooden sign on a post held up by a pile of medium-sized rocks. Amazing that a trail as traveled as this has never had the sign secured a little better because I remembered those same rocks from 15 years earlier when I hiked Cascade in high school. I guess it works if it has lasted this long.

I immediately began my trip over to Porter, which involves dropping down 150' elevation in 0.1 miles to the col and then back up 300' elevation over about a half mile. "I'm in unmarked territory now," I thought to myself as I was hiking over to Porter for the very first time. It was all quite exciting as my adventure continued. Knowing how popular this hike is, I figured the trail would be easy to navigate, and thankfully it was.

This initial 0.1-mile portion of the trail as I dropped down into the col had the most leftover ice on the entire trail, and I kept debating whether I wanted to take out my spikes and put them on—whether I should just stop and take a minute: "work smarter, not harder." It certainly would have made this stretch much easier (and safer), but in the moment I wanted to keep moving, so for better or worse I went without the spikes despite them being in my backpack. I also did not want to take off my backpack and then have that moment of putting the pack on my sweaty back in the chilly air. You know the feeling. It's the worst, isn't it? In the end I opted to just hold some trees and roots and make my way down slowly. It worked out, but in hindsight those times are worth taking a second to put the spikes on my boots and do it right. It only takes one wrong step to suddenly be in a serious predicament in the backcountry. Ultimately, it's never worth the risk. I was still new, though, and learning these lessons is part of the journey.

Once I was in the col, I continued up the trail, which was mostly frozen mud at that point. Shortly after the col I arrived at a giant boulder that was sure to have some noteworthy views, so I wasted no time climbing up to enjoy them. It was totally worth it. A minute or two and a photo or two later I hopped down and continued up the trail up Porter. I was almost there.

After winding through the woods I came out on a rock ledge that felt like the summit, but I wasn't sure if it was the true summit. I didn't see a summit sign or any survey marker in the rocks. I did, however, see a trail sign coming onto the ledge from the other direction (which is the Porter trail coming up from Keene via Marcy Field). Since I didn't have much experience in the High Peaks, I didn't know if I was truly there. So I took out my phone and called my 46'er buddy Josh (who will end up doing many hikes with me) and sheepishly asked him, "Hey! Is there a sign on the summit of Porter? How do I know if I'm there?" He responded, "I don't remember, but you just know when you're there." Well, that's not super helpful, but looking back now it was a fantastic "welcome to hiking the Adirondacks" moment. Most summits here do not have any kind of sign, so you will "just know when you're there." A great lesson and bigger-picture moment for me here on my first "official" High Peaks hike.

It turned out I was indeed standing on top of Porter Mountain, 4,059' elevation for High Peak number 1 of 46. I arrived at 7:25 a.m., 1 hour and 25 minutes after signing in. The summit has spectacular views of the Great Range, Keene, and Cascade mountains. It was a perfectly clear bluebird day. The summit is a medium-sized rock ledge and is a great spot to enjoy a sandwich. The best part of hiking is eating a sandwich on the summit, right? So I ate a PB&J and took it all in. My journey to become an Adirondack 46'er was underway with one peak down. After growing up in Lake Placid, a place where becoming a 46'er is ingrained in the culture, I couldn't believe I was actually going for it. My excitement was real.

It was a quiet day up top, albeit chilly being only May, so after 10 minutes I packed up my gear and headed back toward Cascade. I made great time backtracking through the half mud, half still frozen trail from Porter. I climbed back up out of the col and made it back to the trail junction in under 15 minutes. From the split to the summit of Cascade is just a hop, skip, and a jump away.

A minute or two past the trail junction, the Cascade trail leaves the tree line where you'll embark on a long, open, beautiful scramble to the true summit. Just follow the cairns (rock stacks) and yellow blaze paint on the rocks. It was great, and having been up there a few times in my life, I remembered this summit well. This would be a good time to mention to always stay on the rocks on the summits and don't step on the fragile alpine vegetation. At this point it feels like you're at the top of the world because of the 360-degree views throughout the final approach to the summit. It's a terrific payoff.

I made it to the official summit at 8 a.m., marked by a survey marker in the ground. It was exactly two hours since signing in and 35 minutes from the time I summited Porter. I was back on top of Cascade Mountain, standing 4,098', for High Peak number 2. The summit of Porter was quiet and peaceful, while the summit of Cascade was incredibly windy. Hold-your-hat-so-it-doesn't-blow-away-caliber windy. The summit of Cascade is enormous and amazing, with views of the High Peaks, the Sentinel Mountain Range, and the town of Lake Placid below. Due to the heavy wind, I didn't stay long and headed back toward the tree line to begin my descent.

My spirits were high as I was now multiple peaks into my journey. By definition, "two" counts as "multiple," so I was stoked. My hike down the mountain was fast, and roughly halfway down I started passing people hiking up. Many of them asked me, "Wow, what time did you start?" to which I naturally responded, "Six o'clock." They were always surprised that I started "so early" (remember, this would be the latest that I ever signed in). In general I'm a firm believer that if you're hiking the High Peaks, you should always start as early as possible. The reason being because you never know how much time you'll need out there, and more daylight hours gives the best chance for success throughout your 46'er journey. Plus, hiking in with a headlamp lets you experience the woods as it "wakes up" (which is the best), and don't worry, you will adapt to the light of the headlamp within the first few minutes.

After passing half a dozen groups of hikers heading up Cascade, I made it back to the trailhead and signed out at 9:20 a.m., totaling my day at 3 hours and 20 minutes car-to-car. Cascade and Porter are excellent choices for starting out in the High Peaks, though there are many excellent small mountains below 4,000' elevation in the area that are great to help you find your "trail legs" and gain some Adirondack trail experience before venturing into the High Peaks. So keep those mountains in mind too.

It was a successful day in the woods on my first High Peaks, here on my quest to become an Adirondack 46'er in one summer. Porter and Cascade for summits number 1 and 2 are in the books, and I'm officially on my way. Next time I'll head to the Adirondack Loj with my buddy Josh to tackle Phelps and Tabletop where I'll learn valuable lessons and gain a better understanding of the High Peaks. I will also get a first-hand glimpse of how many unprepared hikers go up Mt. Marcy on a given weekend and learn the importance of knowing the map and your route before you start hiking. My journey to 46 has begun!

# 2 | Phelps and Tabletop Mountains

Phelps (4,161'), Tabletop (4,427')
**Mileage:** 12.3 miles
**Elevation Gain:** 3,766'

Starting at the Adirondack Loj in Lake Placid, this pair of mountains is a great second hike to tackle. It will give you a good idea of what to expect here in the Adirondacks and offers a totally different experience

## PHELPS AND TABLETOP MOUNTAINS

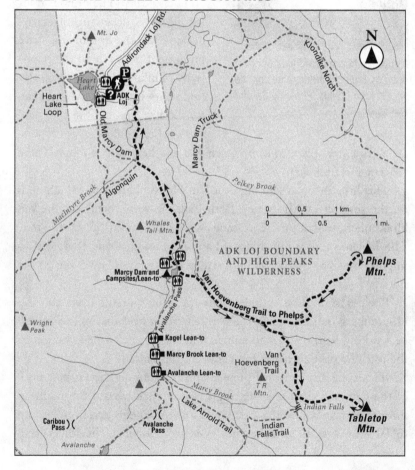

A subzero, frozen beard kind of afternoon on Tabletop before catching the sunset from Phelps. *Photo by Stephan Washburn*

from Cascade and Porter. I often take hikers visiting the ADK for the first time on this hike due to the ruggedness of climbing the herd paths up Tabletop along with the view and summit on Phelps. Hiking into Marcy Dam is always a pleasure too.

If you're not familiar, "herd paths" are non–DEC maintained trails, sometimes referred to as "trailless peaks." The phrase "trailless peak" is deceiving nowadays because all the mountains have prominent trails due to the popularity of hiking them. You will also find yourself going to Marcy Dam for the first time on this hike, and that's a beautiful place to experience. It's a great place to camp too if you get there early enough. There are tent sites and lean-tos.

This hike involves climbing the Van Hoevenberg trail, which ends on the summit of Mt. Marcy. Both trails, however, break off the Van Hoevenberg trail at different points, with Tabletop further up the trail. The Tabletop trail is unmaintained and is in rough shape; therefore it's important to stay on trail and not widen the trail more by going on the sides.

Phelps's summit is a mile from the trail split-off from the Van Hoevenberg trail and gains 1,200' of elevation over that mile. You will be working hard for that mountain, but it's worth it when you get to the top. The summit ledge and views are top notch.

In general, my personal preference is to summit the farthest peak of the day first, then start making my way back toward the trailhead throughout the day. In this case you'd pass the Phelps junction heading to Tabletop first, then make your way back down to the Phelps trail junction, marked by a wooden sign and a boulder with a big tree growing around it like an octopus, just off the trail. This is a good time to tell you—don't get too used to trail signs here in the High Peaks.

You will also notice that there is a summit sign on Tabletop, but not Phelps. All the "trailless peaks" in the ADK High Peaks have brown and yellow summit signs but no trail markers, whereas the DEC-maintained hiking trails have trail markers up the mountains but no summit signs. These trailless peaks have summit signs courtesy of the Adirondack Mountain Club.

## Phelps and Tabletop Mountains

*May 27, 2018. After a great morning a week ago on Cascade and Porter, it was time for my second High Peaks hike, Phelps and Tabletop. Josh was coming with me today on this 12-mile hike with just over 3,800' of elevation gain. Our plan for the day was to hike from the Adirondack Loj to Marcy Dam, then hop on the Van Hoevenberg trail and decide on the day if we were going to split off and do Phelps first or second. Either way, both mountains have trail junctions off the Van Hoevenberg trail, so we could decide later.*

*We arrived at the Adirondack Loj nice and early and signed in at 5:30 a.m. for the first sign-ins of the day. We clicked on our headlamps and off we went into the dark Adirondack woods. From the start Josh was moving fast down the trail, so I asked, "Why are you going so fast?" to which he responded, "Do you know how many times I've hiked into Marcy Dam? We just need to get this portion completed as fast as possible." Now, for me, having only hiked into the dam once as a young kid, it felt like a new place. I typically enjoy the dark walk to the dam. It's a good warm-up, winding through the woods, seeing the forest wake up, walking over several wooden bridges, and not having to turn your brain on too quickly. Fortunately for me, Josh went first, so he caught most of the spiderwebs to the face.*

*To Josh's delight, we made quick time of the 2.3-mile trek to Marcy Dam. The sun started to rise once we made it to the dam, and being my first time there since I was a kid, it was a terrific sight. It's an awesome area at the base of numerous mountains along the Marcy Brook. It's a popular place to camp as well, with both lean-tos and tent sites.*

We went across the new bridge at the dam and then turned right to continue up the Van Hoevenberg trail. This trail runs along the Phelps brook for a large portion. Some gradual elevation is gained as you wind your way through the woods walking on rocks and dirt.

We made it to the Phelps trail junction in much less time than I anticipated. This trail is usually marked by a trail sign, but it didn't have a sign on this day. We decided in that moment to finish with Phelps today and hit it on our way back, which proved to be a good choice. I typically prefer climbing the farthest peaks first and making my way back toward the trailhead throughout the day (as opposed to going further and further away throughout the day).

We continued up the gradual climb on the Van Hoevenberg trail and soon crossed over Phelps Brook as the trail weaved its way through the lush Adirondack forest. After gaining some more elevation, we made it to the Tabletop trail junction. We decided to make our first pit stop of the hike to fuel up before the climb. I enjoyed a quick PB&J, and then it was time to start climbing.

From this junction the summit is only 0.7 miles away. This was, however, my first time experiencing a herd path, also known as an unmaintained trail, and it was a unique view. In some places the trail is extremely eroded a few feet deep in the ground due to a mix of foot traffic and water, and some places it was extremely narrow, getting scratched by tree branch after tree branch. Fortunately, the trail was rather obvious due to the thousands of hikers that come up it every year, and my nerves about this "unmarked trail" concept were slightly put at ease. Of course, I was just blindly following Josh, so I didn't need to navigate, and in fact I didn't even look at the map before hiking today because I knew Josh was coming with me. This was the wrong way to go about things, and it was a lesson I would learn through another hiker later in the day in fact. PSA: Always read the map and know exactly where you're going no matter who you're hiking with . . . don't be like me today. Once again, learning these lessons is all part of the journey.

So we continued through the woods, climbing up the gradual muddy trail to Tabletop, walking on some rugged terrain, some slabs, and getting scratched by the branches that line much of the trail. We made it to the wooded summit of Tabletop Mountain at 8 a.m., the 19th-tallest

High Peak, standing 4,427', for High Peak number 3. It took us exactly 2.5 hours from sign-in to summit. There are some great views of Marcy and the MacIntyre Range on this summit, but today was very cloudy and unfortunately there were no views. The summit is marked with a brown wooden sign reading "Tabletop Mountain" in yellow lettering. Most of the High Peaks with unmaintained trails have brown and yellow wooden signs on their summits (which is helpful). So we took our photo with the summit sign, ate another sandwich and snack, and started back down the herd path toward Phelps.

Just before we got back down to the Marcy trail split, we passed a couple going up, our first sign of human life on the day. We exchanged pleasantries and continued hiking and made it to the Marcy trail junction in what felt like record time. This is the point of the day where my mind would be blown. As we made our way down the Van Hoevenberg trail toward Phelps, we passed dozens and dozens of hikers headed toward Marcy. I knew that's where they were all going because most of them asked us if we went to Marcy already. Having grown up in Lake Placid and seeing Marcy almost every day, I never realized how many people hike this mountain on a given day, and it was only May. There's likely still snow up there, after all, and it's not even summer yet. The alarming part wasn't the number of people climbing it but rather the amount who looked more like they were going to play miniature golf than a 17-mile hike in the High Peaks. I would say 50 percent of them were wearing the proper footwear, and the other half were not. A lot of tennis shoes and Poland Spring water bottles (if they even had water). "Yeah, I'm sure they're all going to make it up," Josh said to me sarcastically. "Just wait until July. There will be double the amount of people," he continued. This was an eye-opening moment to say the least.

The next group we passed were likely college-aged guys, and we referred to one of them as "Sambas" because he was wearing Adidas Sambas, no backpack, no water, with mud completely covering his feet up to his knees, and he looked completely miserable. Next, we met "Blue Jeans." Blue jeans was a woman who was hiking in, you guessed it, blue jeans, but she was sitting on the side of the trail smoking a cigarette, hacking up a lung, and looking like death was unfortunately on her doorstep. She was in rough, rough shape. Fortunately, she was with another person, but I would be shocked if they made it to the summit of Marcy. Hiking up a mountain that is outside your physical capabilities or experience level is not fun, and it's also a recipe for disaster. The ADK is filled with small, gentle mountains to find your "trail legs" and see how capable you are. There's a mountain or trail for every fitness and experience level. Starting out climbing Mt. Marcy if you're inexperienced or out of shape is not the wisest choice. I recommend Mt. Jo. The rangers will thank you too.

We continued along the Van Hoevenberg trail toward Phelps passing Marcy rat after Marcy rat, and we eventually were back at the Phelps trail junction we had passed earlier in the day. I remembered one particular boulder at the junction because there is a tree engulfing it, with its roots like an octopus engulfing a ship. It's always a good idea to take mental notes of the woods and checkpoints throughout your hike.

We took off our packs and fueled up for the mile hike to the summit. This one mile is going to make you work for it thanks to the 1,300' of gain over that mile. While we were enjoying a snack just off the trail, a young couple in their mid-20s passed us, and I saw the guy look at the trail and nervously say, "I think it's this way," as he pointed up the Van Hoevenberg trail toward Marcy. At this point I spoke up and said, "Phelps left, Marcy and Tabletop to the right." He sheepishly turned around and said, "Oh . . . thanks . . . it's this way I guess," as they proceeded to turn around and come back toward Phelps. Then, like a middle-school cafeteria when someone drops their lunch tray in front of everyone, Josh and I both let out a playful "Ohhhhhh." It was all in good fun, and it's good to help one another out so we all have a good backcountry experience. Now, I very easily could have been this dude today because I didn't look at the map before my hike, and I was blindly following Josh, just like his girlfriend was following him. So, thanks to our friend, who was about to take his girl up Mt. Marcy instead of Phelps, I was able to learn my lesson here. The lesson of always doing my own pre-hike homework regardless of who I'm hiking with. Shout-out to that dude for teaching me this valuable lesson today early on in my journey. The proper pre-hike homework should include studying the map, learning the trail junctions you will be looking for, where the rivers and other checkpoints are, and checking the weather beforehand (there are many websites that offer mountain forecasts). Hopefully, she didn't break up with him on top of Phelps for almost leading her deep into the Adirondack Mountains in the wrong direction.

Onward and upward. About 10 minutes after the young couple passed us, Josh and I began our climb up Phelps. Going up Phelps is a steep one, a real gasser. A lot of rock hopping and stepping over trees and small slab climbs and rock scrambles make for a real calf burner. It is an entirely different kind of trail and hiking experience than Tabletop was, which makes this combo of Phelps and Tabletop great thanks to the variety. You've got a warzone-looking herd path with muddy exposed roots everywhere on Tabletop, and then Phelps has lots of rock hopping and steep, rugged slab climbing. It's a great Adirondack hike. We passed a handful of people coming down the trail, and we made it to the summit in just under 35 minutes after leaving the trail split. Phelps Mountain, 4,161' elevation, for High Peak number 4. Phelps is named after a legendary Adirondack guide named Orson Phelps, known lovingly as "Old Mountain" Phelps, the man responsible for cutting the first trail up Mt. Marcy. A fitting name for a mountain that has excellent views of Mt. Marcy.

It was overcast today, so we had some views of the lower elevations under the clouds, which still made for unique views. We shared the summit with another family. I spotted a couple of 46'er patches on their packs, too. "Ah, one day I'll earn that patch and have the experiences to go along with it," I enthusiastically thought to myself. Josh snapped a family photo for them before we sat down to relax now that the hard work had been accomplished. Josh likes to take off his boots and socks on the final summit, and I followed suit since he said it's the best part of the hike. It did feel great I will admit. Although this innocent tradition would prove to have dire consequences for me later.

After about 10 minutes, and after putting on a fresh pair of Darn Tough socks, we decided to head back down the mountain. Switching to a fresh pair of socks after the final summit of the day is a tradition I do religiously, and it makes the hike out much more enjoyable. I highly recommend it. About five minutes into our descent, we passed the young couple from earlier, and he jokingly shouted, "First beer's on him tonight." They were in good spirits and thankfully heading toward the correct summit. Thanks again for teaching me a lesson today as well, my friend!

*The steepness of Phelps had my knees feeling each step on the way down, but what I also started to notice was how terrible my feet felt, particularly the bottom of my feet. Suddenly my shoes just didn't seem to fit right, and the bottom of my feet felt like they were being stabbed with a knife every time I stepped on a rock or a root. It was terrible. I asked Josh, "Hey, do your feet hurt?" and he responded with an enthusiastic, "Nope." Great, so it's just me. Got it. They felt worse and worse with every step. I couldn't figure out why they suddenly hurt so bad. It's likely because my feet swelled up after taking my boots and socks off for 10 minutes on the summit, a realization I would learn a couple of hikes later in the Dix Range when this sharp foot bottom pain came back for round two.*

*Every step hurt more than usual, but we continued along the Phelps Brook and crossed over the low-water crossing this time around. Marcy Dam was close, and then all we had left was the 2.3-mile flat trail back to the ADK Loj, which would have been simple if every step on a rock or root didn't feel like someone was stabbing me in the bottom of my foot. One foot in front of the other and blocking out the pain became the name of the game. Eventually, we made it back to the parking lot and signed out at 12:35 p.m. for a nice early finish. Our day weighed in at 7 hours and 5 minutes car-to-car, with 12 miles of hiking and 3,800' of elevation gain. Another great day exploring and getting to know the mysterious Adirondack High Peaks that I grew up in the shadows of.*

*Another successful day in the woods here on my second High Peaks hike where I summited Tabletop and Phelps for peak numbers 3 and 4 on my journey to summit all 46 in one summer. I wouldn't be able to hike a High Peak again until July due to work travels for the next five weeks. Thankfully throughout June, however, I was able to hike many smaller Adirondack mountains on the weekends, like Hurricane, Pitchoff, Big Crow, Baxter, Catamount, and a few others. I was optimistic about accomplishing my summer's goal, and my eyes were set on July. In the next chapter, Josh and I will head up Whiteface and Esther on July 1 for a climb that will test both my legs and my lungs as I dive headfirst into a month that would have me summiting almost 30 High Peaks.*

# 3 Whiteface and Esther Mountains

Whiteface (4,876'), Esther (4,240')
**Mileage:** 9.5 miles
**Elevation Gain:** 3,820'

Starting at the Marble Mountain trailhead at the Atmospheric Science Research Center in Wilmington, this hike is sure to get your heart pumping and sweat pouring from the start. Good thing you're dressed in non-cotton, moisture-wicking clothing and a backpack with more food/water than you're going to need, right? This hike begins climbing Marble Mountain, which is roughly 1,000' of gain in 0.8 miles, so it's a gasser to say the least. Fortunately the elevation gain eases up a bit on top of Marble (but not too much) as you continue to climb toward the Esther trail split near the top of Lookout Mountain. You will know when you've arrived at the Esther trail split because it's marked by the biggest cairn of all time at the junction (a cairn is a makeshift trail marker consisting of rocks stacked on top of one another). Okay, it's not the biggest of all time, but it's definitely enormous.

Once at the junction, you can choose to tag Esther first or save it for the way back down. Personally, I suggest climbing Esther first since it's a mostly wooded summit; this way you can spend most of your summit time on the magnificent Whiteface summit. Sadly, Esther ranks low on the Summit Sandwich-ability (SSA) Scale, whereas Whiteface ranks a perfect 5/5, offering full 360-degree views and the Atmospheric Science Center. You may even eat your sandwich with people who drove to the summit, since the Adirondack Memorial Highway, aka "the toll road," goes up Whiteface. Drivers will be in awe of you for walking up the mountain. Hiking is hard work, so it's OK to be proud of your accomplishment upon arriving on the summit.

The High Peaks views and the figure-eight-shaped Lake Placid in the valley below make Whiteface one of the best views in the park. It's no wonder they built a road to its summit. Whiteface is the fifth-tallest peak in the ADK, so summiting this peak should give you a nice boost of confidence moving forward on your 46'er journey. Another thing,

# WHITEFACE AND ESTHER MOUNTAINS

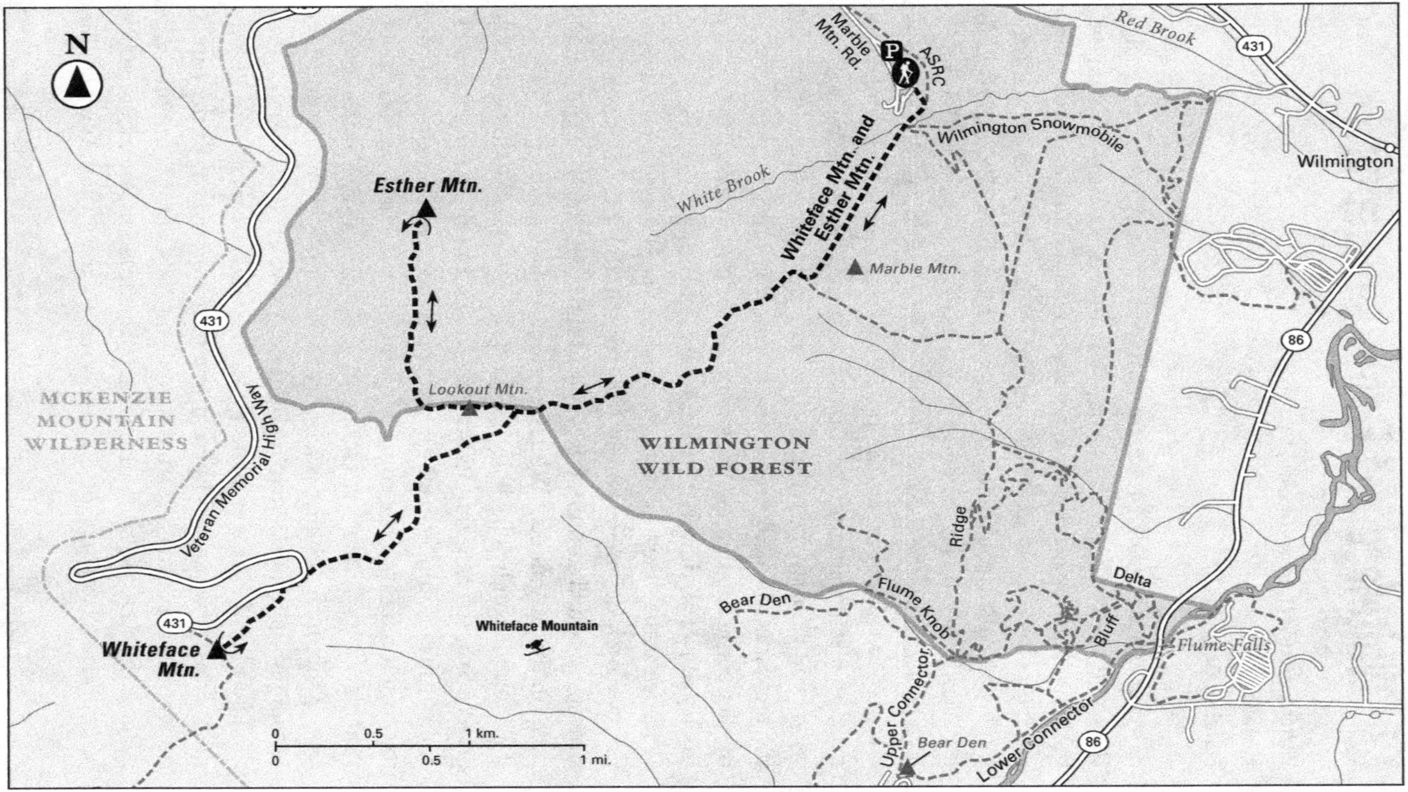

Wilmington

Red Brook

431

86

Flume Falls

Lower Connector

Delta

Bluff

Bear Den

Upper Connector

Ridge

Flume Knob

Bear Den

Wilmington Snowmobile

ASRC

P

Marble Mtn. Rd.

White Brook

Whiteface Mtn. and Esther Mtn.

Marble Mtn.

WILMINGTON WILD FOREST

Lookout Mtn.

Whiteface Mountain

Esther Mtn.

McKENZIE MOUNTAIN WILDERNESS

Veteran Memorial High Way

431

Whiteface Mtn.

N

0    0.5    1 km.
0    0.5    1 mi.

you're looking into Canada from the summit of Whiteface, which is cool.

Okay, settle in for a story about an extremely hot and humid day in the High Peaks climbing Whiteface and Esther. Can't you just feel the heavy breathing and knee pain already? Let's hike . . .

A bluebird Adirondack day on Whiteface overlooking Lake Placid. *Photo by James Appleton*

## Whiteface and Esther Mountains

*July 1, 2018. I'm finally back in the Adirondacks for the entire month and ready to hit the trail hard before I leave again for my next job. My quest to become a 46'er in one summer continues today on the Olympic Whiteface Mountain and Esther Mountain for my third hike and High Peaks numbers 5 and 6. My buddy Josh came with me again on this roughly 10-mile hike. Weather-wise we were experiencing an extremely humid, cloudy, moist, and misty day. It was not my preferred hiking conditions, but I'm home for the month now, so it's go time!*

*Today's hike involves over 3,800' of elevation gain on this out-and-back hike, starting with Esther and finishing on the world-renowned Whiteface Mountain. We snagged one of the few parking spots at the Reservoir trailhead in Wilmington (also known as the Atmospheric Science Center) and signed in at 5:30 a.m. We turned on our headlamps and began walking here in the Wilmington Wild Forest. The first quarter mile of the trip is a nice stroll through the woods, gaining little to no elevation. I enjoy approaches like this to warm up for the day, especially early in the morning. After that, however, the trail starts climbing fast up to Marble Mountain, and this is where it gets real. Hello elevation! The mile climb up to the wooded summit on Marble Mountain is relentless. It's about 900' of gain in 0.5 miles, so it's a quick punch in the lungs to start the day (and in my opinion the most demanding section of the hike). Honestly, all the way to the Esther trail junction is somewhat relentless elevation gain.*

*Due to the humidity we had to stop midway up Marble because Josh was nauseous thanks to the thick, humid weather. I was glad to stop, though, because I was huffing and puffing big time. He eventually pulled it together, though, and still to this day he says it's the worst he's felt while hiking. It sure was hot and it sure was humid. Good ol' Marble Mountain packs a real punch, so prepare yourself.*

*Onward. We continued up the Marble Mountain trail to the Marble summit, which is wooded with some views through the trees, but nothing major. At this point you join the Wilmington trail, which goes to the Esther trail split and the Whiteface summit. The elevation gain on this next section, however, is still plentiful, clocking in at 1.3 miles with 1,100' of gain from Marble to the Esther trail junction. So you'd better grab a swig of water on top of Marble because there's still a lot of work to be done.*

No sign of other people yet, and since we were the first to sign in again today, we wouldn't see any human life until our descent, per usual. Exactly two hours after signing in, and breathing heavily, we landed at the Esther trail split. This junction is humanly impossible to miss. It's a large flat clearing with a boulder and the biggest pile of rocks you'll ever see. Well, maybe not that big, but it is an enormous pile of rocks, not quite a cairn, just a huge pile of rocks marking the Esther trail.

We gulped some water and immediately began the mile trek up the unmarked and unmaintained Esther trail. Like many unmarked trails in the Adirondacks, it's muddy, eroded, and filled with exposed, slippery roots. I personally find tree roots to be the most obnoxious element to deal with while hiking due to the slip factor. Big guys like me don't need to slip and fall to the ground without warning. The earth doesn't need that. I will suffer my share of bumps and bruises at the hands of the High Peaks throughout my journey, and you'll get to read all about them (damn you, Nye Mountain . . . and Dix . . . and Cliff).

After 35 minutes of slipping and sliding in the mud up this mountain, we made it to the wooded Esther summit, marked by a plaque in the ground which reads, "Mt. Esther—4,270 feet. To celebrate the indomitable spirit of Esther Macomb age 15. Who made the first recorded ascent of this peak for the sheer joy of climbing," along with the original 46'er organization logo and "Troy NY." If you couldn't tell, the mountain is named after Esther Macomb, who, as legend has it, first climbed the mountain at 15 years of age in 1839. The story goes that she thought she was hiking Whiteface but ended up on this mountain instead. Imagine being 15 years old in 1839 climbing this rugged mountain where there is no trail or DEC to rescue you. It's incredible. Esther is also the northernmost High Peak, so along with Whiteface it offers very different views than you'll find throughout most of the High Peaks.

After a quick (and wet) summit stay, we headed back to the trail split. It took us 30 minutes to return to the world's biggest rock-pile cairn, which was a welcome sight after climbing this mud fest mountain today. We turned right and continued up the Wilmington trail toward the summit of Whiteface Mountain. The Olympic Whiteface Mountain, that is. Fun fact: Whiteface has the biggest vertical drop east of the Rockies for all you skiers and snowboarders out there. Another fun fact: Did you know that New

York State has more ski mountains than any other state in the country? Now you do.

This part of the trail has a large mix of slabs, narrow stretches, and typical woods terrain. It's a gradual climb from the junction to the summit, tallying roughly 1.5 miles and less than 900' of gain, and the hiking trail eventually comes out to a ski trail since Whiteface is also a ski mountain. It was the "Wilmington trail." Very fitting. This is a blue-square trail for all you skiers and snowboarders out there. Since it's the middle of the summer, I sat on the ski lift and Josh snapped a photo. Of course we're going to sit on the chair lift.

The sun was taunting us with occasional rays before quickly hiding back behind the clouds, but we carried on up the trail and eventually came to the large stone wall at the Whiteface Memorial Highway. It kind of ruins the mountain experience when you come to a paved double-yellow-line road midway up the mountain, but at the same time it's also kind of cool because it's a unique element for this mountain. It's not so bad having one mountain you can drive up, right?

The trail continues along the side of this highway before leaving the tree line for a long, exposed, and fun scramble to the summit. You'll be following the yellow painted lines on the slab for the last 0.3 miles at the end of the ascent. It's quite nice being out in the open and overlooking the ski trails. The summit suddenly appears seemingly out of nowhere as you arrive at the weather center and you're there alongside all the tourists who drove their cars to the summit. It took us 55 minutes to go from the Esther trail split to the Whiteface summit, but we made it to the top and touched the Whiteface Mountain summit sign at 8:39 a.m., standing 4,867' above sea level. It was still quite early in the morning on this rainy, windy, humid, foggy, viewless day, so there were no tourists up there yet. Fortunately for us we had the summit all to ourselves. This makes two High Peaks hikes in a row with little to no views. I didn't mind so much here, however, because I've been up Whiteface in a car several times in my life. On a clear day you can even see into Canada, which is cool.

Since we made it to the summit, you know what that means: sandwich time. Josh and I sat down to eat our victory sandwiches, and it was a unique albeit eerie experience being the only people up at the top of Whiteface thanks to the dark clouds. Visibility was only 10 feet in front of you, creating a spooky mountain vibe. We both sat down close enough for casual conversation, but we couldn't see one another. It was fun.

Once we crushed some food, it was time for the long descent and the beginning of the "pain train." Off the summit, back down the rocks, over the highway, and back to the tree line we went. We made great time getting back into the tree line and out of the misty rain, which is where we passed our first couple for the day. We chatted briefly before continuing our adventures. Whiteface is a tough hike—after all, it's the fifth-tallest High Peak—so that would explain the additional amount of knee and toe pain I experienced on this descent. I was also still building up those hiking muscles . . . and joints.

Speaking of pain, I opted to hike today in my New Balance trail-running shoes, but in reality they're just a beefed-up sneaker. Josh's wife, Emily, hiked the entire 46 High Peaks in the same pair of old tennis sneakers. So, through her inspiration, I opted for comfort today over supportive, waterproof footwear. Unfortunately for me, my toes were getting jammed relentlessly into the front of my shoes during the descent, so much that I eventually lost both middle toenails from it. Coupled with the usual knee pain, this all made for a somewhat painful trip down Whiteface.

We started passing lots of groups climbing the mountain at this point in the day. There was even one group blasting a Bluetooth speaker in their enormous backpacks. So that was awesome. Yes, that was sarcasm. We're all out there to have a good experience in the mountains, and I'm aware we're all at different experience levels in the backcountry, but the Bluetooth speaker is a major pet peeve of mine. Whether you're hiking in the woods or just walking down a public sidewalk, nobody wants to hear your music. Period. I'll just say it: Don't be the dude blasting a speaker on the trail. It's disrespectful to all those around you; the woods and animals don't need it either. If you want to jam some tunes while you hike, then be my guest; just be respectful of others and wear headphones. See how easy that is? That way the rest of us can enjoy the sounds of the woods. After all, that's why we're there, right? The easy solution is to wear one earbud; then you can enjoy the music while still hearing your surroundings and other people on the trail. End of rant. Let's continue . . .

Shortly after the music faded into the distance, we passed a group of girls climbing up Marble Mountain, and they were struggling hard (remember how tough that climb was earlier in the day?). I felt bad because of course they asked that dreaded question, "How much further?" (another pet peeve of mine), but I didn't want to crush their souls. Unfortunately they were multiple hours from the summit. I told them, "It might be a couple more hours." They were less than thrilled about the news. As we parted ways, one of them said, "Enjoy the descent." The descent is actually my least favorite part of any hike. It adds the most wear and tear on my body, especially my poor knees. I'll gladly climb all day long, but descending is harder from my perspective.

Once we got off Marble Mountain, we made a left for the final trek through the woods back to the car. During our descent we decided we had to jump in an Adirondack body of water to finish the day. A humid, sweaty day like this needed to conclude with fresh cold ADK water. I was so sticky I just wanted to jump in with my clothes on, my boots on, even my backpack. Okay, not my backpack, but you get the idea. We made it back to the Reservoir trailhead to our car 2 hours 20 minutes after leaving the Whiteface summit, clocking our roughly 10-mile day at exactly seven hours.

A successful day in the woods once again, summiting Whiteface and Esther, but we still had one more task to complete; we needed to jump in some water. As we drove through the mountains toward Bloomingdale, sandwiched between the Mackenzie Mountain Wilderness on our left and the Wilmington Wild Forest on our right, we found the perfect spot. So we pulled over, stripped down to our shorts, and jumped in the Saranac River. Victory so sweet it almost brought tears to my eyes. Not really, but it sure felt good. A perfect ending to a wet day on the trail on my third High Peaks hike, summiting Esther and Whiteface for peak numbers 5 and 6. My goal to hiking all 46 High Peaks in one summer is well underway. July was the month I was waiting for, and this was just the beginning here on July 1. I would go on to summit a total of 28 High Peaks this month alone, making it one of the greatest months of my life.

Thus concludes the story of my trip up Whiteface and Esther. In the next chapter, despite bruised feet and cranky knees, I'll head up Street and Nye two days later for my first solo hike up unmaintained trails. Time to jump in the deep end and increase my solo-hiking experience level in the High Peaks.

# 4 Street and Nye Mountains

Street (4,166'), Nye (3,895')
**Mileage:** 9.1 miles
**Elevation Gain:** 2,634'

Starting at the Adirondack Loj in Lake Placid, you'll tackle your first day of completely unmarked trails. Don't let that worry you, though, because the trails are relatively easy to follow, and you will build some good confidence. This is one of those hikes where studying the map and memorizing the turns is important because you will pass several trail junctions over the first half mile. You don't want to miss the trail to Street and Nye and end up going through Indian Pass instead.

This hike involves a couple of river crossings, one of which is over the Indian Pass Brook. It can be challenging if the water levels are extra high, so it's worth finding out beforehand. You can do this by calling the DEC, the Adirondack Mountain Club Info Center, or checking online forums.

After crossing the brook you'll be smooth sailing. The trail up Street and Nye is rugged, though, to say the least. There's a lot of blowdown, and it's just plain messy. That makes it fun, though. It's an authentic Adirondack experience and a quintessential example of the phrase "an Adirondack mile."

Once you arrive at the trail junction, you're only 0.2 miles away from the Nye summit and 0.7 miles from Street. I'd recommend tagging Nye first, coming back, then going to Street to hang out and eat your lunch. While neither mountain ranks high on the SSA Scale, Street offers a higher-quality summit experience in my opinion. Nye has minimal views; however, Street offers a unique and worthy perspective of the mighty MacIntyre Range. There's also a good boulder to enjoy that sandwich on.

# STREET AND NYE MOUNTAINS

To Lake Placid

Mt. Jo

Adirondack Loj Rd.

ADK Loj

Heart Lake

Heart Lake Loop

Old Marcy Dam

MacIntyre Brook

ADK LOJ AND BOUNDARY LINES

Indian Pass Trail

Indian Pass Brook

Rock Falls

Street and Nye
Street Mtn. Trail

Nye Mtn.

Chubb River

Street Mtn.

N

0    0.5    1 km.

0    0.5    1 mi.

# Let's Talk River Crossings

Sometimes you may encounter an abundance of herd paths following a river crossing. This typically results from hikers crossing at various points due to water levels. Take your time to figure out the correct trail. GPS apps can be a helpful tool in these scenarios to help you confirm the correct route. Remember when I said peace of mind in the woods is worth its weight in gold?

Another thing to remember regarding water levels is that nature doesn't play by our rules. The river may be significantly higher upon your return than it was when you went up the mountain hours earlier. Always be aware of what the conditions may be like later in your hike and be willing to turn around early if those conditions could become dangerous.

## Street and Nye Mountains

*July 3, 2018. Just two days after summiting Whiteface and Esther I set out solo on my fourth hike to tackle Street and Nye, my first pair of unmaintained trails. I didn't get much sleep the night before, which will become a trend the night before my solo hikes, because I was extra nervous about hitting unmarked trails without the aid of a more experienced hiker. The day was mostly cloudy, but with a nice summer temperature. I parked my car at the Adirondack Loj and started my 8.5-mile hike at 4:30 a.m. Time to hit the trail.*

*My plan for today's light but impactful hike would begin at the Adirondack Loj where I'd walk along Heart Lake before taking the Street and Nye herd path. I'd hike up to the trail split and start with Nye followed by Street Mountain on this 8.5-mile hike with 2,300' of elevation gain. My first solo day on unmarked trails. Here goes nothing!*

*Headlamp clicked on and I was ready to go. I wasn't sure what to expect on this one since the trails weren't marked, but I kept remembering Josh telling me that due to the surge in popularity, all the main trails in the High Peaks are quite apparent. So that gave me some comfort. Thankfully Street and Nye were no exception. I knew the trail for Street and Nye was past Mt. Jo (a mountain I have hiked dozens of times). I headed toward*

Mt. Jo around Heart Lake and my hike was underway. Upon walking next to the Loj at 4:30 in the morning, there was a woman sitting at a computer inside with the window open that I startled extra hard as I walked past the building. I think it was my charm and boyish good looks that startled her, actually.

I continued walking along Heart Lake and passed the main trails heading to Mt. Jo. I was officially entering unexplored territory. I continued on the Indian Pass trail along Heart Lake before signing in at the trail register. First person of the day again. Nice! As you know, I am a firm believer in signing in as early as possible when hiking the High Peaks. I soon came to the junction for the Indian Pass trail and the old Nye ski trail, so I continued straight since I knew from studying my route the night before, and from going through it a million times in my head while I tried to sleep, that I was going straight and not left to Indian Pass. Shortly after this junction, probably 0.1 miles or so, you'll come to the Rock Garden trail junction. A right takes you up the Rock Garden trail for Mt. Jo, and straight starts the "official unofficial" trail to Street and Nye. There was even a sign gently reminding me that nothing is marked from here on out. Perfect. You'll notice within the first mile that you pass several trail junctions; therefore it's important to familiarize yourself with the map. It would be easy to take the wrong trail here.

I was officially on the Street and Nye trail; my first solo trailless hike was underway. It was dark, there were no humans anywhere near me, and I was getting more remote, but I was doing it. It was a good feeling. The first mile is a gentle woods walk gaining very little if any elevation. A nice flowing trail moving along a brook in the woods. A great start in my opinion. Starting this early in the morning, though always preferred, does come with a caveat. The spiderwebs. They were brutal today. I had yet to experience this level of spiderwebs to the face, to my mouth, to my eyes. It was constant, really. Such is life on the trail at this hour, though. Spiders of the Adirondacks, I'm coming for your pre-5 a.m. spiderwebs. Consider this your warning.

Around three-quarters of a mile in I came to the Indian Pass Brook crossing that I was looking for. I knew from my research that this was a checkpoint on the trail. The brook was not too high that day, and after a minute looking around to find the best crossing I was able to find one, hop on some rocks, and make it across. There are cairns marking the crossing area, but people have obviously found different routes on different days due to water levels. At least they put you in the general area, though.

I was feeling good because I was on the correct trail and so far it was easy to follow. That would change, however, once I crossed the river. This river crossing can be high and treacherous in the right conditions or low like a stream. It's one of the main items to be aware of when choosing to hike these two mountains. Fortunately, the water level was low today, so there was no issue crossing. After crossing, though, now the issue was "which way?" There were multiple trails going every direction. Now I needed to figure out which was the correct trail. After a few minutes of auditioning a couple of trails, I eventually found what was clearly the correct one. I later realized these other trails were just herd paths formed from people crossing the stream at different points. Makes sense. Just go right after you cross the river and you'll find the trail. Soon you'll cross a river for the second time, but this time there's an old tree over the water to walk across. The perfect little footbridge.

Still no signs of human life and the sun was up now, so I put my headlamp away. Once past this brook, it's time to finally start climbing. Like many ADK trails, the trail runs alongside a drainage for a good portion of the climb. It's a standard Adirondack herd path trail with tons of slippery roots, very muddy, and moving back and forth across the drainage. This area was mostly hardwood trees, so the forest was open, making for great scenery.

Eventually I made it above the stream around the 2,500' elevation ballpark and was onto the next portion of the ascent. Good-bye drainage, hello blowdown. Since we had a storm for the record books a couple months prior, the blowdown on some of the trails in the Adirondacks was fierce, and I think this trail had more than any others. It's an unmaintained trail, so I suppose that makes sense. This portion of the trail is also a major "elbow scratcher," or more realistically, a "body scratcher." Many trails are narrow where the brush along the side of the trail scratches your elbows, but this trail was exceptionally narrow and scratched your body past your elbows. So narrow that the woods even drew blood once or twice thanks to a branch.

Speaking of minor injuries, as I was climbing over, crawling under, and going around the blowdown, I eventually came to one log that I needed to get past. So I examined it for a moment and thought climbing over would be the best option. I'll straddle the tree and then slide off it (you know the move). So I took my stance. I threw my knee up to get my leg over the log and—boom—I hit my knee at full speed on this little, itty-bitty nub on the tree. It hurt so bad that my mouth dropped, my face turned white, and I couldn't make a noise for a few seconds. I swear I saw stars. It was brutal. I literally kneed a tree at full force. Ten seconds later, when life finally reentered my body, I lifted my shorts and the entire VMO muscle on my quad was already black and blue and swollen to the size of a baseball. Mere seconds after impact the damage was already visible. This was easily the worst pain I had experienced in the woods to date, but I'll take that pain over the five miles of foot pain I'll experience on my very next hike in the Dix Range (but that's for another chapter).

After this horrific event (yes, I'm overexaggerating, but damn did it hurt), I continued up the narrow trail as my quad tightened with every step. I continued up the trail, though, around the giant moss-covered glacial erratic (you'll see it) and through the blowdown-covered woods as the trees switched from hardwood to evergreens. A lot of the elevation has been gained by this point into the hike, and soon I arrived at my first destination, the trail split for Street and Nye. It's impossible to miss. It's the saddle between Nye and Street, so it's a small clearing with a tree that has an S-left arrow and an N-right arrow carved in it. It took me exactly two hours to get here, which coincidentally is the same amount of time it took me on my previous hike up Whiteface to get to the Esther trail split. Two hours to the junction two hikes in a row. Wild.

Typically, I tend to eat my sandwich at the summit, but I was extra hungry this morning so I decided to drop my pack and relax for a moment while enjoying a PB&J. It hit the spot. After five minutes at the junction I decided to go up Nye first since it's only 0.2 miles from the trail split to the summit and most of the elevation has already been gained by this point. Seven minutes later at 6:44 a.m. I reached the summit of High Peak number seven, Nye Mountain. It's a wooded summit marked by a brown and yellow sign with an elevation of 3,895'. Oh, and in case you didn't know, yes, there are multiple High Peaks that are actually under 4,000' elevation. Four of them, in fact. Nye is number 45 on the list of 46 in terms of highest elevation.

So, upon exploring the wooden summit and seeing minimal views through the trees, I hurried back to the junction, which took six minutes to accomplish. Time to head up to Street. This herd path is a little longer at 0.6 miles and more involved. The trail has a lot of blowdown and is again quite narrow in places. The summit has a wooden sign reading "Street Mountain," and a small rock clearing just past the summit is about all you'll get for views up here, but there are indeed High Peaks views to be enjoyed. Good views of the MacIntyre Range in particular. It took me 21 minutes to go from junction to summit, landing me there at 7:15 a.m. standing at 4,166' elevation for High Peak number 8!

I hopped up onto a small boulder and took in the summit views while eating my other sandwich. Yes, my other sandwich. Two summits means two sandwiches, right? I stayed up there for around five minutes before beginning my descent. Since this was a shorter hike, I wanted to get home as soon as possible. Luckily for me the clouds started to shift at this point in the day, too, so I had enjoyable views during the trek down. I even had open views while I climbed over the treacherous log that I busted my knee on an hour prior. Maybe that was the High Peaks giving me a sign? Sunny views at the place that caused me so much pain earlier? The mountains were definitely trying to tell me something.

Anyways, still no sign of life yet and nothing too exciting to report on the descent. I passed my first person of the day when I got back to the drainage. A solo hiker from Canada. We had a quick conversation about the spiderwebs on the trail, which he brought up and made me laugh. Apparently after I destroyed their night's work, they rebuilt. Good for them, I suppose. Less than five minutes later I passed another solo hiker who said, "So you're the fresh footprints I've been following today." Nice guy. He was a trail runner wearing just a chest pack. I'll tell you, walking up mountains is hard enough, let alone running up and down them.

I didn't pass anybody else until I got back to the Indian Pass Brook crossing where I saw a family having the same confusion I did upon crossing. I pointed them to the trail and off they went. That's when I had one of the best ideas in the history of the High Peaks . . . I decided to dunk my head in the river. Having grown up in the Adirondacks, I spent many summers swimming in rivers and waterfalls, like Champagne Falls, Split Rock, the Flume, etc. It had been years since I swam in a river, though, and the second my head went underwater it tasted and felt just as I remembered. It was very nostalgic and brought back many great childhood memories for me. Fast-flowing ADK rivers have that familiar smell, taste, and feel that nothing else compares to. It felt great and was very refreshing.

Shortly after this river refreshment break, I passed a man with four girls between 10 and 12 years old. Seeing parents hiking with their children excites me greatly. The confidence climbing a mountain can instill in a child is unmatched. I hustled down the final flat mile of the trail and soon was back at the trail register to sign out. I arrived back at my car in the Loj parking lot at 10 a.m. on the nose, totaling the trip at 5.5 hours car-to-car.

Well, it was another successful day in the woods here on Street and Nye Mountains for High Peaks 7 and 8. A few bumps and giant bruises on the day, but it was my first time researching, planning, and carrying out a solo trailless hike, and my confidence was building. This would be the start of many more days to come. Thanks for reading my journey as I summit all 46 High Peaks of the Adirondacks in one summer. In the next chapter, Josh will come with me on my first big hike, the Dix Range, a hike where my feet would never quite be the same.

# 5 Giant Mountain and Rocky Peak Ridge

Giant (4,627'), Rocky Peak Ridge (4,420')
**Mileage:** 8.2 miles
**Elevation Gain:** 4,242'

Starting at the Giant Ridge trailhead on Route 73, this short and steep day in the High Peaks is arguably the most bang for your buck in terms of mileage-to-views ratio (along with Cascade and Porter). It's also one of the most popular hikes in the High Peaks because it's amazing from start to finish. The reason I prefer the Ridge Trail over the Roaring Brook trail is because the Ridge Trail frequently comes out of the tree line, offering outstanding views throughout the entire hike. When descending, they're right in front of you looking as glorious as ever. Of course, the Roaring Brook trail goes past the Roaring Brook waterfall, which is cool too. They're both valid choices, but I personally give the edge to the Ridge Trail.

Giant's Ridge Trail, however, is known for being a tough climb thanks to its three straight miles of 1,000' of gain. This mountain will have anyone breathing heavily from sign-in to summit. Sounds fun, right? There isn't a long approach, thankfully, so that keeps the mileage and overall hike time low compared to many other High Peaks.

The Rocky Peak Ridge trail split sits just below the Giant summit. Once there you can choose whether you want to continue to Giant's summit first or on the way back. Both summits are incredible and score a full 5/5 on the Summit Sandwich-ability (SSA) Scale. You will want to schedule adequate summit time on this hike.

The one-mile out-and-back to Rocky Peak Ridge is a challenge as you lose 600' of elevation over half a mile, then climb right back up to the summit. Then repeat on the way back. It's like going to Blake Peak, only the RPR summit is everything you could ever hope for, and Blake, well, leaves a lot to be desired. Poor Blake Peak; you're still cool though in your own way.

Giant and RPR are worth saving for a sunny day, but if you do tackle this on a rainy day, take it slow. This mountain involves open rock

# GIANT MOUNTAIN AND ROCKY PEAK RIDGE

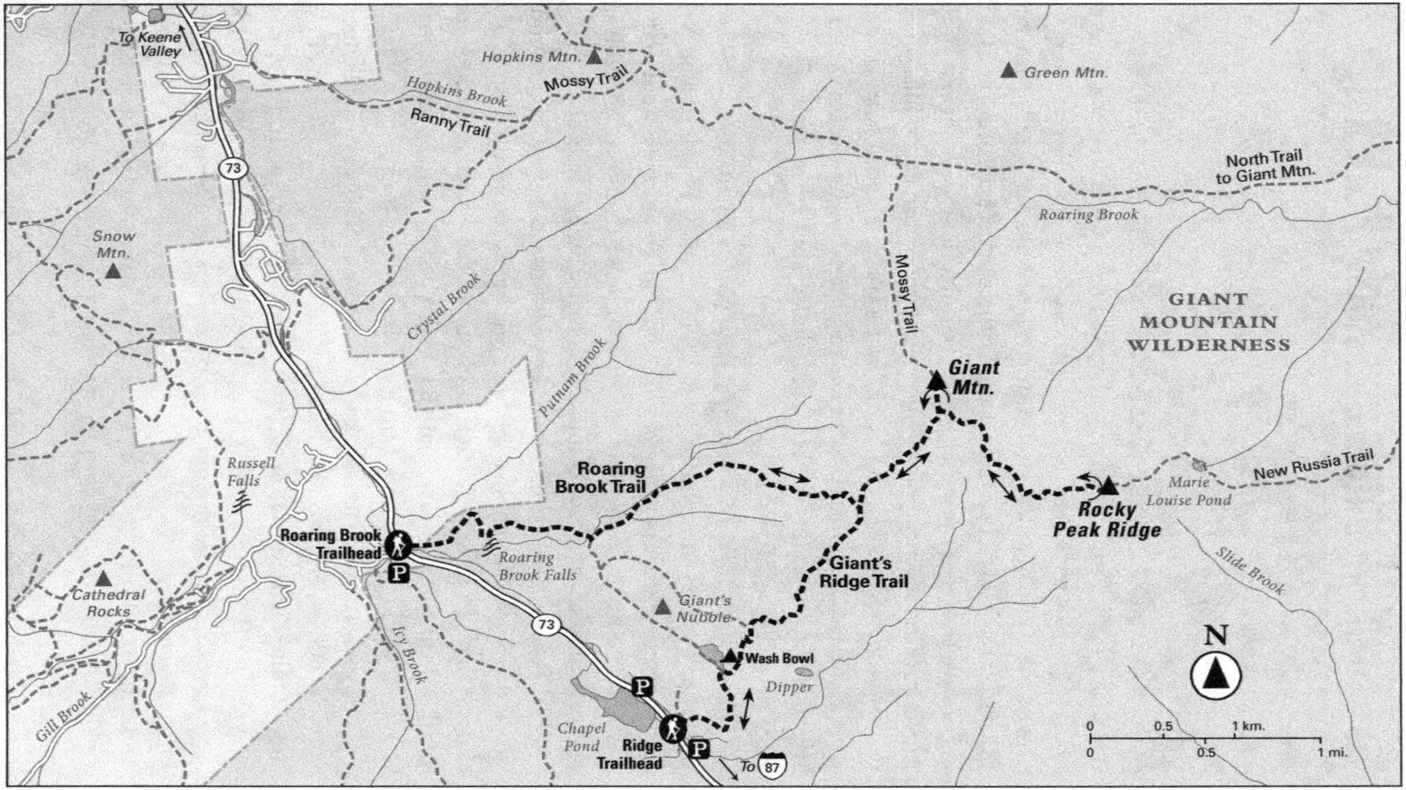

Green Mtn.

North Trail to Giant Mtn.

Roaring Brook

GIANT MOUNTAIN WILDERNESS

New Russia Trail

Marie Louise Pond

Rocky Peak Ridge

Slide Brook

Giant Mtn.

Mossy Trail

Giant's Ridge Trail

Wash Bowl

Dipper

To 87

Giant's Nubble

Ridge Trailhead

Roaring Brook Trail

Putnam Brook

Chapel Pond

73

Roaring Brook Falls

Hopkins Mtn.

Mossy Trail

Ranny Trail

Hopkins Brook

Crystal Brook

Roaring Brook Trailhead

Icy Brook

73

To Keene Valley

Russell Falls

Snow Mtn.

Cathedral Rocks

Gill Brook

N

0    0.5    1 km.

0    0.5    1 mi.

scrambles which, as the saying goes, are slippery when wet. Speaking of slippery when wet, let's find out about my slippery, wet, water-filled-boots day climbing Giant and Rocky Peak Ridge.

The view to the end of the earth from Giant. *Photo by James Appleton*

The Great Range Athlete Marcy Team hike on Giant and Rocky Peak Ridge, summer 2024. *Photo by James Appleton*

# Giant Mountain and Rocky Peak Ridge

*July 23, 2018. Three days after completing the Lower Great Range, it was time for a hike that I planned to do three different times but got rained or "lightning stormed" out of. So I kept pushing it off, but I decided today was the day regardless of the weather. It was a Monday morning, so I also knew the crowds on these popular peaks would be minimal. It was time for the beloved Giant and Rocky Peak Ridge. A shorter mileage day at around eight miles, but it packs a serious punch with 4,400' of elevation gain. The weather called for clouds with only a 10 percent chance of rain, so today was the day. The month was winding down, my next job was starting soon, and it was time to finally summit these two popular peaks.*

As always, that 3 a.m. alarm came quickly, and I was out the door driving from Saranac Lake to the Giant/Ridge trailhead parking just outside Keene Valley along Route 73. I pulled up to the trailhead, and it was very dark, and very empty. There was exactly one car at the trailhead, my car. I kind of figured I might have the whole mountain to myself today since it was a dark, cloudy Monday morning. Once I locked the car and started walking toward the woods, I realized I had forgotten to switch my rain jacket from my work backpack to my hiking backpack. Thankfully it was in my car. So I quickly turned around to grab the jacket, tied up my boots, and entered the woods. The hike was underway.

It took not more than 10 steps into the woods before I started to feel sprinkles of rain. Despite a 10 percent chance of rain later in the afternoon, it was already sprinkling. Even though I figured it would probably stop soon, I decided to throw on my raincoat anyway and take it off in a few minutes. But as luck would have it, that raincoat would stay on for the entire day.

I signed into the trailhead at 4:45 a.m., clicked on my headlamp, and began my hike up Giant. The 3,000' of elevation gain in three miles was underway. The trail begins with light switchbacks and rock hopping. It's a very worn trail, and therefore it's easy to follow and well marked (of course, the thousands of hikers a year on this trail make it hard to get lost here).

The rain continued getting stronger and stronger, and the humidity was getting worse and worse. Eventually I had to put my glasses in my pocket where they'd live for the rest of the day because they were too foggy. It's especially hard to see when you're wearing glasses and it's raining, foggy, and you're using a headlamp. It just doesn't work well.

The climbing continued and so did the rain as I came to the Giant Washbowl, which is a small pond that meets up with the Washbowl trail coming from the Giant–Roaring Brook trailhead. It's a fun spot worth taking a photo or two. I continued my climb up the Ridge Trail and hit another trail junction about half a mile past the Washbowl for the Giant's Nubble trail. It's around this point where this hike becomes very fun. One of the things that make Giant so appealing to hikers is its accessibility right off Route 73, and it's also a great hike. This part of the trail starts to include scrambles that involve coming out of the woods for an exposed scramble, then back into the woods for more trail hiking, then shortly after back out onto an open slab for more scrambling, and then back into the woods. So the views are abundant throughout a huge portion of this hike. It's filled with great places to stop and enjoy the scenery throughout.

Today, however, it was raining and I was in the clouds, so sadly there were zero views to be had (until my descent, thankfully). I kept ascending as the trail continued in the woods, then out of the woods for open rock scrambles, then back in the woods, then back on the slabs following cairns and trail markers up the slabs. It's just an awesome hike. I was getting a little nervous, however, because of how difficult coming down some of these wet slabs was going to be in the rain, but that was a problem for future James to deal with. Present James was enjoying the hike up and imagining how huge these views must be on a clear day.

About halfway up the mountain I arrived at a sign pointing left to go "around the hump" or straight to go "over the hump." I opted to go "around the hump" on the way up and planned to go "over" on the way down. I would end up going around the hump both times, though, because I seemed to miss the sign to go over. Oh well.

So, I went around the hump, which just takes you for a nice walk in the woods. Shortly thereafter you'll meet up with the Roaring Brook trail, and it's time to take a right to continue up the Ridge Trail. This was the final trail junction until the split for Rocky Peak Ridge. So, the first third of the trail was nice woodsy switchback rock hopping, the second third was scrambles coming in and out of the woods, and the final third was a mixture of everything. There are some longer scrambles the higher you get, so pay attention to the cairns. If you're new to hiking, "cairns" are rock stacks acting as a trail marker. You will travel from cairn to cairn.

The rain never let up, and to be honest I didn't even notice it anymore. What I did notice, however, was the wind. The higher I climbed the heavier it got. So much so that occasional gusts would throw me off balance. It was a wild experience.

I made the final scramble up to the trail split for Rocky Peak Ridge, marked by a sign that reads "1.2 miles to Rocky Peak Ridge." Upon reading that, I thought, "I wish it was a lot closer." My plan was to hit Giant first today, so I went left at the junction and continued the 0.1 miles to the summit of Giant. Normally I would summit the farther peak first, but this junction is basically at the summit, so I opted for the quicker win.

I arrived on the summit at 6:50 a.m., 2 hours and 5 minutes after signing in, marking my 26th High Peak. Giant Mountain is the 12th-tallest High Peak, standing at 4,627' elevation. On a nice day, this summit is breathtaking, but today it was heavy rain and wind. There wasn't much to see today so I snapped a quick photo and immediately headed back to the split to start my trek over to Rocky Peak Ridge.

I got back to the split below the summit and started the half-mile hike down to the col. This was certainly a difficult task today as the rain made for wet, slippery, muddy slabs. Getting to the col requires a lot of grabbing onto roots and butt sliding down these slabs as well (at least that's what worked well for me). It seemed never ending, and my feet were getting wetter and wetter with every minute. My boots were advertised as "waterproof" and it's even written right on the boot, but clearly that was not the case today.

It took a lot of effort but I made it into the col, and before beginning my ascent up Rocky Peak I decided to put on a fresh pair of socks. I quickly switched them out in the rain and started the trip up Rocky Peak. From the col to the summit is roughly 600' of gain over 0.6 miles, so it's right on par with the rest of the climbing today. My feet, however, were squishing with every step. Squish, squish, squish. My 10-minute-old socks were already drenched. Great. So I kept climbing up and squishing my way through the woods, and shortly after I made it out of the tree line, I was on the large, open rock summit of Rocky Peak Ridge, standing at 4,420' elevation on my 27th High Peak, just before 8 a.m.

It took me precisely one hour from Giant to Rocky Peak Ridge. This summit is massive and an amazing place to hang out on with 360-degree views. Of course, I was in the pouring rain, and the wind continued to whip fiercely on the summit, so it was a short stay. I quickly retreated into the tree line and out of the wind. Once back in the tree line, I decided to change my socks again (yes, I even had a third pair). This time I also swapped my boot insoles because they were soaked too. I like to carry additional insoles in my pack for this reason and because they weigh nothing but can be helpful in a pinch. I took off my boots one at a time and literally poured water out of each one. The squish life was real. I put the new insoles in, new socks on, and I felt great. Sadly, it only lasted for maybe 15 minutes before the squish returned. Drenched again. At this point I decided, "I'm heading to my car as fast as I can; if I get blisters, whatever. Let's just end this day."

After an hour of climbing back up Giant, grabbing roots and slipping on muddy slabs, I made it back to the trail split. The climb back up to Giant felt like the biggest grind of the day. Now for the fun trek down the mountain hoping I don't slip and take a hard fall on the slabs. Hiking solo in the rain on this mountain, in particular, is not something I necessarily recommend due to the possibility of a big fall. I also feel there are better rainy-day options out there. That being said, I did it, so maybe don't listen to me?

About halfway down I passed my first group of the day, a father and daughter, and they asked how the views were at the top today, and I said, "Nonexistent." I found the question odd considering it was pouring and seemed obvious. The man then told me these are the Adirondack days he and his daughter love to hike in. The wet, humid, muddy days in the High Peaks. It certainly has its own unique vibe and is typically unavoidable here due to the amount of rain we receive. I'll still take those perfect sunny, blue-sky Adirondack summer days over rainy ones. These rainy days give us the very green Adirondacks that we love, though, so I guess we take the good with the bad.

Shortly after, I passed the second and only other people for the day. A couple hiking their first Adirondack mountain. Hopefully they enjoyed themselves enough to try some other mountains, because today was not an ideal day in the woods for your first ADK hike.

As I descended one of the many open rock slabs, I noticed something happening in the sky. Something was moving above me. No, it wasn't a UFO. The clouds were moving! The clouds finally started to open revealing the magnificent Adirondack scenery they'd been hiding all day. I could see Giant Washbowl and the bottom half of the surrounding peaks. Another benefit to climbing this mountain via the Ridge Trail is the constant view in front of you throughout the descent. I stopped at a few different places and took in some views along with some photos. The clouds were moving fast so the views came and went, but at least I got something.

I kept squishing my way down the mountain one step at a time, dreaming of being home, taking a shower, and putting on dry clothes. I finally started to hear the road below and knew I was close. A few more steps and I was back to my car at 10:55 a.m., totaling the wet day at 6 hours and 10 minutes. Ironically, I made it out of this very wet day completely unscathed. No falls and shockingly no blisters. It was a Christmas in July miracle! It's no wonder these mountains are so popular. They offer a fantastic Adirondack adventure.

Another successful, albeit wet, day in the woods complete. So wet that I sent my boots back to Timberland for a new pair. It turned out my boots were in fact defective. There you have it. Case closed. They apologized for my wet day in the woods. It's cool, though, because those days always make for a fun story later, right? I eventually revisited Giant and RPR on a sunny day via the Roaring Brook trail, and I have to say, these summits are a lot nicer in the sun than the rain.

# 6 Dial and Nippletop Mountains

Dial (4,020'), Nippletop (4,620')
**Mileage:** 12.9 miles
**Elevation Gain:** 4,081'

Up next is Dial and Nippletop, two fantastic yet underrated mountains that both score high on the SSA Scale. This hike will begin at the AMR/Ausable Club/St. Hubert's trailhead. Remember, if you're hiking between May 1 and October 31, you will need a parking reservation from hikeAMR.org. I have hiked these mountains in both directions, starting with Dial and starting with Nippletop, and I don't see any disadvantage to either direction. So follow your heart on that one. I will say climbing up Bear Den (if you start with Dial) hits you quick with elevation gain, whereas hiking Nippletop offers a more gradual warmup for the day. Starting with Nippletop, however, involves climbing 1,100' over 0.6 miles up Elk Pass. So, do you want to go up Elk Pass or down it? Pick your poison.

All of that said, I will offer one recommendation as to why starting with Dial is a good choice, and it has to do with the next hike on the list, Colvin and Blake. Hiking the loop clockwise starting with Dial, then over to Nippletop, down Elk Pass, and back to the lake road will have you pass the trail junction for Colvin and Blake at the end. The summit of Blake is 2.5 miles away, and Colvin is even closer. If you have another five-mile out-and-back in your legs and lungs, you *could* add those two mountains since you're right there. It's nice because this route offers a game-time decision based on how your body and mind feel, what time it is, how much food and water you have left, etc. It makes for a big day, but it's very common to hike Dial, Nippletop, Blake, and Colvin in one push. Keep that in mind. It could turn into a two-for-one, four-High-Peaks kind of day. This is what I did, and it became my first big solo day in the High Peaks. Just be aware that those additional five miles and two High Peaks are no picnic thanks to Blake. If you want a big day, you can hike all four, but if you want two manageable days, break them up.

Okay. Lace up your boots and meet me on the lake road. It's time to take you on the first half of my day climbing Dial, Nippletop, Colvin, and Blake. Next stop, Dial Mountain.

## DIAL AND NIPPLETOP MOUNTAINS

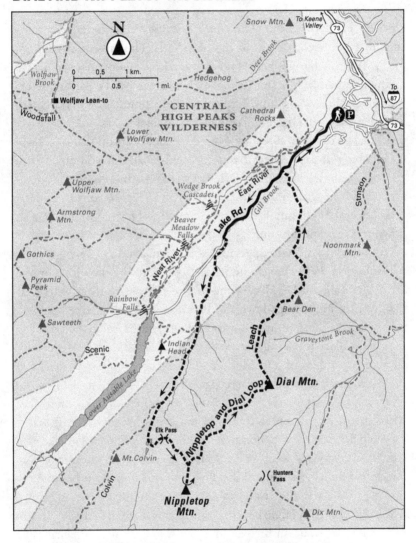

## Dial, Nippletop, Colvin, and Blake

*July 13, 2018. Just five days after hitting the Dix Range, it was time to test myself with my first big solo hike: Dial, Nippletop, Blake, and Colvin. This trip would weigh in at almost 19 miles and over 6,000' of elevation gain, making for another big High Peaks day. My plan for today was to park at St. Hubert's (also known as the Ausable Club or the AMR), walk down the lake road to the HG Leach trail, up and over Bear Den to Dial Mountain, then on to Nippletop, and down Elk Pass. Finally, I would decide in the moment when passing the Colvin trail junction if I was up for adding Colvin and Blake. If I was not up for them, I could complete the loop back to the lake road and come back for Blake and Colvin another day. Knowing I'm the type of person who always pushes myself physically, and knowing I'm the kind of hiker who would rather summit the mountains now rather than come back later, I knew I'd be bagging all four peaks today. So that's exactly what I did. That trip over to Blake Peak, though, that was no picnic. But I'll get to that later.*

I parked my car at the St. Hubert's/AMR parking lot in Keene Valley and began hiking at 4:30 a.m. The "4:30 crew" was just me today, but the start time remained the same. I clicked my headlamp on and started walking up the dark, quiet dirt road toward the Ausable Club golf course. Josh told me what to look for, though, and where to find the trailhead. I remember finding his directions quite confusing. They were as follows: "Park at the St. Hubert's lot, which is across the street from the Giant–Roaring Brook trailhead. Walk up the dirt road past the golf course, and then take a left between the tennis courts down to the trailhead. Can't miss it." Golf course? Tennis courts? I thought I was going to hike some High Peaks? Turns out these directions are incredibly accurate, but it was just strange to hear about tennis courts and a golf course when thinking about hiking remote Adirondack mountains. If I had known what the Ausable Club was, these directions would have made more sense. I do find it to be a unique vibe walking through the Ausable Club to get to these trails. There is a state easement through the property to access public land. Also, dogs are not allowed here on AMR property. Eventually, I came to the golf course on my right, lit up by my headlamp. Ah, all right, so Josh didn't steer me wrong. Next, I made the left between the tennis courts and saw the trailhead up ahead along with the giant wood gate. I was the first person to sign in once again. Nice. I strolled through the big wooden gate to the lake road and my day was underway.

The day begins walking on the infamous "lake road." Love it or hate it, if you hike in the High Peaks, you'll likely hike on the lake road at least a couple of times. It's a dirt road that leads to many different trails up many different mountains. I planned to hike the loop clockwise today starting with Dial, so I was looking for the Leach trail junction on the left-hand side of the road. A quick 1.2 miles after signing in, I came to the green rectangular sign with white letters reading "HG Leach Trail to Dial and Nippletop."

The night before, I decided that I wanted to get in the woods as fast as possible and I was going to save the long lake road walk for the end of the day. I figured by that point I would be fried, and a no-brainer couple-mile walk down a dirt road at the end of the day would be better for me since I was anxious about my first big solo hike. Despite Josh's recommendation of starting the loop with Colvin, I stuck with my game plan and went onto the Leach trail toward Dial. Trekking poles deployed. Let's climb some mountains!

The Leach trail starts by going up Bear Den Mountain (not to be confused with the Bear Den Mountain next to Whiteface Mountain). It's a curvy trail in the woods on soft ground, but it sure does go up immediately. Right from the start you begin gaining elevation quickly. It's certainly a grueling way to begin your day, but I wanted to get on trail as soon as possible. This mostly dirt trail has some small switchbacks and some steeper moments. There's one stretch of the trail surrounded by hundreds of unique trees. They're unique because it's new growth due to a forest fire in 1999 that burned over 90 acres of woods. Yes, forest fires happen in the ADK, and we need to do anything we can to avoid them. The area now has tons of black birch trees growing. You'll know when you're there. It kind of feels like something you'd see in Jurassic Park, to be honest. I assume I was being stalked by a couple of velociraptors. Most of the trail up Dial and Nippletop felt that way to me.

Another sunny and blue sky, perfect Adirondack summer day. Naturally the views and vibes were fantastic today as I made my way toward Dial while the sunshine lit up the woods. The first views of the day came as I reached the top of the Noonmark shoulder, which was also around the time the sun came up. There is a trail sign here letting you know Bear Den is still about a mile away and Dial is 2.1 miles away. I carried on.

The trail dips down as you leave Noonmark shoulder and goes back up to the wooded summit of Bear Den, which is marked by another trail sign stating "Dial Mt. 1.3 Miles, Nippletop 3.4 Miles." The trails today are all DEC marked and maintained trails, and they're easy to navigate (but you still need to do your homework and have a map with you). Getting to Dial took some time since you go over another mountain first, but the Leach trail is fun and diverse, making for an enjoyable hike. Then around 7 a.m., a good 2.5 hours into the day, I arrived at the open ledge boulder summit of Dial. What a view! Dial Mountain, standing at 4,020' elevation.

The summit is a big lookout with fantastic views of the Great Range. First things first, though; let's get that summit sandwich out. I dropped my backpack and enjoyed the delicious views with a delicious sandwich. About five minutes after summiting, I hopped off the summit ledge back on the Leach trail to begin the two-mile trek up the ridge toward Nippletop. The trip down to the col is quick, and then the majority of the mileage is a light, gradual elevation gain up the ridge. The woods during this stretch were picturesque and created the quintessential Adirondack vibe.

Once in the col I decided I needed some more fuel and grabbed a bag of peanut M&M's out of my belt pouch. As I pulled them out, I accidentally dumped the entire bag into the mud. Sadly, I forgot the bag was open, and out they went through the bottom of the bag. Awesome. I picked them all up out of the mud one by one where they went into a ziplock bag and eventually the garbage. The mud they fell into was too questionable to brush off. Plus, I had another bag. I pack a lot of food on the trail.

I made it to the wooden sign at the trail junction for Nippletop and Elk Pass in a flash. The trek between these two peaks is in my opinion one of the easier hikes between any two High Peaks in terms of physical exertion (which is ironic given what awaited me later in the day). At this junction you continue straight the final 0.2 miles to Nippletop. As you would expect, a quick hop, skip, and a jump later I was stepping onto the incredible summit of Nippletop. Talk about an amazing view and place to eat a victory summit sandwich.

The hike took me about an hour to go from Dial to Nippletop, and I landed at my destination at 8:15 a.m. Nippletop stands at 4,620' elevation for High Peak number 15, the tallest of the day. Time to eat another PB&J. I tend to bring one PB&J (or other sandwich) per summit anytime I hike in the High Peaks. So, besides snacks, Shot Bloks, and gels, if I'm summiting four peaks, you better believe I'm bringing four sandwiches. I always eat before I get hungry so that my body is constantly fueled.

Still no sign of other human life yet on the day. After taking in the summit scenery for a few minutes, which includes front-row seats of Colvin and Blake, it was time to head toward those mountains because they were up next. This was one of the more difficult parts of the day in my opinion. Elk Pass is steep! Don't stub your nose. Part of the reason I chose to hike today's loop in this direction was because I wanted to go down Elk Pass instead of up. It's just as difficult physically going up or down, but in different ways. Over the years I'd come to prefer going up these steep trails, but today I descended it. Slowly, but I descended. The one-mile Elk Pass trail is roughly 1,200' of elevation loss in 0.7 miles. Steep!

Toward the bottom of the trail as I approached the ponds I heard voices at a nearby campsite. Okay, I'm not the only human being left on planet Earth anymore. There are others amongst me. Good to know. The bottom of Elk Pass brings you in between a couple of ponds, and after that descent they were a welcome sight. Peaceful little ponds. Shortly after getting to the bottom, as I walked between the ponds on the wooden boardwalks, I passed my first hikers for the day. Two guys in their early 20s who could not believe I had already summited both Dial and Nippletop. I like to start early, what can I say?

After more walking I finally came to the trail junction marking the end of Elk Pass, the Colvin trail, and the Gill Brook trail. I stopped for a few gulps of some water from my Nalgene as a couple of different groups of hikers passed. Every single group asked me how steep Elk Pass was. I think by my slight pause and my eyes getting bigger before answering them they knew what awaited them. Just as I strapped on my backpack to begin the trek up the Colvin trail, another solo hiker walked up, eyeballed the junction signs, and started up Colvin. C'mon. Okay, well I guess I'm going to just stand here for another couple minutes to give him a head start because it's the worst when you just pass someone and then feel like they're on your heels, or vice versa. I gave him a few minutes' head start before starting my climb. I was overly excited to summit two additional High Peaks today. My first big solo day was going well so far.

Up next, however, I had a long five miles ahead of me to get back to this trail junction before hiking out. It was time, however, to finally meet the infamous Blake Peak.

To be continued . . .

# 7  Colvin and Blake Mountains

Colvin (4,057'), Blake (3,960')
**Mileage:** 13.7 miles
**Elevation Gain:** 4,035'

Starting once again at the AMR/Ausable Club/St. Hubert's trailhead in Keene, this hike is another 46'er journey milestone. Blake Peak is often listed on 46'er registrations as hikers' "least favorite" mountain. It's hard to blame anyone, really. It's a tough climb that involves a whole lot of work for a very wooded summit. That's all part of the collective 46'er journey, though. Colvin ranks 3/5 on the SSA Scale, while Blake would score an underwhelming 1/5.

Named after Mills Blake, the right-hand man of great Adirondack surveyor and Adirondack Park legend Verplanck Colvin. These two were childhood best friends and lifelong confidants, so it's great that they still come as a package deal.

The hike from the parking lot to the summit of Colvin is fantastic. A gradual hike on a nice trail that finishes with a fun root climb to the summit of Colvin where amazing views of the Ausable lakes await you. The summit is an open rock ledge with views of Indian Head down below and Sawteeth in front of you.

Once leaving the summit of Mt. Colvin, however, is when the hike takes a turn downhill—literally and figuratively. The never-ending climb down to the col between Colvin and Blake is more than 500' of elevation loss over half a mile. You'll even have Blake gloriously towering directly ahead, taunting you at what's still to come. What's still to come is immediately gaining roughly 500' back up over 0.4 miles to the wooded, viewless, underwhelming summit. This is all part of the High Peaks journey, though, so just lean into it.

Summiting Blake is a lot of work for very little payoff in terms of views or the SSA Scale. Some people love that kind of climb, although I don't believe anyone who says they prefer the summit of Blake to the summit of a High Peak with a view. Yes, I've heard people try to make this claim. They're not fooling anyone.

So, after the haul to get from Colvin to Blake, it's time to do it all over again to get back to Colvin. It's a tough one, plain and simple. It's a rite of passage, though, and always makes for a good story. You'll experience a sense of camaraderie with anyone you pass on that hike.

## COLVIN AND BLAKE MOUNTAINS

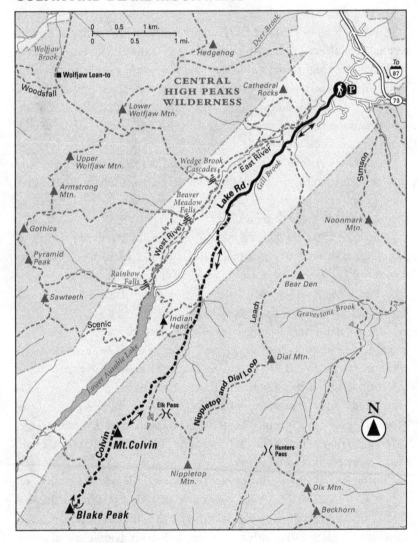

Keep all of this in mind should you decide to add these peaks to Dial and Nippletop. Either way, have a good time out there, and remember, any day in the High Peaks is better than a day at work!

Taking in a glorious High Peaks summer morning on Nippletop. Podcast recorder attached to chest strap for good measure. *Photo by James Appleton*

My hiking partner, Josh Bliss, taking in the magnificent summit of Blake. *Photo by James Appleton*

## Colvin and Blake Mountains

*Continuing from my hike up Dial and Nippletop, next up were Colvin and Blake. From the trail junction, Blake is further away at 2.4 miles, adding up to a 4.8-mile round-trip to summit both Colvin and Blake. Less than five miles to get both peaks? Definitely. Famous last words, though, since I had yet to experience the col between Colvin and Blake. This seemingly innocent five-mile round-trip will make you earn those two High Peaks. Granted you earn every High Peak, but even more so here. It's also a somewhat deceiving sign because while it's less than five miles, it's a hard five miles with a lot of elevation change going from mountain to mountain (and back again). But hiking mountains isn't supposed to always be "easy," right? Onward to Colvin!*

*I began hiking only to pass my fellow solo hiker about five minutes into my trip up Colvin when he stopped to take photos. Then 10 minutes later he passed me again. Then the leap-frogging continued as I passed him for the second time while snapping more photos, only to be passed again by him a few minutes later. I decide to stop and chill for a few minutes and catch my breath, drive a Snickers bar into me, and end this back-and-forth. I would eventually see him again up on Colvin, and then on the way up Blake, but it concluded the constant passing of one another.*

*Carrying on up the Colvin trail climbing ledges and boulders, jumping over mud pits, and enjoying the trek toward this great summit. A great summit named after the leader of the Great Adirondack Survey, Verplanck Colvin. An absolute legend and one of the original champions of the formation of the Adirondack Park in the late 19th century. The climb from the junction to the summit is relatively steep with 1,000' of gain through one mile with lots of slab climbing and scrambling. The hike also ends with a fun rock-and-root climb up to the true summit. A big ledge clearing with fantastic views of the Great Range, Sawteeth, Indian Head, and Ausable Lake. After climbing up those rocks and roots, I finally summited Colvin at 10:15 a.m. for my third High Peak of the day at just under six hours into my hike for number 16 of 46. Another excellent summit to enjoy a sandwich with magnificent views standing 4,057'.*

*The summit had six people on it as I arrived, which made it full but manageable (any more people and it would have been too crowded). It was nice to engage in human interaction and great conversations with* the other hikers after spending the morning solo. One of the hikers, Eli, and I would run into each other again weeks later near Skylight. Not only that, but we would also even go on to hike the Seward Range together and form an actual friendship. It would have been wild to learn what our future would entail upon meeting each other on the summit. You never know what trail friendships will form out in those mountains.

While on the summit, everyone was talking about the number of High Peaks they were at on their way to 46. Everyone else was in their 20s or 30s, which bummed me out because I was only at 16 at that point. So far to go but plugging away little by little every week. It was, however, a good moment to remind myself, "This isn't a race; enjoy the journey."

Speaking of enjoying my journey, after downing another peanut butter and jelly along with a 20-minute stay on Colvin staring out at the Great Range, Sawteeth, and the Ausable River below, I started my 1.3-mile out-and-back hike over to Blake. I wasn't fully aware of how steep it is to Blake until the other hikers on Colvin told me about it. They weren't kidding. Getting to the col means losing a ton of elevation very quickly (roughly 600' down over half a mile and 600' up, then repeat coming back). Down, down, down. Very steep with multiple wooden ladders over slabs. It's slow moving for sure. Throughout the trek down to the col you'll get plenty of front-row seats of Blake towering above you.

Blake Peak is named after Verplanck Colvin's right-hand man, lifelong confidant, and childhood best friend, Mills Blake. So it's only appropriate that these two mountains typically come as one hike. I absolutely love Adirondack history, so it makes me happy that well after their deaths these two ADK legends still come as a package deal. I'm a big fan of Verplanck Colvin, his story, and his legacy in the Adirondack Park.

Once you get down to the col it's time to go right back up, so I wasted no time and began climbing. The woods on Blake consist of mostly evergreens, and the trail, though quite eroded, involves a decent amount of climbing slabs up rugged sections. Be careful and cognizant of where you're stepping and what you're grabbing onto during these climbs.

For anyone going through their journey to 46, Blake Peak is a rite-of-passage mountain. If the mountains were individual movies, Blake would undoubtedly be a "coming-of-age drama about a parent-less child growing up and having to figure out the world, love, and his purpose on his own." It's a tough climb without any reward at the top. Well, I should clarify: it doesn't have a reward in the traditional sense when it comes to big summit views (although the other three mountains of the day all do). The reward on Blake is still a reward; it's just the reward of knowing you made it to the top of a tough mountain. Sometimes the reward at the summit is simply knowing you accomplished the task and a "job well done." More parallels between real life and the lessons we can learn here in the mountains.

About halfway up, I passed a backpack sitting just off the trail. It belonged to my Albany friend that I played tag with ascending Colvin. He dropped his pack to finish Blake in an easier fashion. He was a brave man since this summer had so many bears and Sasquatches stealing people's backpacks. Dropping pack is not my style, personally, but I see the benefit of it from time to time.

So, after lots of climbing and heavy breathing, I made it the 0.5 miles to the summit of Blake standing at 3,960' elevation marked by a medium-sized rock and a trail sign conveniently pointing you back to Colvin (as well as the ridge to Pinnacle). It's a painfully wooded summit with zero views. There's a reason so many people list Blake as their least favorite High Peaks hike. I get it, and I don't blame people for feeling this way. Every mountain has a unique story to tell, though, and collectively they all make the journey special. Some are certainly more enjoyable than others. I summited Blake Peak at 11:30 a.m. Seven hours into the day for High Peak number 17 and four-of-four on the day.

It took me exactly one hour to go from Colvin to Blake and one hour to go back for a two-hour round-trip to Blake. I stayed on Blake for maybe 30 seconds before starting the trip back down. I didn't even take off my backpack. Snapped a photo, looked around, and then turned around.

I passed my new Lake George friends Eli and Josh again just before arriving at the col. We said hello and I wasted no time beginning the trip back up Colvin. I had a nice mental "high" knowing I had summited all four peaks today solo, and that high propelled me energetically back up Colvin.

Up the ledges, up the ladders, and up the trail I went. Once arriving back at the Colvin summit, I decided to eat my final PB&J to fuel up for the hike out. This time there were three guys and a girl enjoying lunch on the summit. She was very chatty, but all three guys sat in silence looking disheveled and miserable. It's hard to be miserable when in the High Peaks on a perfect ADK summer day. The girl was hiking the same route I did today, but she was also adding Sawteeth. She's hard core. Personally, I was more than ready to head back to my car.

I crushed my final sandwich and headed back down Colvin in what felt like record time, back to the Gill Brook trail junction. I was finally on the Gill Brook trail, which would take me out to the lake road where I could zone out and relax knowing I completed navigating my first big solo hike. Getting back to the lake road was the victory moment I thought about all day.

The Gill Brook trail is a nice gradual trail, and I can see why people like ascending this trail because of its gradual nature. I was semi–trail running at this point to make good time. Flying past trees and rocks and ducking and dodging branches. Just straight cruising. I was floating down that trail quite gracefully for a big guy with a big pack. Moments later, however, is when it all came crashing down. Mid-run I stepped on a rock that rolled my ankle. "Oh no, did I just break my ankle?" I thought to myself. This would be a terrible ending to an otherwise perfect day. I stopped and composed myself, standing in one place before beginning to move. So, I looked around and slowly took a step, adding a little more weight, then a little more, and a little more after that, just waiting for the pain to show itself. I was okay, thank God. No pain. I sure dodged a bullet there. At that point I decided to slow down to get to the lake road in one piece. I kept telling myself, "Just get to the lake road." Time to start walking.

I eventually hit the Gill Brook cutoff trail and called an audible. This trail would put me further up the lake road, but it would get me out of the woods and on the lake road quicker, so I decided to take it. A few minutes later I made it to the dirt road known as the lake road. I was thrilled to be there. I still had a roughly three-mile walk back to the trailhead down this hard dirt road where time feels like it stands still, but now I could zone out knowing the hard work and navigating were done.

I was mentally fried and ready to be finished after a mile on the lake road, that's for sure. One foot in front of the other, I soon passed the one-mile marker on the lake road when I suddenly felt it. Oh no! Yup, I was getting a blister . . . on both feet! It looked like I wasn't going to make it out of this day unscathed, and I ended the day with a blister in the middle of both feet that were both developed over the final mile of the hike on the lake road. Damn. Well, I almost made it.

I finally signed out and was back at the Ausable Club walking along the golf course after going between the tennis courts once again. I was out of the woods but not back at my car yet. As I approached the final hill going down to the AMR parking lot, I passed a local gentleman who asked me, "Hey, where did you hike today?" I told him what I did, and he started talking to me and asked where I'm from, to which I answered, "Lake Placid." He then began asking me if I know various people in Lake Placid (coincidentally I did know some of these people). This gentleman was really going for it today with the conversation. As a people person who typically seeks out connection with others, I normally would be all about this chat. However, I was approaching hour 11 on my hike, and I could literally see my car in the parking lot, so all I could think about was getting to that car. I was not going to disengage, though, because that's not my way, especially when someone shows interest in something I'm doing. The conversation eventually ended organically, and I finally made it back to my car, officially ending my day at 3:30 p.m. A long yet enjoyable 11-hour day.

Now it was time to kick off the boots, put on the Crocs, and drive to Stewart's for another post-hike milkshake! Of course, I hobbled into Stewart's because once the boots come off and I sit in a car for 10 minutes, my body shuts down entirely. But the beautiful salty sweet treat made me forget about my sore feet and joints as I devoured a victory milkshake once again. Chocolate peanut butter cup. My go-to flavor.

Another very successful day in the woods as I completed my first big solo trek on my sixth hike where I summited Dial, Nippletop, Colvin, and Blake for peak numbers 14, 15, 16, and 17 on my journey to hiking all 46 Adirondack High Peaks in one summer. A memorable day and a big confidence booster early on in my High Peaks journey. In the next chapter, the weather will change drastically as Josh and I head into the MacIntyre Range up the mighty Algonquin, Iroquois, and Wright.

# 8 MacIntyre Range (Algonquin Peak, Iroquois Peak, Wright Peak)

Algonquin (5,114'), Iroquois (4,840'), Wright (4,580')
**Mileage:** 11.4 miles
**Elevation Gain:** 4,423'

Starting at the Adirondack Loj trailhead in Lake Placid, the MacIntyre Range (Algonquin Peak, Iroquois Peak, Wright Peak) is a fan favorite and is, in my opinion, the most iconic-looking range in the High Peaks. Algonquin can be seen all over Lake Placid in all its glory. It screams power and majesty as it towers high in the Adirondack skyline.

This is one of those hikes that seem a lot more daunting than they are due to the size of the mountains, but the elevation gains at a gradual rate. The views on all of these peaks are indescribable. All three summits score a perfect 5/5 on the SSA Scale. Make sure you bring three sandwiches for this range. The summits on all three peaks are also enormous and above the tree line. After leaving the tree line on Algonquin, it feels like you've entered a different world. It's truly spectacular and unbeatable, especially on a sunny day.

The higher elevation and exposed nature of these summits, however, make them quite susceptible to windy conditions. Be prepared. Follow the cairns and blazes up and down the summits of Wright and Algonquin.

You're welcome to summit Wright before Algonquin or hit it on the way back. Both ways work just fine. The view of Algonquin from Wright is wild. I feel Wright is underappreciated because it gets overshadowed by Algonquin. Then again, it's hard to compete with the mighty Algonquin.

After summiting Algonquin, where views of Colden, Marcy, and more await, it's time to go over to Iroquois. Be aware of the correct trail when you get back into the tree line on your way to Iroquois. It's easy to accidentally take the wrong trail and begin heading down Algonquin. Once you get back to the tree line you'll see a wood sign with

# MACINTYRE RANGE (ALGONQUIN PEAK, IROQUOIS PEAK, WRIGHT PEAK)

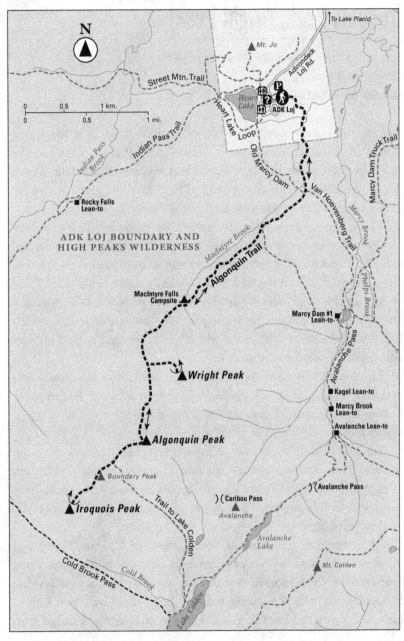

N

To Lake Placid

Mt. Jo

Street Mtn. Trail

Adirondack Loj Rd.

Heart Lake

Heart Lake Loop

ADK Loj

Old Marcy Dam

Marcy Dam Truck Trail

Van Hoevenberg Trail

Marcy Brook

0    0.5    1 km.
0    0.5    1 mi.

Indian Pass Brook

Indian Pass Trail

Rocky Falls Lean-to

ADK LOJ BOUNDARY AND
HIGH PEAKS WILDERNESS

MacIntyre Brook

Algonquin Trail

Phelps Brook

MacIntyre Falls Campsite

Marcy Dam #1 Lean-to

Avalanche Pass

Wright Peak

Kagel Lean-to

Marcy Brook Lean-to

Avalanche Lean-to

Algonquin Peak

Boundary Peak

Trail to Lake Colden

Caribou Pass

Avalanche Pass

Iroquois Peak

Avalanche

Avalanche Lake

Mt. Colden

Cold Brook Pass

Cold Brook

Lake Colden

an arrow pointing left. Do not follow. Instead, go straight. The trail to Iroquois is technically an unmaintained herd path, whereas the arrow sign is pointing you on the maintained Algonquin trail down to Lake Colden. If you start losing elevation quickly you've gone the wrong way. This trail sign can be deceiving, but now you know to watch for it.

After ignoring the left arrow and instead going straight at this junction, you will head through the trees over Boundary Peak and on to Iroquois. On my 46'er registration, I listed Algonquin as my favorite mountain. It will not be hard for you to understand why once you get to the summit.

Okay, let's go have ourselves a wet and rainy day in the MacIntyre Range followed by an unfortunate series of events as Josh and I search for that perfect post-hike meal . . .

An amazing spring morning just after sunrise on Wright Peak overlooking Algonquin to the right and Mt. Colden on the left with Mt. Marcy in the background. *Photo by James Appleton*

## MacIntyre Range (Algonquin Peak, Iroquois Peak, Wright Peak)

*July 15, 2018. Just two days after successfully climbing Dial, Nippletop, Blake, and Colvin solo, I was back in the woods ready to climb the mighty MacIntyre Range—Algonquin, Iroquois, and Wright—arguably the most visually iconic range of them all. Two days prior the weather was sunny and blue, but as it goes here in the Adirondack Mountains, the weather changes drastically and quickly. Today was the opposite, with rain and heavy winds, but the elements added to the experience, making today's hike one of my favorites on my journey to 46.*

Josh came with me on this 11-mile hike with over 4,300' of elevation gain. As always, the 4:30 crew were the first to sign in at the Adirondack Loj to begin our day. Headlamps clicked on, backpack straps tightened, and we were off hustling down the Van Hoevenberg trail in the pitch black. We made great time for the first mile to the trail split for Algonquin, marked by a wooden sign. Algonquin right, Marcy Dam left. So, for the first time I turned right toward Algonquin. Our plan for the day was to summit Algonquin first, then out-and-back Iroquois, and then hit Wright on our way down the mountain. Like most days, I prefer summiting the mountains farthest from the trailhead first and then making my way back throughout the day.

The first portion of the trail is a mix of soft dirt and a lot of rock hopping. These are highly trafficked mountains, so the DEC has done a great job making the trail durable for the hiker volume it receives. In fact, I'd say this trail has even "too many" rocks to walk on going up. It could be considered an "ankle breaker" type trail, but it does help maintain the foot traffic. Every mountain has its own story to tell and experience to share, right?

We wouldn't see any other hikers until later on when we made our way back from Iroquois. It was a nice quiet trip up as the sun began to rise, and we eventually got our first views of the day of some cliffs that Josh told me are a big rock-climbing destination here in the ADK. It's known simply as the "Wright Mountain climbing area." Appropriately named, I would say.

The trail up Algonquin is a gradual, consistent climb leading up to the trail split for Wright, which is marked by a sign at a decent-sized trail junction. This trail junction is 3.5 miles from the trailhead and sits right around 4,000' elevation, while the summit of Wright Peak is less than half a mile away. As tempting as it was to go grab Wright first, we stuck to our plan and went straight toward Algonquin. This is the point where the trail becomes much steeper and there's a lot of slab climbing, so I hope your shoes are nice and "grippy." A little over 1,100' of gain over 0.7 miles is sure to have your heart pumping and your legs burning. This stretch made the climb to Algonquin one of my favorite High Peaks hikes. There's a stretch of slab that is devastatingly long, and once arriving at the top you round the corner and learn you're only halfway up the slab. Soul crushing yet fun all at the same time.

After taking a minute to catch our breath and taking a swig of some electrolytes, we kept on climbing up as the humidity and rain continued to make it impossible to see out of my glasses. To my fellow four-eyed friends, I feel your pain. Eventually I took them off and went without because they were more harm than help.

Despite being the second-tallest mountain in New York State, the hike is relatively quick given the mountain's size. There are many shorter mountains in the High Peaks that are much harder on the legs and lungs to climb. Once the trail leaves the tree line, however, it feels as if you've been transported to another world. The summit felt like a scene from the movie The Princess Bride. Rock slabs and green alpine vegetation all around you as cairns and yellow blazes lead you up to the summit. On a clear day this portion above the tree line is indescribable, but today we were in the clouds. The howling wind and heavy rain continued as we carried on up the final stretch to the summit. It didn't bother me, though, because the vibes the weather offered today created a unique and fun experience all the same. I'll always opt for a bluebird ADK day in the mountains over rain, but sometimes there's something special about climbing mountains in the rain.

Another reason I loved this hike so much was because we arrived at the first summit just around the time into the hike when I was mentally ready to be there. You know when you're hiking and you get to that point where you say to yourself, "Okay, I'm ready to be at the top now"? We arrived at the summit just before my brain got to that point, so that was a great feeling.

We officially arrived on the true summit of Algonquin at 6:50 a.m., just under two and a half hours after signing in for High Peak number 18 of 46.

Standing at 5,114' elevation, Algonquin is the second-tallest High Peak and, in my opinion, the most visually iconic peak in the Adirondack Park. Some may argue Marcy or Colden is, but those people would be wrong. Algonquin is king!

On a clear day the views are stellar in every direction on this enormous, open rock summit, but we were fully in the clouds. Literally standing in the sky in the clouds is fun, though, when you stop to think about it. We slammed a quick peanut butter and jelly sandwich in the rain before starting the mile trip along the ridge over Boundary to Iroquois. On a clear day you can see Iroquois and head straight toward it, but with zero visibility today, navigating off the summit was a challenge. We walked up over the top of the summit and down the backside, following the cairns and yellow trail markers back to the tree line the best we could. It was slow going, but we made it.

Once you get back in the tree line, there's another trail split. This split often gets people lost who aren't paying attention. When you're inside the tree line, you can keep going straight, which takes you over Boundary to Iroquois via the Iroquois trail, or you can go left down the Algonquin trail toward Lake Colden, Mt. Marshall, Avalanche Pass, etc. You'll know you went the wrong way if you start losing elevation rapidly (this Algonquin trail is steep). Also, now that you've read this and looked at your map, if you turned left instead of going straight, that will give you a clue too, right?

The trail to Iroquois involves a quick trip up and over Boundary Peak, which is over 4,000' at 4,829' but due to various technicalities is not considered one of the 46 High Peaks (it's often thought of as a sub-summit of Iroquois). I met a couple of hikers later in my 46'er journey who told me they unknowingly stopped at Boundary instead of going all the way over to Iroquois. So once again, study the map, the trail, and the topography ahead of time the best you can to set yourself up for a successful day in the mountains.

The hike over to Iroquois is easy to navigate and extremely narrow. On a clear day it would be fantastic, with many views to be enjoyed throughout the trek over. After about 40 minutes after leaving the Algonquin summit, we made it to Iroquois at 7:40 a.m., just over three hours after signing in. Iroquois is the eighth-tallest High Peak, standing at 4,840' elevation, and marked number 19 of 46 on my journey.

Due to the heavy wind and consistent rain once again, we just took a picture, gulped some water, and immediately began the trek back to Algonquin. Just below the summit while walking along a boardwalk tucked in between the wet trees, we passed our first humans of the day. They were right on our tracks and signed in at 4:45 a.m., only 15 minutes after us. It was nice to meet some other early birds out on the trail today.

Back up to Algonquin we went. The two-mile out-and-back to Iroquois took 1 hour and 20 minutes round-trip, and by the time we got back up to Algonquin, Josh and I both decided to switch out our socks for some fresh ones. The heavy lifting of the day was behind us, and it was time to ascend toward David Wright Peak. It's not really named after David Wright. David Wright is a New York Mets legend and deserves a mountain named after him, though. Let's go, Mets!

If you recall, on my last couple of hikes with Josh my feet swelled up like a couple of blue whales after taking my boots off. I was trying to avoid the same fate today; therefore, I knew I had to make this sock switch quickly and precisely. So I took my socks out of my bag, lined them up, and prepared for the fastest sock switch the High Peaks had ever seen. I quickly kicked one boot off, pulled off the wet sock, and pulled on the new sock before sliding my foot right back into my boot. Boom! Probably a sub-20-second switch per boot, I'd estimate. I was determined to end this day with healthy feet, and fortunately because I had the reflexes of a cat and the speed of a mongoose, today I was successful in the wet sock transition.

As we began heading back down Algonquin, we passed several hikers on their way up, and we had a quick conversation with one of the Summit Stewards while he hiked up. Down the long slabs of Algonquin we went. We moved quickly despite the slippery conditions and made it back to the Wright trail split where we ran into the largest hiking group I saw all summer. There were at least a dozen hikers spread out across the junction. They were all resting and refueling, but basically blocking the trail because there were so many of them. We said our hellos and quickly scampered around them to start climbing Wright.

As I mentioned earlier, the Wright trail junction is less than a half mile from the summit with about 500' of gain, so we made quick work of it. Fifteen minutes later we were above the tree line climbing up the open slabs approaching the true summit. The summit is similar in nature and vibe as Algonquin. This summit, however, offered something new today that we were not expecting. Something changed in the sky. The rain finally stopped, and the clouds were moving. We had some views! Yes! What an amazing and unexpected treat to experience as we walked onto the summit of Wright Peak, our third and final mountain of the day for High Peak number 20 of 46!

The summit of Wright stands at 4,580' elevation and is yet another huge, open rock summit with full 360-degree views. This range is one of the best because all three peaks are worth spending a lot of time on. Of course, we didn't have those views for most of the day, but we sure got them here as the clouds opened to reveal Algonquin towering above us (literally) while Colden constantly drifted in and out of the clouds. We dropped our packs, sat on a ledge, ate another sandwich, and enjoyed the show the Adirondack sky was putting on for us. The clouds would open for a minute, then cover the mountains, then open again and show us magnificent views, then take them away. It's fun to see Algonquin while standing on Wright and knowing, "I just came from there!" I love that feeling every time.

After enjoying a victory summit sandwich 4,500' up in the misty Adirondack skies, we explored the plane crash wreckage that still sits around the summit before heading down the mountain. On January 16, 1962, a B-47 bomber on a training mission crashed into Wright Peak, killing all four crewmen. Due to inclement weather that night, the bomber veered about 30 miles off course and into the High Peaks region. The crew was likely headed toward the Plattsburgh Air Force Base. There's a memorial plaque, and parts of the plane wreckage are scattered around the summit. It's a haunting vibe as you see the actual wreckage still there to this day, I will be honest.

After exploring we began our descent back to the Loj, passing dozens of groups heading up for the day. Many comments again along the lines of "You're already coming down! Wow!" Of course, because the 4:30 crew needs to get home for their post-hike afternoon nap, right? It's what makes it all worthwhile. I love that nap. It's also never intentional and just happens once I eventually sit down.

While we were hustling down the trail, Josh and I decided we were definitely going to McDonald's after this wet day in the High Peaks. After being rained on for six hours, what sounded better, you know? Oh, and don't forget, calories don't count on hiking days, right? So we had that on our minds fueling our speed-demon ways down the mountain.

There was an expected number of hikers heading up the MacIntyre Range on this rainy July day as we passed them all coming up. We made our way down the endless miles of rocks that make up the Algonquin trail before arriving back at the Algonquin trail split. The final-mile push back to the Loj parking lot was all that stood between us and being dry . . . and hot food. As we sped down the trail, we passed a couple of guys in their 20s who stepped aside and said "Whoa, you guys are cruising!" to which we yelled back mid-stride, "We gotta get to McDonald's!" They laughed, we laughed, but boy did we mean business because I needed those french fries.

Down to the wood bridge, over the bridge, and back up to the final stretch to the trailhead, and soon we were back at the trailhead at 1:35 p.m. Our day on the MacIntyre Range was 7 hours and 5 minutes car-to-car. It would have been longer if we'd had nice weather, but our summit stays totaled less than 30 minutes combined. This is the type of range where every single peak is worth a 30-minute stay. Save this range for a sunny day!

Now that the hike was over, we had more important business to attend to: we had to get to McDonald's for a victory meal. Upon arriving we walked inside to a line literally to the back of the restaurant. When does this ever happen in Lake Placid? This is insane. Now we needed to make a game-time decision to wait in line or go elsewhere despite having our heart set on salty, unhealthy fast food. We decided that since we were going to Saranac Lake anyway, we could just go to that McDonald's instead since this line alone will easily take 30 minutes. So we left.

Ten minutes later we pulled into the Saranac Lake McDonald's where a giant Greyhound bus sprawled across the parking lot. Oh no, not again. Inside we were greeted with chaos. There were dozens of kids lined to the door and scattered everywhere. What is happening! This is the Adirondacks; we don't have lines at McDonald's of all places. It turns out these kids were from a local summer camp. Becoming hungrier by the minute, Josh declared, "I'm not waiting. I need to eat now. Let's just go to the Chinese buffet across the street so we can be eating within four minutes." I didn't want to, but I was also hungry and concurred. So we left. Again.

Going with today's theme of a wet, mostly viewless High Peaks day, our meal was awful, just plain awful. Josh and I didn't even finish our plate. I'm not proud of what happened next. In a moment of pure defeat and utter desperation, I stared Josh in the face and suggested, "I know we just spent this money . . . but let's go back to McDonald's. I bet the line has died down. We can cut our losses and get what our hearts desired." Josh pondered this plan quietly to himself. Then he said the only two words I wanted to hear: "I'm in."

So we did it. Yes, we went back to McDonald's after already eating Chinese and got the meal our hearts desired. The emotions we felt while eating that meal were a mixture of victory, defeat, joy, and self-loathing with every bite. I mean we just had Chinese food and are at McDonald's. To add insult to injury, the food was lukewarm too. Terrible. It was a fitting end to our wet, muddy, rainy day in the High Peaks.

So, another successful day in the woods ended with two different McDonald's, a terrible meal at a Chinese buffet, and then a pathetically fat second meal at McDonald's to finish us off. But today's adventure in the High Peaks, however, was excellent—despite the rain—resulting in some of my favorite peaks of the summer. Algonquin, Iroquois, and Wright for High Peaks numbers 18, 19, and 20. I'm in the 20s and almost halfway on my seventh hike as I tackle all 46 Adirondack High Peaks in one summer. Next time the weather will be the exact opposite once again as I embark on a bluebird summer day on the Lower Great Range where I'll officially pass the halfway point on my journey to 46!

# 9  Lower Great Range (Sawteeth, Gothics, Armstrong Mountain, Upper Wolfjaw Mountain, Lower Wolfjaw Mountain)

Sawteeth (4,100'), Gothics (4,736'), Armstrong (4,400'), Upper Wolfjaw (4,185'), Lower Wolfjaw (4,175')

**Mileage:** 15 miles

**Elevation Gain:** 5,475'

Starting at the AMR/Ausable Club/St. Hubert's trailhead, the Lower Great Range, with the addition of Sawteeth, may be the quintessential Adirondack High Peaks hike. This is what I consider a "big" hike due to the mileage, gain, and nature of summiting five official High Peaks and one bonus peak in a single day. While it is considered a "big" day, it's more doable than some may think. The beauty about this hike is that once on top of Gothics, it's smooth sailing to Armstrong, Upper Wolfjaw, and finally Lower Wolfjaw because it's roughly one mile between each of those summits. It's a lot of bang for your buck going from summit to summit to summit with minimal climbing and mileage. Half a mile down, half a mile up, half a mile down, half a mile up. It's a great hike. The SSA Scale is off the charts with Gothics ranking a full 6/5. Yes, it's that good. Sawteeth, Armstrong, and Upper Wolfjaw all score a 3/5, while Lower Wolfjaw finishes the day with a low 2/5. Bring a whole lot of sandwiches on this range.

I recommend walking the full three miles down the lake road to Ausable Lake and climbing Sawteeth first. I've taken both the Sawteeth-Scenic trail and the Weld trail past Rainbow Falls, and I preferred the Scenic trail due to the abundance of lookouts. Both are good choices, though, so you can't go wrong.

Climbing up to Sawteeth is a challenge at 2,200' of gain over a couple of miles. Oddly enough, the hardest part of the day will be climbing over Pyramid Peak on your way to Gothics. There's a good 900' of gain over a half mile up Pyramid. It's all there on that mountain. It's fitting

# LOWER GREAT RANGE (SAWTEETH, GOTHICS, ARMSTRONG MOUNTAIN, UPPER WOLFJAW MOUNTAIN, LOWER WOLFJAW MOUNTAIN)

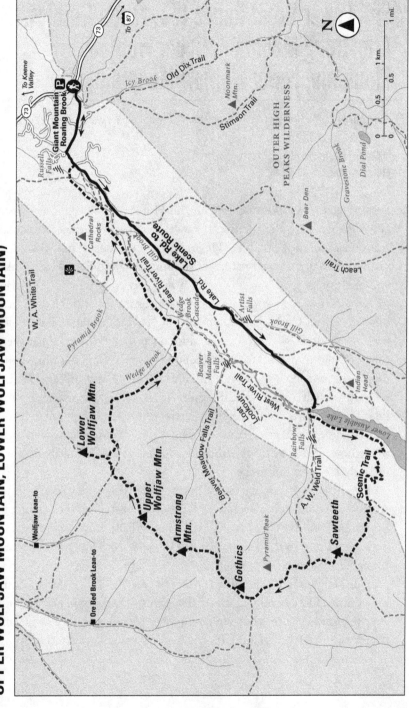

that the nonofficial High Peak is the hardest part of the day—yet also offers arguably the best view . . . there's definitely a life lesson in there.

Once you summit Gothics, the "hard" work is done. Next, you'll enjoy a delightful stroll along the Lower Great Range all the way to Lower Wolfjaw. Obviously there is still elevation and climbing to be done, but the dopamine highs of tagging peak after peak in a short time becomes a constant morale booster.

Once finished with Lower Wolfjaw, all that's left is a long five-mile walk down the mountain and back to your car. Classic Adirondack hiking, am I right? On a nice sunny day, the Lower Great Range is the best of the best. A truly beloved High Peaks hike.

**NOTE:** The hike up Sawteeth, over Pyramid, and onto Gothics can be an entire day in and of itself. If you want to break up this hike into two days, I'd suggest doing Sawteeth and Gothics one day and Armstrong, Upper Wolfjaw, and Lower Wolfjaw another. The whole range is often completed in one day but can be split up. There are also many bailout points throughout the hike, so consult your map and plan accordingly. It's not a bad time to do some camping either.

Time to go have an amazing bluebird Adirondack adventure on the Lower Great Range, but first, the lake road . . .

Looking back at Gothics on our way to Armstrong. A memorable winter day in the High Peaks. *Photo by James Appleton*

## Lower Great Range (Sawteeth, Gothics, Armstrong Mountain, Upper Wolfjaw Mountain, Lower Wolfjaw Mountain)

*July 20, 2018. On tap today was one of the classic High Peaks hikes, the Lower Great Range. Gothics. Armstrong. Upper Wolfjaw. Lower Wolfjaw. And though not technically part of the Great Range but a popular addition to this hike, Sawteeth. Roughly 15 miles, with 5,500' of elevation gain and five High Peaks (plus one bonus peak). Another big day was on tap. Fortunately, the forecast called for a sunny bluebird day here in the Adirondacks. I was told to save this range for a sunny day, and that day arrived. Per usual, my 3:00 a.m. alarm went off, I took a quick shower, and I was out the door heading to Keene Valley back to St. Hubert's, also known as the Ausable Club, or the AMR. It sure has a lot of names, doesn't it?*

*I left my car at exactly 4:30 a.m. and started up the dirt road toward the golf course to make a left between the two tennis courts toward the trailhead. My plan for today was to walk the entire three miles of the lake road in the dark to the Sawteeth-Scenic trail. Then I would head up and over Sawteeth to Pyramid Peak and on to Gothics where the Range trail would take me over Gothics, Armstrong, Upper Wolfjaw, and to Lower Wolfjaw. I'll head back down via the Wedge Brook trail to the West River trail along the Ausable River and back to the trailhead.*

*The day began with the three-mile walk down the flat dirt road known as the lake road. Nothing to report other than it was dark, and it was a dirt road. I decided to listen to some music during this initial stretch, so I popped one earbud in and listened to some music to pass the time as I walked toward the Lower Ausable Lake. I passed many different trail junctions on both sides of the road, but I kept on walking since none of those were on today's agenda. Having just been here to hike Dial, Nippletop, Colvin, and Blake, it was good to see these trails again and continue familiarizing myself with the area. The more we see things, the better, right?*

*I made it to the Lower Ausable Lake at 5:40 a.m., 1 hour and 10 minutes after leaving my car. I left the lake road behind and walked over the long wooden bridge and quickly came to the trail junction I was looking for, the Sawteeth-Scenic trail. A left onto the trail, and now the hike really began. The Scenic trail is exactly that, scenic. It begins for a good half a mile walking along the Ausable River over rocks on the dirt trails, all while showcasing nice views along this iconic ADK river. After a half* mile or so, the trail comes to outlook 2 of 5. This is the point where the climbing begins.

There are five outlooks on the way up Sawteeth (hence the name "Scenic trail"), and they're all great spots that help break up the ascent with views to enjoy. Once up Sawteeth, the bulk of the major elevation gain for the day is accomplished, so while it did have me huffing and puffing, I made it to the top at 7:45 a.m., 3 hours and 15 minutes after leaving my car. High Peak number 21 of 46.

Sawteeth stands at 4,100' elevation and has a smaller summit with trees you'll have to look over, but like every mountain today, it has excellent views. In fact, this range has some of the best views you'll experience in the Adirondacks or anywhere. I ate my first of many summit PB&Js today, gulped some electrolytes, and started the 1.5-mile trip to Gothics. I went over the summit onto the Sawteeth trail before meeting up with the A. W. Weld trail. First things first, however, I still had to go up and over Pyramid Peak to get there. Pyramid isn't considered one of the High Peaks for technical reasons (it doesn't have enough prominence from Gothics), but it does have arguably the coolest view of the day in my opinion. It's also one of the most physically demanding portions of the day with its 900' of elevation gain in just a half mile. Those legs and lungs better be ready to work!

It took me a little under an hour to go from Sawteeth to Pyramid where the front-row views of the Gothics slides awaited me. Going down Pyramid and up to Gothics was fast, however, and I knew that once on Gothics it would be smooth sailing for the rest of the day because this range hike is basically four peaks in a row of "half mile to the col, half mile to the summit, half mile to the col, half mile to the summit." There's a lot of bang for your buck on this range hike, which is what makes it such a fan favorite.

Gothics was one High Peak I had climbed previously. Many years earlier, Josh and I had hiked this with our buddy Jon and Jon's father. I have great memories from that day and of devouring a Noon Mark Diner pie after the hike.

So, having been up Gothics once before, I recognized the last portion of the climb once the Weld trail met up with the Range trail for the final push to the summit once you leave the tree line. Leaving the tree line is great on a sunny day with those 360-degree views. Gothics is easily one of the best summits in the High Peaks. I finally made it to the true summit, marked by a geological survey marker in the ground, at 9:05 a.m. I was 4.5 hours into my day and feeling good standing 4,736' above sea level and on top of High Peak number 22 of 46.

It's important on this summit (and any summit with vegetation) to stay off the alpine vegetation and stay on the rocks when traveling. Gothics' summit is large and has lots of different areas to sit and enjoy the views. It is the place to have a summit sandwich, that's for sure. Speaking of summit sandwiches, I actually opted to forgo my sandwich on Gothics. Crazy, right?

I had the summit to myself for a few minutes before a nice family made their way up the cable route from the Saddleback side. This was their first Adirondack hiking experience. I chatted with them for a few minutes before carrying on with my journey across the range because I was less than a mile away from being halfway to 46. Up next, Armstrong.

It's just under a mile over to Armstrong and is one of the easier parts of the day as far as terrain, elevation change, and time between summits. Due to this minimal elevation loss/gain, I made it to the col quickly and back up at a good pace before stepping out onto the summit lookout, or as I like to call this summit, the Amphitheater of the High Peaks. I was officially halfway to 46 standing on Armstrong Mountain, 4,400' elevation, for number 23 of 46.

I was officially halfway to 46. It felt great, and Armstrong will always have a special place in my heart. I arrived at this amphitheater-like summit at 9:50 a.m., roughly 40 minutes after leaving Gothics. Since I didn't eat my summit sandwich on Gothics, I decided to have a quick PB&J now. After five minutes I started hearing faint voices in the distance. It was the family I met over on Gothics coming up the trail, so I decided to carry on and give them the summit. I took my sandwich to go and continued hiking. Onward to Upper Wolfjaw.

It's basically a mile between summits once again, but getting to the col between these two peaks is one of the more challenging portions of the day. It's steeper than the other peaks and has one major cliff you climb down (or up depending on which way you're hiking) that requires being extra cautious since you can easily get hurt, or even fall to your death if not careful. But again, it's not too bad. There is a helpful wooden ladder toward the bottom, though. I made good time heading to Upper Wolfjaw, and 35 minutes after leaving Armstrong I arrived at the boulder summit at 10:30 a.m., standing at 4,185' elevation. Six hours after signing in I was standing on my fourth High Peak of the day and number 24 of 46. I was officially over the hump.

There was a gentleman and two teenage girls enjoying lunch on the summit when I arrived. They were hiking the range in the opposite direction that I was today. The man was a very experienced Adirondack hiker as I could tell by listening in on his conversation with the girls while he pointed out each mountain and continued telling stories about each one. I remember thinking to myself, "I hope I will be able to point out all these mountains one day." Imagine if someone had told me in that moment that one day I'd be writing a book about climbing these mountains, let alone pointing out each one. Life is wild sometimes.

After a few minutes enjoying the view as the hikers left the summit, I decided to change my plan and unload my secret weapon for the day. Something I had planned for the final summit, but since I had the summit to myself now, I figured "it's time." I took off my green EMS "school bookbag style" backpack (yes, I didn't have a fancy hiking backpack until long after finishing the 46 High Peaks), and I pulled out the most perfectly crafted turkey sandwich on a toasted everything bagel the world has ever seen. I was thinking about this bad boy all day. It was a great choice to stay for lunch and a great sandwich. I worked at Subway for three years in high school, so I kind of know my way around a sandwich. I was in the industry. My purple Subway shirts didn't have "sandwich artist" embroidered on the sleeve for nothing . . . that's all I'm saying.

Once I came back down from the heavens as I finished my bagel sandwich, it was time to head toward my final peak of the day, Lower Wolfjaw. I suited up and climbed back down the boulder summit to the trail where I ran into two uniquely dressed hikers. The first guy was wearing sandals. Yes, sandals. Not flip-flops but more like a medieval-looking sandal. His feet were filthy. We caught eyes, and I said to him, "You have to be comfortable, right?" to which he laughed and nodded his head in agreement. Then about 20 feet behind sandal man was his friend who was dressed in his Sunday best from head to toe. Nice dress pants and a tucked-in long-sleeved button-up shirt buttoned to the top. He looked slick, to be honest, but it was certainly an outfit you wouldn't expect out here in the muddy backcountry. As we passed one another, I asked him, "So does your friend always hike in sandals?" to which he laughed and responded, "Yeah, he's insane though."

I continued down the 1.4-mile trek along the range trail toward Lower Wolfjaw, which from Upper Wolf looked like it was 100 miles away. It's around a mile to the trail junction for Lower Wolfjaw before a half-mile climb up. It was steep getting off Upper Wolf, and then steep again going down the backside of the hump the trail goes over until you come to the col and a trail junction with multiple trail options. Left is the Wolfjaw trail, which comes from a different direction to access the Wolfjaws; right is the Wolfjaws Notch cutoff trail (which is a faster route straight to the Wedge Brook trail); and straight is the W. A. White Trail, which goes to the summit of Lower Wolfjaw. Straight is the correct answer today. Time to climb.

From here it's a half mile to the summit and you'll gain over 500' elevation, so even though it's short you're going to work for this summit. I made it to the top in exactly 30 minutes at 11:50 a.m., 7 hours and 20 minutes into my day. Five High Peaks and one bonus peak summited before noon? Not too shabby for High Peak number 25!

The summit stands at 4,175' and is tree covered with a lookout view over the tops of some trees. Probably the smallest and least exciting summit of the day in my opinion. As I walked around the summit, I realized my decision to eat my victory bagel sandwich earlier on Upper instead of Lower Wolfjaw was the right choice because there wasn't an ideal spot to sit and enjoy it. It's the little things in life, am I right?

After a few minutes exploring the summit, I turned around and began the long journey home, starting with the 0.5 miles back to the trail junction to hit the Wedge Brook trail. After making quick work of that steep, eroded half mile, I took a left onto the Wedge Brook trail. Since my day was finished from a summit perspective, I hurried down the mountain at a fast pace, passing hiker after hiker just starting their day. It's an oddly satisfying feeling knowing I summited five High Peaks while others were just getting started. Perks of those early starts.

The Wedge Brook trail goes down the mountain along the, you guessed it, Wedge Brook. So, if you need to refill some water for the trip out, this is a good spot for that. This trail up the mountain winds and weaves through the woods and is a gentle but consistent climb. Once making it down the mountain you'll come to the West River trail where there is also an abundance of more delicious Adirondack river water. This is a soft dirt trail that eventually comes to the West River trail where I took a left to head back to St. Hubert's. This is a nice, flat woods walk for almost two miles, which was welcomed at this point in the day.

I was ready to be out of the woods, so this portion of the hike felt endless. After crossing over a wooden bridge, I finally made it back to the trailhead. What a day! I waited in line to sign out, and again it was a great feeling watching people just sign in for the day as I was waiting to sign out after already summiting five High Peaks. A victory moment, really. I quickly hurried back through the AMR property back down the dirt road to my car and arrived at 2:30 p.m., clocking my day at exactly 10 hours car-to-car. What a perfect day. And no blisters! Just the usual light knee discomfort, but what can you do! After all, this is climbing mountains. Nothing a little sleep can't fix, right?

Another very successful solo day in the woods hitting five High Peaks and one bonus peak for numbers 21, 22, 23, 24, and 25 on my quest to summit all 46 High Peaks in one summer. Sawteeth, Gothics, Armstrong, and Upper and Lower Wolfjaws in the books. I'm officially over halfway to 46.

# 10 Dix Range (Dix Mountain, Hough Peak, South Dix, Grace Peak, Macomb Mountain)

Dix (4,857'), Hough (4,400'), South Dix (4,060'), Grace/East Dix (4,012'), Macomb (4,405')

**Mileage:** 15.2 miles
**Elevation Gain:** 5,200'

The Elk Lake trailhead is the most popular place to hike the Dix Range. However, the Round Pond trailhead on route 73 in Keene Valley is a valid option but comes with a higher mileage. The Dix Range is notorious for lost hikers. It's a range to take very seriously (they all are, but extra serious here). It's also a good "big hike" to tackle and earn that post-hike, extra-thick Stewart's milkshake. This hike will also put you on five different ADK summits. If you're looking for a weekend of camping and hiking, the Dix Range is a great place to do it.

The entire range is often completed start to finish in a single day hike, but you could easily break it up into multiple days if you prefer. More importantly, let's talk summit sandwiches. Every peak in this range offers a great place to have a summit sandwich with a view, and as a range it ranks a collective 4/5 on the Summit Sandwich-ability (SSA) Scale. They're all good. Okay, let's get into the hike.

My recommendation is to hike the loop starting with Macomb first due to the Macomb slide. The Macomb slide is a giant rockslide, and it's the real deal. I feel that going up this is much safer than coming down, so I recommend starting with Macomb. Just be extra cautious, but enjoy the adventure because the Macomb slide is a unique stretch of trail on your 46'er journey.

Once at the top of the slide, you're almost at the Macomb summit. At that point, going from peak to peak is relatively quick and fun. From Macomb you'll head over to South Dix, then an out-and-back to Grace Peak, back to South Dix, and just past it you'll find the trail to Hough. The climb to Hough and from Hough to Dix has decent elevation gain, but the real challenge of the day will be the hike down the Beckhorn trail off Dix Mountain. An elevation loss of over 2,500' in under two miles makes for a steep and slow trip down a seemingly never-ending mountain. Once off the mountain comes the 4.5-mile walk back to your car at the trailhead. These long ADK approaches are the real killers at the end of the day, but that's what makes the Adirondacks special.

The Dix Range is a big day and a milestone for one's 46'er journey. Do some extra homework before tackling this range. Study the map well and take note of the various trail junctions so you stay on the correct trail. With that said, this day can be a dream on a sunny day as you work your way around the range with views that are hard to beat. Start early.

Speaking of sunny days on the Dix Range and starting early . . .

## DIX RANGE (DIX MOUNTAIN, HOUGH PEAK, SOUTH DIX, GRACE PEAK, MACOMB MOUNTAIN)

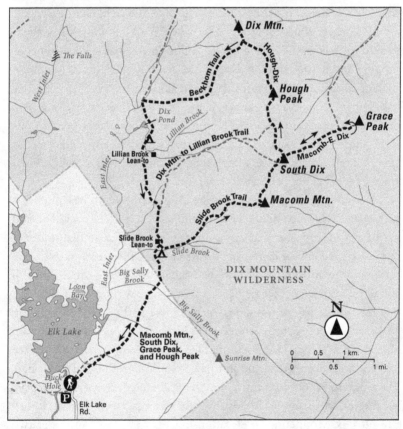

# Dix Range (Dix Mountain, Hough Peak, South Dix, Grace Peak, Macomb Mountain)

*July 8, 2018. The Dix Range. Macomb, South Dix, Grace Peak, Hough, and Dix. My first big hike, and in a wilderness notorious for lost hikers and search and rescues. I told Josh, "Let's do a big hike this weekend!" and the Dix Range immediately came to his mind. Five High Peaks in one day, over 15 miles of hiking with more than 5,000' of elevation gain. I asked for a big hike, and I got one.*

*We set out from Saranac Lake at 3:30 a.m. and drove to Newcomb to the Elk Lake trailhead where we got the only remaining parking spot at the trailhead. Hallelujah! When this tiny lot is full, the only other parking lot is a quick three miles back down the dirt road, which you will then walk to the trailhead, adding six miles of road walking to an already long day. Sure, who wouldn't want that, right? Needless to say, I was beyond thrilled there was an open spot at the trailhead.*

*It was a beautiful sunny day in the Adirondacks. Blue skies, no wind, low 70s—a classic ADK summer day. After the hour-and-a-half drive to the trailhead, we gathered our gear and signed in at 5:00 a.m. For once we didn't need our headlamps, and it felt strange starting a hike after first light. Dammit, Josh, I knew we should have left at 3:00 instead of 3:30!*

*Our plan for the day was to hike in via the Hunters Pass trail and take the right onto the Slide Brook trail to summit Macomb, then South Dix, Grace Peak, back to South Dix, over to Hough, and finally over the Beckhorn to Dix. We would take the Beckhorn trail down Dix back to the Hunters Pass trail to the car. The day would weigh in at just over 15 miles, 5,200' of elevation gain, and five High Peaks. A big day was upon us.*

*We began our hike on the Hunters Pass trail, which is a flat woods trail for a couple miles until you come to campsites and a cairn marking the beginning of the Slide Brook trail. It's a little awkward because the campsites are basically on the trail, so you end up walking through the middle of someone's campsite. There were many campers still sleeping at this hour, so we quickly and quietly walked through to the cairn and began the climb up.*

*This part of the trail up Macomb has a nice, gradual elevation gain. It's very easy to follow, so Josh had me lead because I needed to get the experience leading and navigating. The Slide Brook trail is about a mile* and a half to the summit of Macomb, but first you will come to the epic and infamous Macomb slide. Once the trail takes you out onto the slide, it's a fun and unique Adirondack experience. This slide is the real deal, though. There is a lot of loose rock and slippery sand, so this slide needs to be taken with extreme caution because one can easily be hurt on this slide with a wrong step. With that in mind, it is a fun stretch of trail and a real calf and quad burner. Josh moved much quicker up this slide than I did. Since you can see the top of the slide, you'll find yourself looking up often, only to think, "It doesn't feel like I'll ever get there." You will, eventually.

We both walked across the slide and hugged the right side as we went up, which seemed to be a good option. We met one other solo hiker climbing the slide. A nice guy from Massachusetts. He passed both of us, and we wouldn't see him again for the day. What I found challenging about the slide is that since you always see your destination every step of the way, it feels like it takes forever to make any progress. Then once you finally get to the point you've been eyeballing, you turn the corner and you're still not even close. Good times, though, right? I promise it's a fun stretch of trail. I highly recommend going up this and not down, because I feel the risk of danger going down is much greater. People do it both ways, but to me the best option is ascending the slide.

It took us 35 minutes to climb the slide followed by another 15 minutes to the Macomb summit where we arrived at 7 a.m., exactly two hours from sign-in to the summit. Macomb stands at an elevation of 4,405'. There is a wooden summit sign with a nice ledge lookout to the Great Range and the other peaks here in the Dix Range. Each summit offers a new perspective of the Dix Range, showcasing where you're going and where you've come from today, so I found that enjoyable as the day went on. We both slammed a quick peanut butter and jelly before continuing with our hike, since this was only the beginning of our big day in the High Peaks.

We were now on the Dix Range trail heading to South Dix, also known as Carson Peak, named after Russell Carson, a former president of the Adirondack Mountain Club. This part of the trail was quick since it's less than a mile between Macomb and South Dix, so it took us around 30 minutes to the top of South Dix. Before the summit of South Dix, you will come to the Lillian Brook cutoff trail, which is a good bailout point if you need to. There aren't many signs on this range, so it's important to know the map, know your route, know what turns you're taking, and know when to take them. It's no wonder so many people get lost and turned around on this range.

The summit of South Dix stands at 4,060' and is marked by a tree with an "X" and "S. Dix" carved into it. It's just past the Hough trail split and has another rock ledge lookout. Every mountain today has great views, which makes the Dix Range one of the best in the High Peaks. We took in those views for a good five minutes before continuing on the trail. We went past the "S. Dix X" tree to the East Dix trail, now known as Grace Peak trail. East Dix was renamed Grace Peak in 2014 after the beloved Grace Hudowalski, who in 1937 became the first female Adirondack 46'er and the ninth person ever to complete all 46. There are over 15,000 finishers now. Amazing.

This trail to Grace is an out-and-back from South Dix, so after getting there we will be coming right back to South Dix to connect with the trail to Hough. This stretch of the hike also took us roughly 30 minutes summit-to-summit to go the one mile. The trails are narrow throughout the Dix Range in general, but they're all visible and easy to follow in my opinion. There are just various trails, so the wrong-turn factor is what gets people lost. That's why it's especially crucial on this range to study the map before the hike, because that wrong turn down the wrong trail could spell disaster. With this said, however, we eventually came out on the summit of Grace Peak, a fantastic open ledge summit standing 4,012'. No summit sign or marker here, but you can tell when you're there. It's a great summit to spend some time on overlooking a picturesque cliff. So take off your pack, grab a snack, and enjoy the view.

Since we had to go the mile back to South Dix and then go to Hough, we only stayed a few minutes before starting our way back. After suiting up, tightening our packs, and with trekking poles in hand, we realized something: "I don't remember seeing this big boulder when we came out of the woods." As we excitedly walked onto the summit 10 minutes earlier, we had forgotten to take mental notes of where we exited the woods onto the summit. We scanned the woods but couldn't find the trail that led us onto this giant rocky summit. After a good five minutes of looking around, Josh eventually found the trail, and then it all came back to us. A good lesson learned—don't get so excited when summiting that you forget to take mental notes of where the trail came out of the woods.

We hurried back to South Dix, passed the "S. Dix X" tree, and were back on the Dix Range trail heading the 0.75 miles to Hough. The col between South Dix and Hough is cool, and the ascent up Hough has some steeper, rugged stretches. There's even a mini rock climb I found enjoyable.

Despite the short mileage between peaks, this portion of the hike was not as quick as the other mountains were today. Probably the 500' of gain over 0.3 miles had something to do with it. We eventually made it to Hough at 10:20 a.m., almost five and a half hours into our day. Hough (pronounced "huff") is a mostly wooded summit with a rock ledge lookout marked by a yellow trail marker that says "Hough" written in sharpie. Hough stands at 4,400' and offers a great glimpse of the Beckhorn on Dix that you're about to climb. Up until this point in the day, we had only passed our Massachusetts friend going up Macomb and one trail runner on our way to Hough. A quiet day for hikers on the Dix Range despite the perfect July weather.

When Josh and I hike, we both struggle to relax because there's usually still work to be done, so we summit, eat a quick snack, and keep going around five minutes later. We're always moving. Knowing Dix was our destination to relax more than usual, Hough was our shortest summit stay of the day at just a couple of minutes. We continued along the Dix Range trail toward Dix, but first we had to climb up and over the Beckhorn, a big knob on the southern slope near the summit. The trip between these two mountains was tough and one of the harder parts of the day physically for me. Climbing over the Beckhorn to the true summit of Dix wasn't going to be easy this far into the day, nor should it have been. There are two humps you hike over before the final climb over the Beckhorn to the true summit.

At this point Josh and I had been moving basically nonstop for over seven hours, so what happened next is no surprise. While climbing up a steep section, I climbed up onto a boulder and, thanks to both fatigue and my backpack throwing me off balance, I took a tumble backward. After losing my balance, I was forced to jump off the boulder I was on and fell. It was a good five-foot drop, but thankfully I landed feet first before rolling. It could have been much worse, but fortunately I didn't even twist an ankle. I was lucky. At 240 pounds, I would have made it very difficult for Josh to carry me out. Though he probably would have just left me for dead. Every man for himself at that point. It was at this moment that I knew, "We need to stop and take a good 30-minute break when we get to Dix," which Josh was fully on board with.

As we got to the Beckhorn and started our final push to Dix, we began to see these little red circles on the trees. What are these little discs? Trail markers! The Dix trail is a DEC-maintained trail, so once you get to the Beckhorn, you're officially on a DEC-marked hiking trail. From here we quickly made it to our destination for the fifth and final summit of the day, Dix Mountain. The sixth-tallest peak in New York State at 4,857'. Can you believe it? I did it. All five peaks of the Dix Range in a day. My first big hike for numbers 9, 10, 11, 12, and 13. Hot damn, I'm into the teens now on my journey to 46! Now this feels real.

Okay, now we can relax since the major work for the day is behind us. So, in Josh fashion, he kicked off his boots and socks, then I followed suit, and we ate some summit sandwiches while enjoying the beautiful open views. A perfect Adirondack summer day in the Dix Range. We did it; the day is basically over, right? . . . Right? . . . Right? Wrong. We had many miles back to the trailhead, with a trail entirely too steep and a whole lot of foot pain still to experience between there and the car. But I'll get to that soon.

I mentioned in the chapter on Phelps and Tabletop how my feet were killing me after Phelps because I took my boots off for 10 minutes on the summit, resulting in my feet swelling up. Well, after a good 25 minutes without boots on, my feet swelled up even more than usual, and after putting them back on with a fresh pair of Darn Tough socks, my boots were snug . . . a little too snug.

After a long, enjoyable summit stay, we had to say our good-byes and head back. Back we went toward the Beckhorn trail, which we passed earlier just before arriving at the summit of Dix. Josh had warned me throughout the day of how steep this roughly two-mile trip down Dix is, and my God, he was right. This trail is by far the steepest, longest trail straight down of anything I've experienced here in the Adirondacks. It's comically steep, and when dealing with trails that steep and technical, it doesn't make the mileage pass very quickly. Dropping over 2,500' of elevation in 1.8 miles has that effect, you know?

About 15 minutes into the trip down is when it all started to change. What had been a flawless ADK day was about to take a turn for the worse.

I started to have that same bottom-of-the-foot pain that I experienced on Phelps. I could feel every rock and root in the center of my feet like I was being stabbed. It felt that way on every step. Truly awful. It got worse and worse as the trek went on. I haven't experienced such foot discomfort in my entire life, and thankfully wouldn't again because this is where the lightbulb went off in my head. "Of course your feet hurt, you fool. They're swollen because you took your boots off for half an hour." Too bad I still had 6.3 miles back to the trailhead. I would never make this mistake again. Some people can air out their feet on the summit without issue, but clearly I am not one of those people.

Toward the bottom, about 1.5 miles into our descent, we came across an older gentleman with his adult son and dog. Covered in sweat and breathing heavily, they asked the dreaded question, "How much further?" Like my group of female friends from Whiteface a week prior, they were not close. They were not even close to being close. I get it. They just began the two miles of relentless climbing, and it's hard. Today, however, sadly we had to destroy the man's soul by telling him about the climb that awaited them. The "Oh no, what did I get myself into?" look on the poor man's face said it all. I did not envy them at this point in the day. Make no mistake, people, the Beckhorn trail up Dix is steep as hell, and it's no joke no matter which way you're hiking. Weighing in at just under two miles with over 2,500' of gain (or loss depending on your direction), it's all there. Climbing up this trail should be reserved for those experienced hikers in great cardiovascular health. It's a serious beast.

Shortly after our interaction with our two friends and their canine companion, while every swear word in the book blasted through my mind as my feet throbbed with every step, we made it off Dix and arrived at the Hunters Pass trail. Hell yes. I was then greeted by a trail sign gently informing me that my car was another 4.3 miles away. Hell no. Another 4.3 miles. Kill me now. Okay, that settles it. I can't make it. I took out my giant knife and begged Josh to put me out of my misery and just cut off my feet. I was going to live here on the Hunters Pass trail from now on. I'm now Peg Leg Jimmy, and I was ready to become the crazy, peg-leg hermit who roamed the woods of the Dix Range. I needed to stop fighting my destiny. This is who I was meant to become. I was ready to make this land my home. Josh selfishly turned down my request, though. He's a bad friend like that. The remaining 4.3 miles might as well have been 54.3 miles because it felt like an endless amount of walking. The day started out so well and slowly became so rough. What else could we do, though, but just keep walking, right?

So we kept moving slowly but surely, and wouldn't you know, we eventually came to the campsites from this morning where the Slide Brook trail starts, and I knew from that point it was two miles and about 45 minutes to the car. It was a morale boost, I must say. We even picked up our pace at this point, and I was doing everything possible to block out the pain as we hurried down the trail. On the way back, Josh and I started talking about what we were going to get to eat at Stewart's in Keene on the way back, which took the edge off. Dreaming of some delicious hot food. Maybe I'd get a slice of pizza, maybe some chicken tenders, but probably both. We decided we were also going to get some milkshakes (something I haven't had from Stew's in years). An extra-thick, chocolate peanut butter cup Stewart's milkshake was going down, and it was going down hard. This was the day the post-hike Stewart's milkshake tradition was born!

We continued walking, quietly lost in our own minds, and then a few steps later we saw it. Like the Griswold's family Christmas tree with a beam of light shining down from the heavens, we saw the trailhead parking lot. Hallelujah! After dreaming for hours of the moment I could finally take off my boots and slip on my Crocs. We made it against all the odds. Okay, no odds were against us, but you can all imagine the joy my heart felt arriving at that trailhead. Off with the boots, off with the socks, and on with the Crocs. Yes, it was everything I dreamed it would be. So was that Stewart's milkshake, I might add.

Well, we did it. The mighty Dix Range. Done! We made it back to the car at 3:05 p.m., totaling 10 hours and 5 minutes car-to-car. Another very successful day in the woods despite the rough ending, but a hike that would give me the confidence to start tackling longer days. Five High Peaks hikes down and peaks 9, 10, 11, 12, and 13 in the books here on my quest to summit all 46 High Peaks in one summer.

# 11  Mt. Marcy, Mt. Skylight, and Gray Peak

Marcy (5,344'), Skylight (4,926'), Gray (4,840')
**Mileage:** 17 miles
**Elevation Gain:** 5,069'

Time for the big one—Mt. Marcy and the gang. Starting at the Adirondack Loj, time to climb the tallest, fourth-tallest, and eighth-tallest peaks in the park. Sounds like a big day, right? It is, but it's more manageable than you may think. By this part in your journey, you're more than ready.

Marcy is a mountain people often hike by itself, but I think that's the wrong way to go. Here's why—Mt. Marcy alone is going to be a 15'ish-mile day no matter how you slice it. If that's the case, then why not add a mere two miles to the day and hit Skylight (0.5 miles to the summit off the trail) and Gray Peak (0.5 miles to the summit off the trail)? This allows for a nice loop and summiting two other amazing High Peaks on the day. Sure, you could enjoy a 15-mile out-and-back of Marcy alone on the Van Hoevenberg trail, but your adventure can be so much better with minimal added effort. That's my opinion on the matter.

It doesn't matter which direction you hike this loop in, but you will want to determine when you want to tackle the infamous (or beloved, depending on who you talk to) "floating logs." The floating logs are literal floating logs in a mucky, watery mess. Personally, I recommend saving them for the end of the day when most of the work is complete. Thus, my recommendation is to hike up Marcy first via the Van Hoevenberg trail to Marcy, over Marcy down to the

A winter sunrise on Marcy. One of the most memorable hikes of my life.
*Photo by James Appleton*

# MT. MARCY, MT. SKYLIGHT, GRAY PEAK

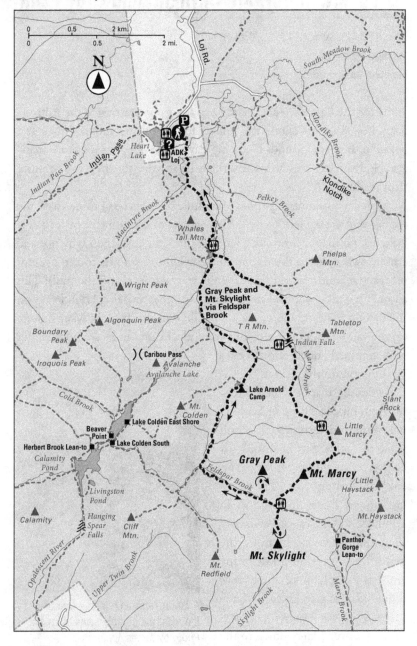

Four Corners trail junction where you'll break off for the one-mile out-and-back of Skylight. After Skylight you'll come back to the Four Corners junction and head down the Mt. Marcy trail toward Lake Tear of the Clouds, aka the start of the Hudson River. Here you'll find the cairn marking the herd path to Gray Peak. Like Mt. Skylight, Gray Peak is also a one-mile round-trip out and back.

After summiting Gray and making your way down back to the Marcy trail, you'll continue down Marcy to the Feldspar Brook camp-sites where you will then turn right onto the Lake Arnold trail. The Lake Arnold trail will take you home. After you pass through the floating logs, of course. Then you'll hit the Avalanche Pass trail and complete the loop at Marcy Dam. From the dam it's the classic three-mile walk back to the Loj. Yes, this is a big day, but it will be a memorable one.

I recommend saving this hike for a sunny day because the SSA rank-ing is off the charts for Marcy and Skylight. After all, Marcy is the tallest point in New York State, so it should be awesome. Gray scores a lower 3/5, but the other two are 6/5 (I told you they were off the charts).

Now, I would be doing you, the reader, a disservice if I didn't take a minute to talk about "the floating logs" in a little more depth. This is a boggy area along the Lake Arnold trail, just north of the Feldspar Brook lean-to, that has literal logs floating around as makeshift foot bridges. I've traveled this stretch of trail when the water was low, and it was a nonissue. I've also traveled it when I was quite literally surfing logs across two-foot-deep water. I got extremely wet that day . . . twice. Therefore, it's hard to really "recommend" anyone traveling this stretch of trail, but it is what it is. I suppose it's another rite of passage on one's 46'er journey. Hopefully you enjoy the experience.

Marcy, Skylight, and Gray is a big day and one of my favorite hikes in the Adirondacks. I've even had the pleasure of enjoying a sunrise on top of Mt. Marcy in both winter and summer. Those were mornings I'll never forget.

Time to get into the hike. You will see as you read my trail story that I spontaneously decided to add two other High Peaks to the day while I stood atop Mt. Marcy. It was an interesting choice to say the least, but let's get into it. I don't want to spoil the surprise too much . . .

Heading over to Skylight just after sunrise. *Photo by Jonathan Zaharek*

# Mt. Marcy, Mt. Skylight, Gray Peak, Cliff Mountain, and Mt. Redfield

*July 29, 2018. My 10th High Peaks hike and my 8th and final hike of July. The month is about to end, and I'm gearing up to leave home again for a couple of months of work, so the pressure was on to summit as many High Peaks as I could this month. After today I would be at the big 3-0 on my journey to 46. That was the plan, anyways, but plans often change out there in the woods.*

*My low goal for July was to get into the 20s, but preferably to 23 of 46. My stretch goal was to get into the 30s on my quest to hike all 46 High Peaks this summer. With that in mind, I had already hit my goal of 23, and this hike would accomplish my stretch goal. So today I planned to hit the big one, Mt. Marcy, the highest point in New York State. The plan was to also summit Skylight and Gray, the fourth- and seventh-tallest High Peaks, respectively. Needless to say, it was a big day, which makes my mid-hike audible even more . . . foolish? Interesting? Adventurous? I don't know; you be the judge. So buckle up, because today is going to be the longest day I've ever spent on the trail . . . by far.*

*Marcy, Skylight, and Gray weigh in at just over 18 miles with an elevation gain of over 5,000'. The plan was to begin at the Adirondack Loj and take the Van Hoevenberg trail into Marcy Dam, then go right onto the Avalanche Pass trail to the Lake Arnold trail, and finally to the Marcy trail. I would head up the Marcy trail and out-and-back Gray first via the Gray herd path, then continue up the Marcy trail to the Four Corners, go right to summit Skylight, then back to the Four Corners and up to Marcy. I would then loop back down via the Van Hoevenberg trail to Marcy Dam and back to my car at the Loj. That was the plan today. Those plans would change, however, once I got to the top of Marcy, but let's not get ahead of ourselves.*

*As always, my day started with a 3 a.m. alarm. I flew out the door to the Adirondack Loj where I signed in at the trailhead at 4:30 a.m. on the dot. I love being at the Loj at this hour. Pitch black, silent, and the aroma of the woods at that hour is unbeatable. I clicked on my headlamp, tightened my backpack, and was off to the races down the 2.4-mile trail to Marcy Dam. Through the forest, over the wooden bridges, winding through the woods, destroying spiderweb after spiderweb with my face.*

I eventually came out to the dam, and it's always an exciting moment no matter how many times a person has been there. It was a quiet morning; the sun was starting to rise once I was at the dam. I went over the bridge and passed a few tents filled with sleeping campers before arriving at the trail split. I went right onto Avalanche Pass trail and continued hiking.

This section of the trail skirts along the Marcy Brook. So far the elevation gain was minimal on the day, mostly just flat woods walking with a lot of rock hopping on the Avalanche Pass trail, but then I came to a wooden bridge, lean-to, and campsites just before the Lake Arnold trail junction. The bridge takes you over the Marcy Brook and is a great spot to grab a gulp of water and admire the scenery. At this trail junction you can go right and stay on Avalanche Pass or go left onto the Lake Arnold trail. Left it was today. Marcy Dam was checkpoint 1 today, and the Lake Arnold trail was checkpoint 2.

Time for the elevation gain to begin. The Lake Arnold trail begins with a good mile and a half of constant elevation gain going from boulder to boulder as you travel up the northern flanks of Mt. Colden. I would say it's more difficult mentally than physically because it's a good mile straight where every step looks exactly the same. It is, however, a part of the trail that you can make great time on and push harder, so that's a plus and that's what I did today.

Soon I came to several wooden plank bridges before arriving at Lake Arnold and the trail split for the L. Morgan Porter trail up the eastern side of Mt. Colden. I hit this trail split at exactly two hours into my hike at 6:30 a.m. Coincidentally, on my very next hike I would be taking this exact trail up to Colden. I would also arrive at the trail junction almost to the second in the same time it took me today.

After passing Lake Arnold, you'll head down the ridge for a bit, winding through the woods along a drainage. This point into the hike was where it felt like I was entering no-man's-land, and I love that feeling. You'll lose elevation during this portion of the hike as you make your way down into the col between Gray and Mt. Colden. Then I finally arrived. I was there. I had read about it. I had heard the horror stories about it. I was at the floating logs (cue the scary movie music). The bog was in front of me. It was time to delicately choose my path across, attempting to remain as dry as possible.

This notorious part of the trail goes through a swampy mess involving walking across and balancing on literal floating logs to get across. Some people find it fun. I personally do not. Crossing this stretch of infamous High Peaks trail added a good 30 minutes to my hike because it took me a long time to find a path that wouldn't involve me falling into the water (easily up to my waist that day). I hopped, skipped, and jumped from log to log. As you step on each log, they sink into the water; therefore it sometimes looks like a good step until you put your weight on the log, and then before you know it your whole boot is underwater. Fun, right?

It didn't take long for a step to sink my boot as the water went past my ankle and filled my boot. At that point I just sent it because what else could I do? Once over and back onto dry land, I decided to stop and switch socks before the inside of my boot got too wet. I untied my boot, took off my sock, rang it out, and put on a new one. "Okay, much better," I thought to myself. Sadly, I continued a few steps up the path only to realize I wasn't finished with this bog yet. Then, as luck would have it, my boot went in again. I'm wet again! The same boot! Fed up, annoyed, and wet, I decided to just send it across once again. I was ready to get wet and deal with it later. In my head the floating logs will forever be known as "Satan's bog." I did not find it enjoyable, and at that moment I swore I'd never come down this trail again. Fortunately, I'd be looping out via the Van Hoevenberg trail down the other side of Marcy, and therefore I wouldn't be back here later today (it's funny how things work out sometimes; keep reading). Once I had completed this cursed stretch of ungodly floating trail, I switched my sock again. I took the one dry sock from each pair of socks and put them on my feet. So I had two different socks on, but both feet were relatively dry. Dry'ish.

Shortly after changing my socks post–floating logs, I came to a campsite where I saw my first group of people for the day at Feldspar Brook. They were awake and prepping for the day as I passed them. We chatted for a moment, and I started the ascent up the Marcy trail. Time to climb some mountains!

The trail runs along the Feldspar Brook all the way up to Lake Tear of the Clouds, aka the start of the mighty Hudson River. The Feldspar lean-to is a popular camping location because it's a great access point for many different peaks in this Lake Colden area, like Marcy, Skylight, Gray, Colden, Cliff, Redfield, and Marshall, to name a few.

The Marcy trail gains a lot of elevation quickly, but with such a long approach I was ready to climb. I was a few hours into my day now, and I began seeing lots of hikers on my way up the Marcy trail on this beautiful sunny day.

After ascending 1,000' of elevation over 1.2 miles along the Feldspar Brook, I made it to Lake Tear of the Clouds and the herd path for Gray Peak, marked on the left by a small cairn. Thanks to the seven-mile trek to get back here, on top of my hellish floating logs experience, it was a long morning and I was very ready to summit some peaks. So, with no hesitation or stopping, I turned left and started up Gray.

The Gray trail is unmarked and is a typical herd path, but it is only a half mile from the cairn to the summit. The trail is very worn, with lots of exposed roots, mud, and climbing slabs by the roots along the side—the types of slabs that often involve butt sliding on the way down.

With 500' of gain over the half mile, this last stretch had me breathing heavy, but I arrived on the mostly wooded summit in 25 minutes at 9 a.m., 4.5 hours into my day. Gray Peak stands at 4,840' elevation, marked by the same brown wooden summit sign with yellow lettering found on most unmaintained High Peaks. The seventh tallest and my 28th High Peak of the summer.

The summit has a couple of good clearings for views, but it was cloudy this morning resulting in minimal views (on this peak, that is; that would change drastically soon). I only spent a few minutes up here, just long enough to devour my first PB&J of the day, and then I started back down the herd path.

Back down the mud and slabs I went. About halfway down I slipped and abruptly fell backward. Fortunately I caught myself with one of my trekking poles. Unfortunately, however, I bent said trekking pole to a 90-degree angle. You've got to be kidding me! The bottom section was at a right angle, rendering the pole useless. I'm a big guy and I maxed that pole out today, that's for sure. I bent the pole back the best I could against a rock, and it was good enough to continue with my day. (Side note: Black Diamond Equipment sent me a new section of pole to replace the bent one, no questions asked. So their customer service did well by me.)

I made it back to Lake Tear of the Clouds at 9:35 a.m. and took a left to continue up the Marcy trail, and a quick quarter mile later I made it to the Four Corners trail junction. This junction had lots of hikers going in all different directions when I arrived. It was busy, but it showcases how the Adirondack Park truly is a giant outdoors playground. Different people hitting the same mountains starting from very different places having all sorts of adventures along the way. What an amazing place.

I took a right and began another half-mile trek to another top-10 High Peak summit, Skylight. This trail has a mix of slabs and woods trails, and the summit is unbelievable. This peak is like Algonquin in that once you leave the tree line, it feels like you've entered a different world. It also has an exposed scramble for the last portion. Sadly, I was in the clouds again, so I was a bit bummed upon arrival because I wanted today to be epic, but I made it to the enormous rock summit at 10:15 a.m. Skylight stands at 4,924' elevation for High Peak number 29!

The summit is marked by an enormous pile of rocks that hikers have created because folklore has it that if you throw a rock on the pile you will have good weather. Knowing this beforehand, I grabbed the smallest little rock along the trail just after Marcy Dam and planned to toss it onto the pile. I know we should leave no trace, and this is the opposite of that, but at the time it's what I did because I simply didn't know any better (although I believe this practice has since stopped).

I stayed up there for a few minutes immersed in the clouds, and then a miracle occurred: the clouds started lifting. No way! The legend is true! I kid you not; the clouds all started to lift and move rapidly, and within 10 minutes of tossing the stone onto the pile, I had clear 360-degree views that included Marcy, Haystack, Redfield, Allen, and so much more. Skylight is often listed as people's favorite High Peak, and it's not hard to understand why. It's amazing. Now that views had cleared up, I took off my pack and decided to stay another 10 minutes to take it all in while enjoying my second peanut butter and jelly sandwich. I shared the summit and a nice chat with a group of college kids with their dog. The clouds were moving fast, and once they lifted and revealed Marcy towering above, I knew it was time to get over there. I said good-bye and hurried down the slab and back into the tree line. On my way back to the Four Corners, I passed another hiker that I saw three times today coming down each peak. More from him later.

*I made it back to the Four Corners in no time, walked across the junction, and began the 0.8-mile climb to the tallest mountain in New York, Mt. Marcy. This trail has it all, from dirt to slab climbs, to an enormous, long exposed scramble to the top. Once leaving the tree line you'll follow cairns and yellow markers on the rock for quite a while. This is fun because you leave the tree line rather quickly, and it's a long climb so you get a lot of bang for your buck, with views all around you. You'll see little specks up in the distance, which are hikers in front of you further up the trail. A fun portion of the day. By the time I made it to the top, my quads and calves were on fire, but after growing up in Lake Placid and seeing Mt. Marcy in the skyline millions of times, I had finally made it to the top. 5,344' elevation, the tallest point in New York State.*

*It was 11:15 a.m. for High Peak number 30. I did it. My stretch goal of getting into the 30s was accomplished. The weather even cleared up, making this moment, a month in the making, even more special. Full, clear, 360-degree views. You couldn't ask for anything better. I whipped out my victory summit sandwich to take in the views. A bagel sandwich with roast beef today, and I feasted like a king. Fun fact: Did you know that then–*

*vice president Teddy Roosevelt was climbing Mt. Marcy when he found out President McKinley was about to die from his assassination attempt? So, he basically learned he was about to become the president while on Mt. Marcy. That's so Teddy Roosevelt.*

*While I was enjoying my sandwich and those Marcy views, I began thinking to myself, "I really don't want to hike in through those floating logs again for Cliff and Redfield" (again, some people love those logs, so don't let my experience steer you from them if you want to experience it yourself). Then a crazy plan started brewing*

The floating logs in all their floating glory. Yes. Seriously. *Photo by James Appleton*

The floating logs floating less. *Photo by James Appleton*

in my head as I looked down at Cliff and Redfield from the top of Marcy. I was feeling good, and it was still early in the day. While chatting with the Summit Steward, I asked him, "Do you think I'd be nuts if I added Cliff and Redfield today since it's still early?" He gave me a look that said it all. The look was half "Yes, you'd be kind of crazy" and half "Well, it is still early . . ."

It was happening. I called my wife from the summit and said, "Hey! I'm on Marcy. I'm going to add Cliff and Redfield today!" Having no real understanding of what this decision entailed, she said, "Sounds good, text me when you can." She then called her 46'er brother, Josh (yes, the same Josh who hikes with me), and told him what I was doing, to which he responded, "Wow, that has to be like a 27-mile hike." My marathon day was literally becoming the length of a marathon.

I gave it one final thought as I stared down at Cliff and Redfield from the top of Marcy (everything looks close when you're standing on top of Marcy, you know?). I looked at my map again and thought, "Okay, I just hike back down to the Four Corners, go all the way back down to the Lake Arnold trail, go left 0.5 miles further down that trail (which seemed *like nothing at the time, but it's still another mile round-trip . . . stupid), and then Cliff is just under a mile and Redfield is only 1.2 miles." Piece of cake, right? Wrong. What failed to occur to me at the time was that I had to double all that mileage. Clearly my excitement clouded my common sense. Then, after all those miles, there was that pesky little seven-mile trek back to the Loj once I finished these bonus mountains. In hindsight, it was probably not the best decision for me to add these two into the mix, but spontaneous adventure excites my soul, and I was going for it. I felt great and it wasn't even noon yet, so why not, right? I picked up my bent trekking poles and started walking back down Marcy the way I came up. "Okay, I'm doing this. I'm adding Cliff and Redfield. No going back now!" As I was leaving the summit, I asked the gentleman I passed two other times if he wanted to join me, to which he jokingly responded, "No way, you're crazy!" I was crazy, but I love spontaneous adventure. All right, Cliff and Redfield, I'm on my way!*

*To be continued . . .*

# 12 Cliff Mountain and Mt. Redfield

Cliff (3,960'), Redfield (4,606')
**Mileage:** 18 miles
**Elevation Gain:** 4,101'

Depending on which approach you prefer, this hike can begin at the Adirondack Loj trailhead or the Upper Works trailhead. Since so much time is already spent at the Loj, it may be a good time to start from the Upper Works to experience that glorious approach. Just browse the map and do what works best for you. With that said, starting at the Upper Works trailhead in Newcomb, you'll enjoy a nice four-mile approach on the Calamity Brook trail as you pass the Flowed Lands before getting to Lake Colden. This approach is quite scenic and is an alternative way to approach what I call "Lake Colden Land." It will be good for your 46'er journey to get the full experience by utilizing this trailhead too (though, again, you can hike these mountains from the Adirondack Loj as well).

Once arriving at Lake Colden, the 1.5-mile trek up to the Cliff and Redfield split is also quite scenic in my opinion. Most of the mileage for the day is the approach to and from the trailhead because the climbs up each mountain are minimal, with Redfield weighing in with a 1.2-mile ascent and Cliff just under a mile. The trail junction for these peaks is marked by a single cairn, with Redfield's trail to the left and Cliff's to the right—where a football-field-sized mud pit awaits your boots. Damn you, Cliff.

Cliff was not named for this reason, but there is coincidentally a cliff/slab that must be climbed on this peak. You should be fine at this point into your journey, but it's something to be cautious of. There is also a false summit on Cliff, so don't be fooled. There is also a lot of mud. A. Lot. Of. Mud.

The hike up Redfield is enjoyable as you climb in the river (Uphill Brook), going from rock to rock, boulder to boulder. Just follow the cairns. After leaving the river, you're about a half mile from the summit.

# CLIFF MOUNTAIN AND MT. REDFIELD

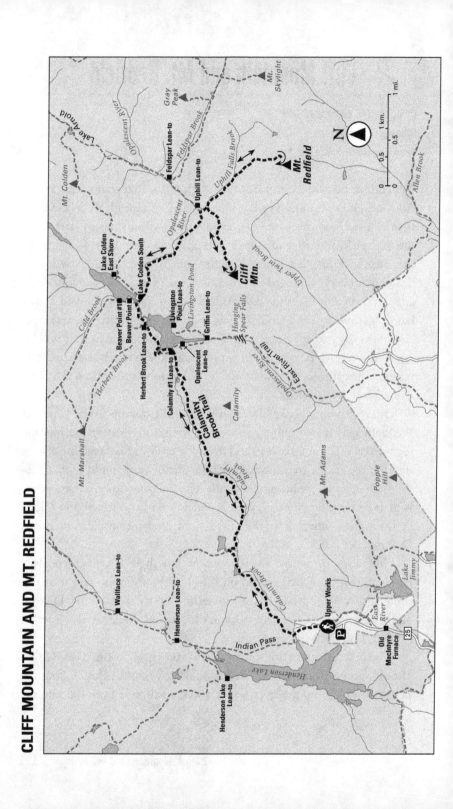

Both summits are marked with brown wooden signs with yellow lettering and offer some minimal views. The SSA Scale is low for this hike, ranking a 2/5 for both peaks. Redfield offers some views, but you'll be standing up to see them while you enjoy that summit sandwich.

This hike isn't a bad choice to tackle on a rainy day. You're going to have some wet days in the High Peaks, and since the views are minimal, it's a decent choice when raining. Remember, those wet days in the High Peaks are all part of the experience. In closing, be ready for a lot of mud on Cliff. Did I mention Cliff is muddy?

On the summit of Cliff Mountain—my archenemy. *Photo by James Appleton*

### (Mt. Marcy, Mt. Skylight, Gray Peak) Cliff Mountain and Mt. Redfield continued . . .

*Marcy, Skylight, and Gray are in the books, and now it's time for part 2 on this spontaneous bonus adventure. Cliff and Redfield, let's go!*

*Once I got back down to the Four Corners, I hiked with an older gentleman for a quarter mile down to Gray. He was almost finished with his 46. Hiking with him for that short stretch was one of the highlights of the day—not just because when hiking solo it's nice to chat with someone, but because he was very pleasant and shared a lot of wisdom. He'd hiked all 48 of the White Mountains and was on 43 of the Adirondack High Peaks. The 10 minutes as we hiked together was a real morale boost. He complimented me on my grit for adding these mountains to the day and confidently declared, "Yeah, you'll be fine." His confidence in me was reassuring that I wasn't making a terrible mistake here. Soon we hit the split for Gray and said good-bye as I continued down the Marcy trail.*

Minutes later I passed a familiar face coming up the trail, a hiker I met on the summit of Colvin a couple weeks ago. We both recognized each other and chatted for a minute. His name is Eli. It's the first time I had a second run-in with someone on a trail. We chatted for a few minutes, and we'd go on to form a friendship after finding each other on an Adirondack hiking page. We would even go on to climb the Seward Range together a few weeks later. I love seeing friendships formed on the ADK trails. Eli also thought I was nuts for adding these two mountains to the day, but I was doing it.

I continued down the trail and was soon passed by a group I had passed earlier. I was shocked they'd caught back up to me. I don't know why I move so slowly on descents, but I do. Soon I arrived back down at the Lake Arnold trail. Round 2 of the day was officially underway. Time to turn left and continue the adventure. Cliff and Redfield, I'm coming for you!

The trail to the unmaintained Cliff and Redfield herd paths is a flat woods trail with nothing much to report, but I made good time because I was determined. I had a major second wind and had the energy as if I had just started for the day. Plus, I desperately wanted to get to these trails to start climbing.

I had not yet decided which mountain to tackle first. Cliff was shorter mileage, but the gentleman I hiked down to Gray with said he remembered Cliff being the harder of the two. I opted to get the longer mileage out of the way first and chose to start with Redfield. I figured I'd save the harder one for the end when that's all there is left to do.

I made it to the Cliff and Redfield herd paths. They're marked by a medium-sized cairn. Left to Redfield, right to Cliff. Left it was to start the 1.2-mile trip up Redfield. This herd path trail runs along, across, and even in the fast-flowing Uphill Brook for the first half of the trail before veering above the drainage. It's a fun stretch of trail going in and out of the woods, climbing on boulders in the river as you ascend. It was enjoyable and one of the better unmaintained High Peak trails. This river is also bigger and faster than many drainages that run along many High Peak trails. It's called a "brook," but it has more of a "river" feel. The water was flowing fast today, too. If you're worried about following the trail while it's in the river, don't be. It's very apparent due to all the scratches on the rocks from microspikes and trekking poles, along with plenty of cairns to follow. Once *leaving the water behind, the final third of the trail is a classic, very worn and soft, exposed-root dirt trail to the summit.*

*At this point I passed the only people I'd see on Redfield, a young couple in their 20s and their dog. The guy said there wasn't much of a view at the top, while she told me it was great. So given those mixed reviews I didn't know what to think, but there was only one way to find out, right?*

*I found myself moving slower and stopping for a breather more than usual up Redfield. I was somewhat exhausted, but more so bored if I'm being honest. I really wish I had someone to chat with, but such is solo hiking. I feel experiencing the trails with other people always beats going at it alone.*

*Due to my slower hiking, it took me longer than I anticipated to summit, but I made it up to the wooden Redfield summit sign at 2:30 p.m., almost three hours after leaving the summit of Marcy. The ascent from the trail split took about 1 hour and 15 minutes. I was no speed demon up this mountain today. Mt. Redfield, named after William Redfield, who organized and participated in the first recorded ascent of Mt. Marcy, stands at 4,606' elevation. It has a mostly wooded summit with some views if you're tall enough to see over the trees. It's not the type of summit to sit and eat a sandwich while taking in the views, but any mountain summit is better than no mountain summit.*

*I only stayed a few minutes on Redfield before heading down the trail because Cliff still awaited me. Once I made it back to the stream, I ran out of water. The five liters of water I brought for the day was gone. It was time to pump some water for the very first time and experience drinking this delicious Adirondack backcountry river water. Fortunately, a few days before this hike I had purchased a small low-profile water pump from EMS. It was $50 and my wife wasn't thrilled about me spending the money, but I told her, "If there's ever a time on the trail that I need to pump water, I'd rather have this pump than an extra $50 in the bank account." That was the case today. I filled up my two water bottles and a portion of my three-liter bladder and carried on. I also popped a couple of electrolyte tablets into the bottles. I highly recommend having these in your backpack because when you're dehydrated, water alone won't fix the problem; you need electrolytes and salt.*

It felt like it took an eternity to get down from Redfield today, and then seemingly out of nowhere, boom, I was back at the trail junction marked by the big cairn. So that was a pleasant surprise, and a morale boost, when I finally arrived.

Okay, Marcy, Skylight, Gray, and Redfield are done. Time to bag the final peak of the day, Cliff.

Now let me start off by saying that I listed Cliff as my least favorite peak on my 46'er registration. So, with that in mind, this hike didn't go too well for me (and my love for this mountain has never quite increased). From the start there is about a good 50 yards of pure 12-inch-deep swamp mud. Mud so deep you better hope you don't lose your boot. And there is no way to avoid it. No good logs in the mud to step on, no bridge, no down trees. A real train wreck of a stretch of trail. Both of my feet went in up to my shins at different points while traversing through this mud pit known as the Cliff Mountain trail. Once you finally get past this football field of muddy filth, the next quarter mile is still some of the muddiest trail I've experienced. It's not the same depth of mud the first portion is, but it's still way more than usual. Mind you, I'm physically and mentally exhausted at this point and my body is slowing down, so there's a good possibility that I've blown all this way out of proportion in my head due to my circumstances, but I'm not exaggerating on the caliber of mud on this trail.

After a quarter mile, the trail starts to climb up literal cliffs and long exposed slabs. Just before I got to the cliffs, I accidentally scared a group of four ladies hiking who did not expect to see me. I always knock my trekking poles together when approaching someone to avoid startling them, but I must not have been loud enough. The woman in front nearly jumped out of her boots when she saw me. Sorry, ladies!

They told me multiple times to be careful hiking alone on this mountain and warned me about the climbing that was to come. Having never hiked this peak, I wasn't entirely sure what they were talking about, but it became known as soon as I came to the slabs. I grabbed some roots along the side of the slab and started climbing. I ended up off trail at some point and had to do a quick bushwhack to get back to the trail. Fortunately, I found it after a few minutes. Getting lost out here at this point in the day would have been terrible.

Once at the top of the cliffs I started feeling like I was at the summit, and you know how when you feel like you're at the top you let a little "steam out of your system"? You release the "pressure valve" inside a little bit? Well guess what, I wasn't there. I was pump-faked hard by this false summit. I could have killed someone. Being tired, super muddy, and admittedly starting to get cranky, I was really hoping to see that Cliff Mountain summit sign, but as the trail started going down I stopped and took out my map. Yup, I still had to go over this ridge, down into the col, and then back up to the true summit. Damn. The information was there, so it shouldn't have come as a surprise, but I obviously didn't do my usual homework for the spontaneous addition to this day's adventure. It bit me in the ass a bit. Well, emotionally, anyways. Maybe a little physically too. But mostly emotionally . . . and spiritually.

Anyways, I carried on hiking down and up the final 0.1 miles to the summit. After this huge day and all that work in the mud pit, there awaited me a huge open summit with views for days, right? . . . Right? Nope. A completely wooded summit with minimal peaks popping out over the trees. It was a fitting finish for my Cliff Mountain experience. Nevertheless, I made it. I arrived at the Cliff Mountain summit sign at 4:50 p.m., 3,960' elevation, almost 12.5 hours into my day for my fifth High Peak of the day for number 32. I surpassed my month's stretch goal by multiple mountains with weeks to go. I was stoked. Exhausted, but stoked.

Cliff Mountain ranks 44th out of the 46 High Peaks elevation-wise, so it's one of the shorter mountains. I impressed myself today with what I could do when I kept pushing and didn't quit. One foot in front of the other. It was hard, but I was here. It didn't take long, however, for reality to set in about what was still ahead of me. "Great job, James! You summited Marcy, Skylight, Gray, Cliff, and Redfield today. Good work! Too bad you still have eight miles back to the Loj." Dear God. Eight more miles? Just kill me now. The thought of that eight-mile walk back to the Loj, including another trip through the floating logs, was not what I wanted to do. But like any hike, there was no choice in the matter because my feet had to take me home. Sure, I could have taken other trails to avoid the logs, but that would have added more time and mileage so that wasn't happening. Time to keep going, one foot in front of the other.

Upon arriving on Cliff, I snapped a photo and then called my wife to tell her I made it before immediately starting back down the trail. This was a quick Blake Peak–length summit stay today. Short and sweet.

Descending Cliff felt much faster than going up, and I got down off the cliff faces without issue, thankfully. My broken trekking pole was even holding up, and I was moving at a good pace. I passed a man and his dog on my descent as they were climbing up. I warned him about the cliffs and to be careful with his dog (even though dogs tend to do better than we do in those situations). He was camping tonight down at the Uphill lean-to. Oh yeah, camping. I often forget that people camp out here and make the days much more reasonable instead of always being long day hikes in and out. I should try that sometime.

I told myself that once I got to the mud pit at the bottom of the trail I was just going to send it straight through. Hot and fast. So, with the same focus, determination, and inner rage with which I approach a 600-pound deadlift, I was just going to plow through that section of trail, mud be damned. And so I did. And it was muddy! It did prove to be a faster and even somewhat more efficient way across, though. My feet were wet, muddy, and gross. I wasn't going to change my socks, however, until I got past the floating logs. To me that was the appropriate time.

I made it back to the cairn and was officially off Cliff. Hallelujah! It took about an hour up and an hour down for me. Now for the 0.5-mile walk back to the Marcy trail junction, and then the long walk back to the Loj—a roughly seven-mile trip home via the Lake Arnold trail, to the Avalanche Pass trail, to Marcy Dam, and then to the Loj. Let's do this! Oh, if only I knew what awaited me just up the trail. Let's continue . . .

Shortly after I passed the Marcy trail junction for my third time of the day, I walked across a wooden bridge over the Opalescent River that I was positive I went over about 12 hours earlier on my hike in. However, nothing looked familiar, and I couldn't find trail markers, just campsite signs. I was a little out of sorts for a moment. "I swear I came this way this morning," I thought to myself. After a few minutes of looking around and realizing, "I just don't remember anymore," I walked back over the bridge and for the first and only time on my 46'er journey, I asked for directions. Thankfully some campers graciously pointed me back on the trail toward the Loj. It turns out I didn't go over that bridge this morning; I just went past it. At this point I could feel my body wanting to shut down both physically and mentally, but I couldn't let that happen since there was still so much hiking left to go. I fueled up with the last piece of food in my pack, a king-size Snickers. Hungry? Why wait? Grab a Snickers. If any of you readers work for Snickers, I would love an endorsement.

I was back on the right trail now and carried on. A few minutes later I was back. I was back for my revenge on the floating logs. It was time to conquer or be conquered. So I planned my attack. I'd go from this log to that log to the land over here. Then step over there, get wet on that log, and finally change my socks after. Okay, I had a game plan. Time to execute.

I followed my plan, and it was working beautifully. I was actually crossing the bog and remaining dry in the process. Then on my final step back to dry land, it happened. Snap! The log I was standing on snapped in two as my entire back leg dropped straight down into the water while my front leg stood on dry land. Half my body was submerged in the water up to my waist as I literally straddled the Adirondack backcountry. Desperate to not fall backpack first into the bog, I grabbed on to the tiniest root sticking out of the ground. This little-root-that-could held strong as I held on for dear life. Without that root I would have become 100 percent submerged in the water. Good-bye to both my cell phone and my dignity, right? But thank the Lord this godsend little root held strong and I pulled myself out of the water and onto dry land. Thankfully only half my body was soaked. From what could have happened, I'll take it.

Remember when I said "conquer or be conquered" earlier? Well, lesson learned today. Nobody "conquers" anything about these Adirondack Mountains. The mountains allow you the opportunity to experience them. It is a privilege to explore their woods, summits, lakes, and rivers. They are to be respected and revered. They will always do the conquering. The mountains are not calling you. The mountains don't care about you. I learned that lesson today. Shout-out to the High Peaks for once again teaching me more valuable life lessons. Thank you.

After falling victim to the floating logs (again), I was finally over them, and now I could change my socks one last time. What a great feeling it was. The worst was over now, and it was time to get back to the Loj. I moved as fast as I could, but I was moving rather slowly.

Just before the Colden trail split, I passed a young couple hiking into "Lake Colden Land" for some camping and hiking. I think they thought I was a little weird because I was that solo hiker who was "all too excited" to see and chat with another hiker. After all, it was a long day solo in the woods with no one to talk to but myself. At this hour I didn't expect to see anybody else either. They were hiking in to the Feldspar lean-to for the night, but thanks to those two for engaging me in conversation, because I was definitely borderline insane at that point in the day.

Once I came to the Colden trail split, I had a split-second thought cross my mind: "Do I dare?" Fortunately, I still had some sense of intelligence and said, "No way, leave it for another day. You'll probably die up there because your body hates you right now." Imagine if I did, though. This story would be even longer than it already is.

I kept hiking as I started down that long gradual stretch of rock hopping in the valley of Colden. This stretch was killing my feet at that point because they were just toast from the day. My brain wanted to shut down, but I couldn't let that happen because I still had a lot of hiking left to do. That became a minute-by-minute battle like late-night drives where you have to keep yourself awake.

Once I made it back to the Avalanche Pass junction, I had a great conversation with a camper who was taking in the evening air on the bridge over Marcy Brook. Once again, I likely came off as the insane hiker who is overly excited to talk with someone, but he was alone too, so we had a great conversation. Out of curiosity, I asked him why he chose this campsite over others since he was planning to hike Cliff and Redfield and there are so many closer options. He looked me in the eyes and let out one word, "Bears." "Bears?" I responded. "Yes. There've been a lot of reports of bears in campsites up there this summer and even bears taking people's packs at their campsites." I imagine it was probably Sasquatch stealing people's packs and not bears, but it was good intel nonetheless.

Soon we parted ways, and I was back on the Avalanche Pass trail heading toward Marcy Dam when I got a text from my dad that said, "Are you back on level ground yet?" I responded, "I am back to Marcy Dam, but then I still have 2.4 miles back to my car." I was still a few miles from my car, but I kept walking slowly as I was dying on the inside. Not really, but I *was ready to be back. Shout-out to my mom and dad for always checking on me during my hikes and for caring. I am a blessed man.*

*Once I saw the Marcy Dam campsites, I received a surge of energy because I was near the dam. Yes! The final checkpoint of the day was upon me. It was another morale boost, and I needed it because the sun was starting to set. Despite the darkness taking over, I had an argument in my head with myself that went something like this: "I refuse to take off my backpack to get my headlamp. . . . I will not hike out with my headlamp. . . . No! . . . I'm going to make it back before it's too dark." The mountains laughed at me and responded, "Sure, James. Nice try. Watch this!" as the woods were overtaken by the dark, night air.*

*I got to the dam and mustered all the energy I could to pick up my pace to beat the darkness. I made it all the way to the Algonquin trail split before finally giving in. The mountains won. Again. I took off my pack and grabbed my headlamp with only one mile to go. The woods had been pitch black for a good 10 minutes now, so it seemed like the right choice. My day started in the dark and ended in the dark.*

*Overwhelmed with joy and moving slowly, I made it back to the trail-head and signed out at 9:30 p.m. A big 17-hour day with 27 miles of hiking and climbing five High Peaks, including the tallest, fourth tallest, and seventh tallest. What a day!*

*While I feel very accomplished and proud of this day, in hindsight adding Cliff and Redfield was not the wisest choice. Thankfully I made it out okay without any serious issues. Well, aside from the emotional trauma suffered not once but twice at the hands of the floating logs, along with the entire trip up Cliff, of course. It's good to push yourself, and the mountains are a great place to "see what you're made of." This was a bit early in my journey and experience level, though, to tackle such a big day solo. With that said, I was proud of the day.*

*Now that I was out of the woods I had one thing on my mind—hot food. Having not eaten "real" food since 11:30 a.m., I was famished. I said to myself, "I'm going to McDonald's." Let's go!*

*I quickly kicked off my socks and kicked on my Crocs and drove to McDonald's in Lake Placid, ready to feast. I pulled up to the drive-thru to order. I sat there in anticipation of ordering half the menu. A minute went by. Followed by another minute. Nothing but the gentle sound of my idling* engine filled the night air at the drive-thru. "Hello? . . . Hello?" I said into the neon screen. Silence. "There's no way they're closed at 9:45 on a summer night," I said to myself. Sounds of my rumbling stomach grew louder and louder. Desperate to order and getting hungrier by the minute, I drove around to go inside. I walked up to the door, and taped on the glass was a handwritten note in black sharpie that read, "Closed at 8 p.m. tonight. Sorry for the inconvenience." YOU HAVE GOT TO BE KIDDING ME! How does this keep happening to me? Like after my day in the MacIntyre Range, I called an audible and immediately headed to Saranac Lake's McDonald's. I drove like a race car driver down Route 86 determined to make it there before they closed. I pulled into the drive-thru, and then I heard the most angelic, glorious sound of my life: "Hi! Welcome to McDonald's. What can I get for you today?" Hallelujah! Let's just say I hit that drive-thru pretty darn hard that night.

A few minutes later I pulled into my driveway and hobbled up the steps into my house where my wife greeted me after my longest day in the woods to date. I actually had a hard time unwinding and falling asleep that night because my body did not want to shut down. I had certainly pushed my limits that day and challenged myself, but I made it home in one piece and that's what truly matters.

Another extremely successful day in the woods where I summited Marcy, Skylight, Gray, Cliff, and Redfield for High Peaks numbers 28, 29, 30, 31, and 32. Today's hike surpassed my stretch goal for the month of getting into the 30s on my quest to summit all 46 Adirondack High Peaks in one summer. This hike would finish off July for me, a month in which I climbed 28 High Peaks, averaging almost one High Peak a day. I told myself that after this hike I needed to take a break for a couple of weeks. Funny how we say things like that to ourselves, isn't it? I would end up right back on the trail to tackle Colden and Marshall just five days later. Thanks for coming along with me on this monster 17-hour, 27-mile, 5-peak day. Next time I'll revisit a huge chunk of today's hike on my way up Colden and Marshall as I hike around Lake Colden and through Avalanche Pass for the first time.

# 13 Mt. Colden and Mt. Marshall

Colden (4,714'), Marshall (4,360')
**Mileage:** 18.3 miles
**Elevation Gain:** 4,677'

Starting at the Adirondack Loj in Lake Placid, this is one of those hikes that could be broken up into two individual hikes or tackled as one day. I feel pairing these two mountains makes for a fun, diverse Adirondack experience. It's important to do your homework with the High Peaks map to learn the route so you know how and where to connect the trails.

Colden is one of those mountains with a big open rock summit with unbelievable views of Lake Colden below and the MacIntyre Range directly in front of you. It also offers a fun climb. Marshall is a more rugged experience with a wooded summit. Combined, these two peaks offer a diverse ADK experience in one package. SSA Scale rankings favor Colden with a 5/5 while Marshall ranks a 1/5. They can't all be 5/5, right?

Once Marshall is complete, the hike will take you along the backside of Lake Colden, past the Colden trap dike, over the hitch up Matilda, and through the fan favorite Avalanche Pass. Another reason I enjoy this loop is because most of your day involves new trails. This keeps things interesting throughout the entire hike.

You're welcome to do the loop in either direction since there isn't a real benefit one way or the other; just study the map and choose your preference. If you do break up the hike into two days,

Mt. Colden and its slides as seen from Wright Peak. *Photo by James Appleton*

there are several ways to tackle Colden, and even a couple for Marshall. Since they're both deep in the wilderness, however, you'll end up traversing a lot of the same land twice (but that's not always a bad thing). Overall I think these are great peaks to pair together.

Okay, enough talking about it. Story time. Mt. Colden, you're up next!

## MT. COLDEN AND MT. MARSHALL

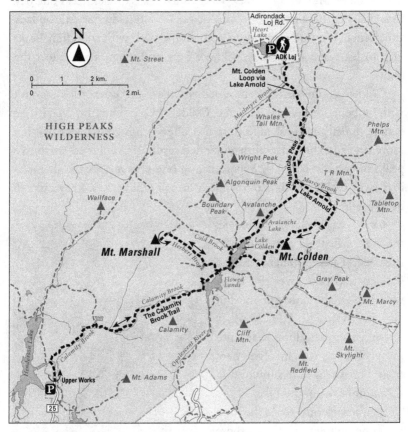

## Mt. Colden and Mt. Marshall

*August 3, 2018. Just a mere five days after I swore I was taking a few weeks off hiking following my 27-mile, 17-hour solo day climbing Marcy, Skylight, and Gray, along with the spontaneous addition of Cliff and Redfield. But as the mountains so often do, they drew me back in. It only takes a day or two away to feel the need to return to the woods. So back to the Adirondack Loj I went. This time to climb fan favorite Mt. Colden and the often confusing, unmaintained Mt. Marshall. It was a Friday morning, but I was leaving for work on Sunday for a couple of months so I had to squeeze in as many days on the trail as I could. Off to the mountains!*

My plan today was to revisit the same trail I hiked five days prior while also traversing an abundance of trails I've yet to experience. I would start at the Adirondack Loj to Marcy Dam, then take the Avalanche Pass trail to the Lake Arnold trail up to the L. Morgan Porter trail to climb Colden. I would descend the other side of Colden via the Colden trail back to Avalanche Pass. I would walk along the shores of Lake Colden toward the southern tip of the lake where I'll eventually take a left onto the Calamity Brook trail just after the wooden bridge at the edge of the lake. From there I would head for the Herbert Brook trail to ascend and descend Marshall. My loop would continue via the Lake Colden trail along the western side of the lake until it eventually met back up with the Avalanche Pass trail, which I would take all the way back to Marcy Dam, and then the Van Hoevenberg trail back to the Loj. So that was my itinerary for the day. A lot of trails making for one big ADK adventure!

The first five miles of my route were fresh in my mind since I had hiked it five days prior. That's why I decided to start extra early today. I also wanted to finish earlier since I was leaving home soon for work. I wanted as much time at home with the family as I could get while also continuing to push toward this goal.

Due to the typical pre-hike jitters I always experience the night before a solo hike, I barely slept. My mind would not shut off as it went through my route repeatedly. That did make it easier to wake up at about 2 a.m. though. I was out the door and signed in at the Loj at 3:30 a.m. The first sign-in of the day once again. I clicked on my headlamp and began hustling down the trail toward Marcy Dam. Through the woods, over the bridges, and face-first into the spiderwebs as the sounds of the dark

*Adirondack woods surrounded me. I knew from my previous hike that the trip to the Morgan Porter trail up Colden would be exactly two hours, so I anticipated this whole portion to be in the dark. It was.*

*I crossed over Marcy Dam and went right again onto Avalanche Pass trail, where I traveled along the Marcy Brook. I'm pretty sure I startled some campers at the Lake Arnold trail junction who were not expecting to hear someone coming down the trail at this hour. I saw the flashlights turn on in the tent and could hear someone whispering frantically. I quickly took the left at the junction and began the trail up the long but gradual trek toward Lake Arnold. This part of the trail involves almost all rock hopping and is one long constant elevation gain. Dare I say even a little monotonous?*

*It was a humid, cloudy, and misty summer day. Thanks to the humidity, mist, and sweating, my glasses were fogging up nonstop once again. Foggy glasses and a headlamp do not mix, so off they went. Ah, much clearer now . . . kind of.*

*I finished the climb up to the wooden planks at the Colden trail junction at Lake Arnold almost to the second that it took me five days prior. Literally a five-second difference. Wild. If you're wondering, it took two hours, landing me there at 5:30 a.m. The sun was starting to rise, but it was still relatively dark in the woods. So this time I turned right and began my trip up Mt. Colden. Colden is a mountain people often save for their number 46, but for me it would be number 33. Scottie Pippen's number. The ultimate sidekick.*

*This trail up the eastern side of Colden gains elevation gradually and is a mix of dirt and slabs. A lot of elevation is gained by the time you arrive at the Porter trail. There's still plenty to go, of course, but the Porter trail starts at 3,700' elevation.*

*Just before I climbed another rock slab I decided to take a breather and eat a PB&J. I don't often stop for a pre-summit sandwich, but I could feel the hunger in my stomach. Fueled up and ready to go, I hurried up the slab and quickly came out onto what I thought was the summit. A big, exposed open rock face that felt very "peaky." As I walked around, I thought, "Hmm, that mountain next to me looks like the summit of Colden." I was right; it was a false summit. It took me a minute or two to find the right trail over this rock ledge because I missed the yellow painted* trail markers on the rock when I thought, "I'm at the summit!" My excitement took over prematurely.

It took me 45 minutes to get from the Colden trail junction to this false summit. The summit looks miles away on this ridge, but it's closer than it seems. I hopped back on the trail and continued up toward the Colden summit. It only took another 15 minutes to the summit, landing me there at 6:30 a.m., exactly three hours from signing in at the Loj and one hour from the Lake Arnold trail junction.

I was standing on top of one of the most iconic mountains in the High Peaks. Mt. Colden, 4,714' elevation, the 11th-tallest High Peak for number 33. It has a cool summit with amazing views, and it's a great place to pencil in sometime. It was cloudy on this day, so my views were a five out of ten. Not terrible, but not as spectacular as they could be. What is cool on Colden, however, and unique is seeing the valley with Lake Colden and Avalanche Lake below.

Since it was cloudy and humid and I had just eaten a sandwich 20 minutes before on the trail, I only stayed for 10 minutes. Since my plan for today was to go up and over Colden, I descended via the Colden trail toward the Avalanche Pass trail at Lake Colden. The view as you make your way back to the tree line is awesome because you have the mountains, the valley, and the lake down below on full display.

The trail down Colden is consistent in terms of elevation loss/gain, but what makes it unique is that the majority of the trail is a rock slab. There are some dirt portions, especially down low, but the large majority is rock. On this day it was very wet, though, so that made for slippery conditions. There were a few slips and a lot of grabbing onto roots while butt sliding down. There's even an awesome stretch with a long wooden staircase. Shout-out to the trail crews who built those stairs; they're great. I'm willing to bet you'll probably snap a photo or two while going down the stairs. This trail would be a fast one to ascend or descend on a dry day thanks to the slabs, making the hike more like walking on pavement than dirt, but since today was wet, it was slower.

I eventually made it down to the Avalanche Pass trail at the bottom and went left to begin walking the shores of Lake Colden. The trail around the lake has you constantly stepping from rock to rock and climbing over giant boulders. Around the eastern edge of the lake I went. I eventually came to a wooden bridge at the southern tip of the lake leading to a wood ladder to climb up to the trail above. In my brain this was the unofficial start to phase 2 of the day, the Marshall phase. Also, the views down here at the tip of the lake of Mt. Colden towering above are unbelievable.

I climbed the ladder and went left toward Mt. Marshall. This trail is called the Calamity Brook trail, and it goes all the way to the Upper Works trailhead. A lot of people access this area of the High Peaks from that direction. Not long after walking in the woods and along some rocks I came to the cairn marking the beginning of the Herbert Brook trail, a herd path to the top of Mt. Marshall. As I arrived at the cairn, I passed my first humans of the day. The hikers in their early 20s camped just up the trail and were climbing Colden, Cliff, and Redfield today. Then, if time and energy allowed, Mt. Marshall as well. Talk about a huge elevation day. All the way up and all the way down three to four different High Peaks. We chatted about the mud that awaited them at the beginning of Cliff. I was still a little salty about that mountain. Oh, Cliff Mountain, maybe one day we will be friends. It wasn't going to be today though.

I started up the herd path that hugs the Herbert Brook, hence the name. I was extra cautious about staying mentally focused because Josh warned me that this mountain is a little confusing and to be attentive to the trail. The older gentleman I met coming down Marcy also told me he took the wrong trail on Marshall resulting in not summiting. These warnings kept my mind focused on the path.

The beginning winds and weaves through the woods following the brook, like many Adirondack trails. With this being an unmaintained herd path, the trail has the exposed roots and muddy areas due to all the foot traffic. Marshall is a rugged mountain not unlike many High Peaks, and I made it up to the wooden summit sign at 9:50 a.m., just under 6.5 hours into my day. My total ascent time was 1 hour and 15 minutes. Mt. Marshall, named after original 46'er brother Robert Marshall, stands at 4,360' elevation for High Peak number 34.

The summit is wooded with some small views at various points around the summit. It is not the most popular hike for views though. Now, by this point into my journey you know the rules: one sandwich per summit. So I took off my backpack and refueled for the long walk back to the Loj with another delicious peanut butter and jelly sandwich. Triple-deckers today, too. I summit sandwich at a very high level.

While I was up here, I remembered a friend of mine telling me about a plane crash site near Mt. Marshall. At the time I had no idea where it was so I didn't go looking around, but it's something to keep in mind when you're planning this hike. The plane crashed on August 10, 1969. Today was August 3, 2018. Therefore one week from today marks 49 years since the plane crashed. The pilot survived the crash, thankfully, despite a body of broken bones. The rescue story is worth looking into as well. In fact, it would make a fantastic movie. The pilot was lucky because his plane landed in a small grove of pine trees, narrowly missing boulders that would have caused a very different ending.

If you are curious, the plane crash is located just off the Indian Pass trail in the valley between Marshall and Iroquois. This trail can be difficult to follow at times, but the crash is roughly 100' off the trail. There is no specific marker for the plane crash, but when you reach the valley between Marshall and Iroquois, keep your eyes peeled for a large distinct boulder sitting directly on the left side of the trail (assuming you're coming in from the Lake Colden/Avalanche Pass area). The plane crash is visible from behind the boulder if you look carefully. I'll have to check it out sometime, but today wasn't the day.

I summited both peaks of the day, and now it was time to head back home. It took me about 1 hour and 20 minutes to descend the mountain, and I went back down the way I came, via the Herbert Brook trail. I got back to the cairn and went left toward Lake Colden where I continued around the western edge of the lake on the Lake Colden trail. This trail passes the ranger outpost at Lake Colden. So if you're ever in need of help, there's typically someone there. Just follow the Lake Colden trail around the lake and you'll come to the ranger outpost cabin.

Once past the lake and the trail up the backside of Algonquin, the trail merges with the Avalanche Pass trail heading toward Avalanche Lake. This is all flat woods walking, so one can run and make great time on it. It's very remote out here too, and you can feel it.

Still no sign of other people today besides the two guys at the base of Marshall, so I had the woods to myself. Once I got to the Avalanche Pass trail I was able to relax since I was on the trail that would take me back to the familiar territory of Marcy Dam. This stretch along Avalanche Lake is scenic, with amazing views of Mt. Colden to the east and Avalanche Mountain to the west.

As I walked along the lake, climbing up and over boulders, I randomly remembered the Colden trap dike. "Crap!" I thought to myself, "did I miss the trap dike?" Then I looked directly across the lake and, boom, there it was in full glory. I was literally directly across the lake from it for a perfect photo op. I like to think the mountains were in my head saying, "James, don't just walk fast with your head down. Stop and enjoy the scenery sometimes!" They were right, and the scenery was amazing. Another good life lesson from the Adirondack High Peaks.

Shortly after passing the trap dike, I walked over a stretch of trail I've seen many photos of over the years, known as "Hitch-Up Matilda." This stretch has the trail walking over the lake via a wood bridge attached to the side of Avalanche Mountain. Picture steel frames drilled into the side of Avalanche Mountain with wooden planks laid across the beams forming a bridge hovering a few feet over Avalanche Lake. It's an iconic stretch of trail here in the High Peaks. You'll be sure to take a photo, I can guarantee that.

The name "Hitch-Up Matilda" comes from an old story about Bill Nye, an Adirondack guide whom Nye Mountain is named after, while guiding Matilda Fielding, her husband, and their niece in 1868. Originally, this stretch consisted of floating logs chained together like a raft, allowing the trail to continue along the lake. This bridge was replaced in the 1970s with what we see today. Beyond Hitch-Up Matilda, the walk around Avalanche Lake involves a lot of rock hopping and climbing up and down ladders and boulders along the lake.

I started to pass group after group around noontime as hikers walked in for their summer weekend adventures here in the Adirondack backcountry. I found myself slightly bored from being alone with just my thoughts all day once again. I like good conversation with others on the trail, and that was lacking today. Then I passed a father and his little boy out for a hike. They weren't hiking any mountains this weekend; they were simply going camping and being in the woods together. It's not always about climbing mountains; it's about the sheer joy of the great outdoors. What a great way to live.

*Once I got back to the Lake Arnold trail junction, I walked over the wood bridge to begin the final trek toward Marcy Dam followed by the 2.4-mile walk from the dam back to the Loj. I continued passing dozens of campers walking toward the dam for a weekend of adventure as my day's adventure was coming to an end. Another amazing day it was.*

*I made it back to the trailhead and signed out at 2:15 p.m., totaling my day at 10 hours and 45 minutes. A good long day with these two peaks for High Peaks number 33 and 34. I certainly earned them here on my 11th High Peaks hike on my quest to summit all 46 High Peaks in one summer. Mt. Colden and Mt. Marshall complete, and to quote New York Mets radio broadcaster Howie Rose, "Put it in the books!" I'd be back on the trail just 36 hours after signing out as Josh and I headed to the Upper Great Range to climb Haystack, Basin, and Saddleback, snagging the only remaining parking spot at the Garden at 3:45 a.m.*

# 14 Upper Great Range (Mt. Haystack, Basin Mountain, Saddleback Mountain)

Haystack (4,960'), Basin (4,827'), Saddleback (4,515')
**Mileage:** 18.5 miles
**Elevation Gain:** 5,207'

Starting at the Garden trailhead in Keene Valley, this will be a monumental day in the High Peaks, a group of mountains that possess a magical quality about them. Two of these mountains are in the top-10 tallest in the ADK Park (Haystack and Basin), and it's a long nine-mile trek to Haystack, but that adds to its magic. You earn these summits, and trust me, they're worth the effort.

Haystack is like Mt. Marcy's younger brother. They sit next to one another and are close in size and stature, with the magnificent Panther Gorge between them. The day continues with Basin and Saddleback. The Upper Great Range scores a perfect 15/15 on the SSA Scale, each peak landing a 5/5. Pack those sandwiches!

Starting at the Garden, you will hike three miles to John's Brook Lodge where you will begin and end the day's loop. I strongly recommend hiking this loop starting with Haystack (then to Basin and ending on Saddleback) for one reason: the cliffs. Climbing up both Basin's and Saddleback's cliffs is arguably safer than climbing down them. People hike this range in both directions, but that's my recommendation.

It's extra important to study the map meticulously because there are a few trail junctions that can throw a hiker off track if they aren't paying attention. So make sure you study up before this hike (like you always do).

It's a long hike to the first summit of the day, the mighty Haystack, totaling nine miles from trailhead to summit. These nine miles aren't without views, though. Once you arrive at the Marcy trail junction, you'll be near Little Haystack and see Haystack towering above. The last mile of the ascent is above the tree line and offers an unbelievable experience. It will be a welcome sight as the Adirondack High Peaks fill the sky. It will feel like you're on a different planet.

After Haystack, you will climb back over Little Haystack into the tree line. Next, it's down to the col, where you'll pass the Sno-Bird campsite (the highest campsite in the Adirondacks, sitting just over

## UPPER GREAT RANGE (MT. HAYSTACK, BASIN MOUNTAIN, SADDLEBACK MOUNTAIN)

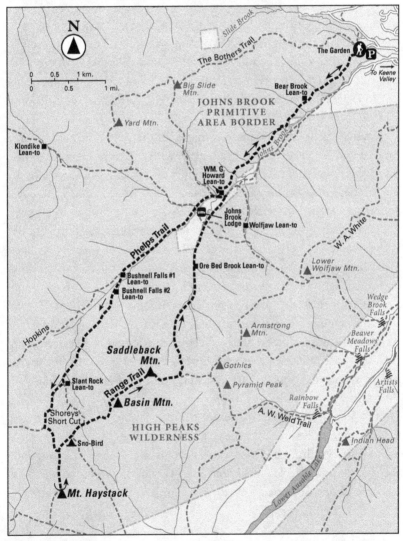

4,000') as you head up Basin. The climb up Basin has some sketchy moments as you climb slabs via tree roots on the side, so use caution. It's a mile up from the col to the summit and almost 1,000' of gain. It's a solid climb, but you'll be met with an open rock summit and amazing views—the best type of summit.

Heading down the backside of Basin toward Saddleback is also a bit rough at times, so take it slow and be safe. The beauty here is once you make it to the col. You're very close to the summit of Saddleback thanks to the Saddleback Cliffs.

By now you've probably heard all about the Saddleback Cliffs. This is an actual rock climb—a short one—but a climb, nonetheless. You'll be scaling cracks, always keeping three points of contact, and climbing a rock face. It is not to be taken lightly. In that same regard, it is also not to be feared. You can do it. If heights or a small rock climb frightens you, you *could* always tackle this range in multiple days via different trails to avoid the Saddleback Cliffs. I think you're better off tackling your fear and overcoming the challenge, though. I'm willing to bet you will say "That wasn't so bad" when you finish. Most people do. By this point in your journey, you should have a lot of confidence built up.

**NOTE:** The trail signage at John's Brook Lodge can be confusing. There is a mileage sign pointing you to Haystack, but that direction involves going over both Saddleback and Basin first; therefore, it's the opposite direction of the loop outlined in this guide. Following that sign will have you going down the Saddleback Cliffs, which I'm try-ing to help you avoid. At this junction, look at your map and continue straight on the route you've been climbing toward Marcy and do not go left. It is technically an accurate sign because you can get to Haystack that way (eventually), but in my opinion it's an extremely deceiving sign that can lead to major safety concerns for some hikers not expecting to go down those cliffs. Something to keep in mind upon arriving at JBL. Follow the map and take note of the junction at John's Brook Lodge.

Time to get into my perfect bluebird summer day on the Upper Great Range.

The mighty Mt. Haystack during a summer Great Range Traverse. *Photo by James Appleton*

### Upper Great Range (Mt. Haystack, Basin Mountain, Saddleback Mountain)

*August 5, 2018. It was a Sunday morning, and later today I would be back on the road for another stretch of work. This amazing month of hiking was over, but my 46'er journey was still very much underway. Less than 36 hours after finishing Colden and Marshall, I was driving to the Garden trailhead in Keene Valley with Josh to squeeze in one last hike before leaving home for a couple of months. The Upper Great Range. Haystack, Basin, and Saddleback. Arguably the most epic hikes of all the High Peaks. A crowd favorite. And we had another perfect, sunny, bluebird Adirondack summer day.*

Knowing I had to drive to New York City after our hike, Josh obliged me, so the 4:30 a.m. crew got an earlier start than usual. We drove separate cars, and I left my house in Saranac Lake at 3:00 a.m. and headed to Keene Valley. Given how busy the Garden parking lot is, we decided to park one of our cars at the Roostercomb lot then hop in one car and drive up to the Garden. We got to Roostercomb and it was packed, leaving me worried the Garden would be even worse. But I parked my van and hopped in Josh's truck. We drove up to the Garden and snagged the only remaining parking spot at the trailhead. Thank God! So the hike was on. It was very dark and very quiet, but it was time for another adventure. We clicked on our headlamps and signed in at 3:45 a.m. Time to hit the trail.

No more than three steps into the woods, we both heard something very large just outside the glow of our headlamp move through the woods, and it stopped Josh and me dead in our tracks. "Hello . . . ?" I called out into the dead silence. Whatever moved had stopped moving. "What was that?" I whispered to Josh as we both gave each other a nervous look. Since neither of us wanted to be the wimp, we shook it off and continued down the trail. We moved quickly through this first section, though, I will admit.

Our plan for the day was to walk into John's Brook Loj and head toward Marcy to summit Haystack first. After that nine-mile stretch from trailhead to summit, we would continue the loop past the Sno-Bird campsite and up to Basin, followed by Saddleback, then back to JBL and back to the parking lot. The day would be around 18.5 miles, with just over 5,000' of elevation gain. Although, after my recent trek up Marcy, Skylight, Gray, Cliff, and Redfield, anything under 20 miles seemed like child's play. The Upper Great Range, however, is still a big day, no matter how you slice it.

We continued the 3.5-mile walk to John's Brook Loj, winding through the woods on a pleasant dirt trail. A nice, easy start to the hike. If you're not familiar with John's Brook Loj, it's a Loj with campsites people can rent out. It's a great spot and I recommend it.

Thankfully we didn't hear any more large noises in the woods this morning. We made it to JBL and crossed over the brook via the high wooden bridge just as the sun was beginning to rise. I had only been to JBL once in my life before today, and that was on a sixth-grade field trip. The field trip was an overnight trip where you learned team-building skills with your classmates. One of the other class trips was cut short, however, when one student threatened another with a knife before pulling out said knife. Field trip over. Middle school, am I right?

So, after arriving at JBL we walked around and took a stroll down memory lane for a minute before following the signs toward Marcy. Now if Josh were not here, I likely would have fallen victim to the confusing trail sign here, the same way a French Canadian man we met later in the day did. The sign is correct, but it's confusing and misleading in my humble opinion. Allow me to explain. At JBL there's a sign pointing you left and telling you the mileage to Haystack. If someone's brain is on autopilot, it's easy to go that way. After all, that direction is pointing you to Haystack with the correct mileage. What is misleading and confusing, however, is that that route involves going up and over Saddleback and Basin first to get to Haystack. If you're planning to do the loop clockwise starting with Saddleback, have at it, but today we wanted to start with Haystack. I would have gone the wrong way if it wasn't for Josh already knowing about this sign. It's accurate, yes, but a little misleading, and in a way that I feel could easily be fixed by adding a few words to the sign to accommodate hikers. It would also be safer, too, considering the whole Saddleback Cliffs conversation.

Anyways, we went toward Marcy from the Loj and continued along the brook as we gradually began climbing up to Haystack. The sun was out so we put our headlamps away and had open blue skies above us. This trail is long and feels like you're never going to arrive when you know it's nine miles from the trailhead to the summit. But we kept plugging along the trail, walking through the woods, some climbing and a little mud. The typical Adirondack hiking terrain.

We eventually came to Slant Rock, which is literally an enormous slanted rock. We grabbed a gulp of water and a snack. Up until this point, I wasn't feeling great on the day. I felt "off" from the moment I woke up this morning and couldn't understand why; however, at Slant Rock I decided to fuel up with one of my "share size" bags of peanut M&M's. In case you're wondering, no I did not share my share-size bag with Josh. I ate the entire bag at Slant Rock, and from that point on the "off" feeling I felt was gone. I felt great. M&M's to the rescue.

We suited back up and carried on up the Phelps trail where we came to the shortcut trail. Josh took it the first time he and his wife hiked this trail and said it's super steep and he didn't want to take it today, so we stayed on the Phelps trail. If you're heading to camp at the Sno-Bird campsite, one of the only campsites above 4,000' elevation in the park, I'd recommend taking that shortcut trail.

We finally came to the next trail junction and the checkpoint we were looking for. Left to Haystack or right to Marcy. Left it was today. This begins another gradual climb up for about half a mile heading toward Little Haystack and the junction for Haystack. Once we arrived at the trail split, we went right toward Haystack. Very quickly you will come out on the summit of Little Haystack where you get front-row views of Haystack in front of you. A massive mountain indeed. Now that we could see the summit, that nine-mile journey didn't seem so bad.

The trail goes up and over Little Haystack toward Haystack where the final climb is all above the tree line, the best kind of hiking, as you follow the cairns and yellow paint markers. This is another one of those mountains where it feels like you've entered a different world, like something from The Lord of the Rings or The Princess Bride. The final ascent from Little Haystack to the summit is a third of a mile and looks longer than it is, but we hustled to the top and then we were there. High Peak number 35. Haystack, the third-tallest High Peak, standing at 4,960' elevation in the perfect blue Adirondack sky.

We summited at 8:30 a.m., clocking in at 4 hours 45 minutes from sign-in to summit. One of the longer hikes to the first summit, that's for sure. Time for a sandwich. Today I decided to treat myself on each summit and instead of my usual PB&Js I brought a turkey and provolone sandwich to eat on each summit. My fuel level was going to be good today. Haystack's enormous, open rock summit has lots of space with 360-degree views all around, and on a clear day like this it was perfection. The summit had a few different groups on it when we arrived, and they were the first people we saw today. We enjoyed some friendly conversation as I am wont to do with my fellow hikers.

After hanging out for 20 minutes, we began the trek back down to Little Haystack, up and over it, and finally back to the Range trail junction. Onward to Basin. Getting to the col between Haystack and Basin wasn't too bad. It's a lot of rock hopping with a gradual descent. Nothing like what going down the next mountain would be, but let's not get ahead of ourselves.

We passed the popular Sno-Bird campsite and soon made it to the col and immediately began the ascent to Basin. Halfway up there's a big rock slab climb. Get ready to grab some roots along the edges and hold on tight as you climb. Upon reaching the top of this slab we heard the strangest accent yelling to us from up the trail. It was a very nice French Canadian man who was extremely excited to see us. He was solo, and as a solo hiker most of the time, I can relate to the desire for human connection on the trail. A quick conversation can be a big morale booster for solo hikers. It is for me, anyways.

Turns out this hiker went left toward Haystack back at JBL and fell victim to the confusing and semi-misleading-though-still-technically-accurate sign I discussed earlier. He was hiking the loop backward from how he planned to. He meant to go the same way we did. We chatted for a minute, and he told us to be careful going down the backside of Basin, which was my first hint that it was going to be brutal.

We carried on up Basin and made it to the summit one hour after leaving Haystack at 10:15 a.m. High Peak number 36, standing 4,827'. High Peak number 36! Wow, only 10 more mountains to 46! This was the first time where I could start to see the finish line of this journey. It was a great feeling.

Basin is a smaller summit compared to Haystack, but it is still open, spacious enough, and offers full 360-degree views. This whole range is unbelievable, to be honest. This was also a great summit to enjoy another great summit sandwich. So I did exactly that. We sat down, and since we had the summit to ourselves, we relaxed for a good 20 minutes before our "must keep moving" mentality kicked back in.

Now it was time to head to Saddleback. Getting down Basin was the most physically challenging part of the day. The entire descent from the summit to the col is very technical. It's the type of trail where you calculate every step before you take it. "Okay, I'll grab those roots, then step down to that rock. Then I'll hold onto that tree and swing down there to that rock." That sort of thing. It's fun, though, but it's slow going.

We both experienced a few slips on the wet muddy slabs but thankfully nothing serious. Once we made it to the col, I was thrilled because my knees were pounding and my brain needed a break from that descent. Once in the col, you're only a quarter mile from the summit, since most

of the mileage is spent descending Basin. In between you and the summit, however, are the infamous Saddleback Cliffs. This is literally a rock
climb. It's a light rock climb, but it's a climb nonetheless. You don't need
harnesses and rock-climbing gear, though some days I imagine you might,
but you'll be hanging onto rocks and climbing up. So be mindful if that
sounds like something that may be tough for you. With that said, I feel
these "cliffs" are blown out of proportion within the High Peaks hiking
community. It's a short climb, and in my opinion there are harder slab
climbs in the High Peaks. Just remind yourself that people do it every day
and you can too. You got this!

Once you stand up after climbing the "cliffs," you're at the summit.
Boom, there it is. Big open views once again with a similar-sized summit as Basin. You can enjoy the terrific views of the mountains you just
came from. Like Basin, this hike also took one hour summit-to-summit.
We landed at 11:25 a.m., for High Peak number 37. Saddleback, 4,515'
elevation. All three peaks summited before noon once again. Awesome. I
feel it's a great accomplishment to be standing on the final peak of the day
before noon. One other note about the Saddleback Cliffs: I imagine going
down the Saddleback Cliffs must be difficult, which is why I would recommend doing this range loop the direction we did. People climb these
mountains in every direction, though, so just follow your heart. Also, if
you want to avoid the cliffs altogether, you can break this range up into
two hikes from various directions. Just browse the map and create a plan.

We had the summit to ourselves again, but knowing the drive ahead
of me, we didn't stay long. I don't usually talk about "enjoyable descents"
because they usually destroy my body (and my soul), but I will make a
sweeping declaration and say the descent off Saddleback was my favorite
of any High Peak. Why, you ask? Because it has so many different types
of terrain. This change keeps it interesting both visually and physically.
One minute you're climbing down slabs by the roots, then you're in a
new section of dirt trail, followed by some rock hopping for a while, then
you're walking down an enormous wooden staircase down the side of a
huge slide. It was awesome, and props to the trail crew who built that long
wooden staircase. There are some amazing raspberry bushes at the end
of the staircase, too. Raspberries are much more emotionally satisfying in
the wild than from the store.

*After the staircase we were back on level ground for the long walk out to JBL and eventually the Garden. Shortly before JBL we crossed a river and decided to stop and refill our water for the walk out. Delicious ADK river water, you just can't beat it.*

*We made it to JBL and continued a fast pace through the woods back on the Phelps trail toward the Garden. Since it was Sunday afternoon, Josh and I decided to make a friendly wager on the way back. The bet was "Will there be more or less than 15 people coming down the trail from the garden?" I took the over, Josh the under. The stakes were "winner buys Chinese food." Which we planned to eat on top of Big Slide for my 46'er finish. What a way to celebrate, right?*

*The stakes were set, and it was time to start counting. Bring on the hikers! We walked for a good 10 minutes without passing a single soul. I began thinking, "Of course, it's Sunday afternoon; no one is coming in here at this point." Shortly thereafter a few hikers trickled in, and then a few more. Now I'm thinking, "Okay, this is more like it." Meanwhile, Josh was very confident we would not see more than 15. Then moments later, it happened. Like a scene from a movie in slow motion with triumphant music blasting. Up the trail came a group of 12 teenage boys hiking in for an exciting couple of days at JBL. And the winner by knockout is James Appleton. As we passed this group of boys, I thanked them one by one for choosing to go camping today. Chinese food won is better than Chinese food paid for . . . or something like that.*

*We made it back to the Garden trailhead and signed out at 2:55 p.m., totaling our day at 11 hours 10 minutes. A long yet enjoyable day on the trail with arguably the best views and summits of all the High Peaks. My day, however, was far from over. Sadly, I still had to drive back to New York City for work at 6 a.m. tomorrow morning. I remember standing on top of Basin and thinking to myself, "I'm standing on top of Basin right now, yet I'll be going to sleep tonight in Brooklyn." A wild realization, really. Josh had a great suggestion and said I should jump into Chapel Pond on my way out of town and then change my clothes for my drive. A truly amazing idea that checked all the right boxes. If you've never swam in Chapel Pond, add it to your list. It's on Route 73.*

*We packed into Josh's truck, and he dropped me off at the Rooster-comb parking lot where the inside of my vehicle was 101 degrees. That's* what sitting in direct sunlight all day will do. Then we went our separate ways. I drove down the street and jumped into the Chapel Pond. It was heavenly. I got out, changed my clothes in my van, and drove to Brooklyn. Roughly five hours later when I arrived at the apartment, I got out of my car and was immediately greeted by the smell of hot garbage, fumes, and the loud JMZ train running directly over my head. I just wanted to die in that moment. Nine hours ago I was standing on top of Saddleback, and now look where I am. Oh well. I'll be back home this weekend.

So, another very successful day in the woods where I summited Haystack, Basin, and Saddleback for High Peaks 35, 36, and 37 on my 12th hike here on my journey to climb all 46 High Peaks in one summer. A perfect sunny bluebird day to cap this five-week Adirondack adventure. I gave it my all during this time off. During this five-week span from July 1 to August 5, I summited 33 High Peaks.

What an adventure it was! My journey wasn't finished, though. I would get some hiking in throughout August on the weekends when my work schedule, traveling back from New York City, and family time allowed for it, because I had a goal to accomplish, and I was going to do it!

Next weekend, after begging Josh to hike this range with me and him ignoring my cries, I had to suck it up and go at it alone. The mighty Santanoni Range was up next. I had put this range off long enough, and it was finally time to visit the infamous Couchsachraga bog.

Looking back in the middle of the Great Range Traverse. *Photo by James Appleton*

# 15 Santanoni Range (Santanoni Peak, Couchsachraga Peak, Panther Peak)

Santanoni (4,607'), Couchsachraga (3,820'), Panther (4,442')
**Mileage:** 17 miles
**Elevation Gain:** 4,612'

Starting at the Santanoni trailhead on Upper Works Road in North Hudson comes the final stretch of your 46'er journey. Some may call these "the hard ones." These ranges tend to be pushed off to the end of people's 46'er journey for one reason or another, but they are the Santanonis, Sewards, and Allen. We will start with the Santanonis, yet another rite of passage on your 46'er journey. It's a range that gives hikers anxiety because they've heard about it from others, and they know how tough (and remote) it can be for even the most seasoned hikers. The big reason for this anxiety can be summed up in one word: Couchsachraga.

It's no wonder Couchsachraga is a Native American word translated as "dismal wilderness." That's exactly what it is out there. Looking at the map you'll notice how far you travel to "Couch" (pronounced *kooch*) from the other mountains. It's an out-and-back that rivals the Blake out-and-back, but it's a lot muddier thanks to the infamous Couchsachraga bog. The bog is a wet, muddy, dismal mess to put it bluntly. Make sure you have some extra socks to put on after crossing back over the bog the second time. I mentioned it's an out-and-back, right? So, lucky for you, you get to cross it twice! Fun. The Couchsachraga summit is also quite underwhelming, but there is a summit sign to take a photo with. I've noticed those Couchsachraga summit photos usually aren't as smiley as other summit photos. I wonder why.

Other than Couchsachraga, this range is a typical High Peaks hike. Both Santanoni and Panther have great views and summits, way better than they get credit for, and score respectably on the SSA Scale. Panther 4/5. Santanoni 3/5. Couchsachraga, well, a dismal 1/5. The Santanoni

# SANTANONI RANGE (SANTANONI PEAK, COUCHSACHRAGA PEAK, PANTHER PEAK)

Express trail is steep and slow going, but it's nothing you haven't already experienced by now.

I've hiked this range looping it in both directions, and I don't feel one was more beneficial than the other. They both have their pros and cons. Panther has a fantastic open summit, the best of the day. I do love the view from Santanoni, though, because you get a unique perspective of the MacIntyre Range, but Panther is ultimately better for sitting down and relaxing. If you want to turn this hike into a weekend camping adventure, the Bradley Pond lean-to and campsite are a convenient option right off the trail. One last thing: bring an extra extra pair of socks. Trust me.

**NOTE:** Be extra careful here, study that map, and know the trail junctions. I know multiple people who got lost on this range and had to spend the night or be rescued. Having that extra GPS tool and knowing the junctions beforehand will help minimize that possibility.

A nice view from the summit of Panther looking at Santanoni. *Photo by James Appleton*

## Santanoni Range (Santanoni Peak, Couchsachraga Peak, Panther Peak)

*August 12, 2018. A dozen day hikes in and 37 mountains down. Time for lucky number 13 on my quest to hike all 46 High Peaks of the Adirondacks in one summer, and what a range to make number 13. The Santanoni Range was up next. Panther, Couchsachraga, and Santanoni. I repeatedly asked Josh to hike this range with me because I was nervous, but he wasn't interested. So it was time to hike solo yet again on this 16-mile trek with roughly 5,000' of elevation gain.*

*My itinerary was to hike in toward the Bradley Pond lean-to on the Bradley Pond trail, go up Panther first, then Couchsachraga, back to Times Square, and over to Santanoni where I'll go down the Santanoni Express completing the loop, and back to the parking lot. A simple itinerary and a range that is anything but simple.*

*Like every night before a solo hike, I went to bed early, but I could barely sleep due to nerves and constantly going over the route in my head. I decided at 1 a.m. that it was time to just get up because quality sleep clearly wasn't going to happen. I also knew I had a 90-minute drive to the trailhead, so getting a head start wasn't a bad idea.*

*I was out the door earlier than ever this morning as I drove from Saranac Lake to the Santanoni trailhead on Upper Works Road. Upon arriving, it was as you'd expect, dark and quiet. As I prepared my pack, I started to feel something weird . . . a killer up inside of me. A killer that went from 0 to 60 in mere seconds. For the first time ever, I had to go "number 2" in the woods. There was no denying it. This was happening. So I went far into the woods, around 200' from the parking lot, and took care of my business. And I must say it was a more delightful experience than I anticipated. Cue toilet flush sound.*

*Anyways, I went back to my car, grabbed my gear, and it was time to go. I signed in at 3:55 a.m. and started walking down the dirt road into the wilderness. It's around 1.5 miles down this road until taking a right into the woods onto the Bradley Pond trail. I must say, due to the hour, the range I was in, and being solo, I found myself more nervous out there than usual. Hearing every noise in the woods around you. Knowing that if something goes wrong, you're far from any sort of help. The woods just felt different today. Eerie and strange.*

I grabbed my earbuds and threw one in my left ear and listened to some music to calm my nerves. Despite having done so many solo hikes and always starting around 4:30 a.m., there was just something different about today. The music helped tremendously during this approach, and I eventually came to the Bradley Pond trail without issue. I turned right off the road and went into the woods. Time for the hike to really begin.

The Bradley Pond trail runs along the Santanoni Brook. It's a nice dirt trail with gradual elevation gains throughout, along with some wooden bridges here and there. Some rock hopping and welcome plank bridges in extra muddy spots. Since it was still the middle of the night, I could only hear the brook but I couldn't see it.

I soon came to the trail junction for the Santanoni Express, which is marked by a cairn. Since my plan for today was to start with Panther, I went right at the cairn toward Bradley Pond. Around half a mile later I was at Bradley Pond where a small cairn and a nice wooden sign pointed me left to Times Square. The sign looked relatively new, and I found it interesting that it doesn't say Panther but says Times Square, which is just a nickname for a trail junction. If you arrive at a lean-to, you've gone too far. Turn back around.

I began my ascent on the Panther Brook herd path. Time for the real climbing to begin after making my way around the northern edge of Bradley Pond. The trail was a good mile and a half of constant elevation gain. A classic Adirondack herd path trail with exposed slippery roots and mud as it weaves though the forest. I was fortunate today that I had sunny weather because in my head I always pictured hiking this range in rain and crappy weather. So it was great to have a sunny day.

There were a couple of moments I remember having to look around to make sure I was still on the trail, but overall it was easy to follow. Once getting above the Panther Brook, it's about a half mile to Times Square. You'll know you're close once you're above the river. I made it to Times Square in relatively good time. There are two rocks with carvings in them; one says "P" for Panther, with an arrow pointing right, and the other says "TS" for Times Square, with an arrow pointing left. So I went to the right. Time to summit some mountains.

Panther is only about 0.2 miles away from Times Square, so it's a great mountain to go snag first and build momentum for the day, or good to save for after Couch because it's easy to grab on your way back. Regardless, I was starting with Panther today.

Once I came out of the tree line onto the 4,442' Panther summit at 7:32 a.m., roughly 3.5 hours in for High Peak number 38, I was thrilled at the unexpected views and the summit itself. It's great! I don't know why people say there are no views in the Santanonis, because this summit feels like a miniature version of Skylight or Algonquin. Much smaller, of course, but still way better than I expected and better than many Adirondack summits. It was a nice surprise. It might even be my favorite summit out of all the unmarked mountains.

Unlike most herd path mountains, there was no summit sign on the top of this peak this day (it's since been replaced). I had a feeling this would be the best peak of the day, so I dropped my pack and ate a sandwich. I stayed up there for around 15 minutes enjoying the views of Santanoni and Couchsachraga in front of me. You likely know by now that some High Peaks are actually below 4,000', and the smallest, Couchsachraga, seems obviously below 4,000', especially when looking at it from Panther.

I finished up my sandwich and then it was time to move on. The sun was shining, and my nerves were gone, so now it was business as usual on the trail. It felt like any other day. No sign of other people yet, and I hurried back to Times Square past the carved stones to the actual junction, which was a lot less grand than I anticipated. With a name like Times Square, I felt like it would be a big, grand destination, but it's just a flat spot, maybe a 20' radius, and some trail junctions. But it's still cool. Up next was the infamous Couchsachraga, so I took a right at the junction. Time to head down to the bog.

It's a three-mile round-trip out-and-back from Times Square to Couchsachraga, so summiting this mountain took some time to accomplish. The trip down to Couchsachraga goes down . . . and down . . . and down . . . and down . . . and down some more as you descend the western flanks of Panther. It's only a mile with 800' of elevation loss from Times Square to the bog, but it felt endless. There are some nice openings that offer some great views at various points, though, so that's a bonus.

Around 30 minutes of hiking later, I was there. No, not the summit. I was at . . . the Couchsachraga bog (Cue ominous horror movie music). I was staring this godless stretch of trail right in the face. It's a giant football-field-sized, swampy mess with no good route across, but it was time to experience this notorious bog for myself. I was determined not to fall victim to this bog like I did twice at the floating logs. So I took some time and mapped out my plan. I went to the left and found a few decent logs and began the trek through it. It was go time. Midway across, however, I came to a point of no return and I was stuck. Crap!

I looked around and saw no good route, so I decided to backtrack a few steps and hop another log that made all the difference. I made it across unscathed and not too wet. Thank God for trekking poles, because I don't think I would have been successful without them.

I made it across the bog and was ready to climb the wooded trail up to the shortest High Peak of them all. The hike down to the bog is the main chunk of mileage on this out-and-back, so once across the bog it's a quick half mile to the summit. A lovely gradual climb in the woods. Twenty minutes later I walked onto the wooded boulder summit of Couchsachraga, High Peak number 39. The shortest of all the 46, standing at a mere 3,820'. It was 9:20 a.m. for my second peak of the day. This one was tough, I'm not going to lie. For being the shortest High Peak, it certainly makes you work for it. The summit has a sign and is mostly wooded, with some views over the trees if you're tall enough. This mountain is often listed as people's least favorite High Peak on their 46'er registration form, and I can't blame them. It does have some unique qualities, though. As I've said in the past, every mountain has its place, and collectively they all make up the unique adventure that is the Adirondack 46'er journey.

Knowing I had to cross back through the bog, I was anxious to get moving, so I didn't stay long. Quickly I came to the bog, and for reasons I still don't understand today, I took a different route back across. I have no idea why since the first route had proven successful. I went right down the center this time. Right up the gut. This time I decided to use my waterproof boots to my advantage and thought, "If my boot goes under for just a couple seconds, I'll be okay." So I moved fast across the bog where my boots went in the water on every other step. It was almost as if I was jumping across a swamp filled with alligators, stepping on their heads one by one as fast as possible. I made it across much faster than the first time, though.

The bog was officially behind me, both literally and figuratively. Now I had to regain all that elevation loss from before, grabbing roots and climbing up while periodically turning around to enjoy the nice view. About halfway up I came across my first human of the day. A teenager from my hometown of Lake Placid, New York, who was hiking in muddy tennis sneakers with a JanSport backpack. He also started before sunrise, but he went up the Santanoni Express and hiked the range in the opposite direction. Nice kid. We had a quick chat, and he informed me how steep the Santanoni Express trail is and that it would be tough to go down it. So now I had that thought in my mind and started to second-guess my itinerary. Oh well, too late now.

We went our separate ways and wished each other a successful day. I was almost back to Times Square when I passed a couple in their early 30s asking if they were almost at Times Square. "You guys already passed Times Square; this is the trail toward Couchsachraga," I said. "What?" she responded. "How did we miss it?" she asked her husband. Since I was almost back up there, they would have just missed it. I explained what it looked like, and he responded, "Yes, that's just back there. Wow, I guess I expected Times Square to be much bigger." My thoughts entirely. They planned to hit Couchsachraga first, then Panther, then Santanoni, which isn't a bad plan. Getting the farthest peak accomplished first is usually a great strategy.

Moments later I arrived back at Times Square, exactly three hours after I left the summit of Panther. That Couchsachraga out-and-back was no joke. I went around the giant boulder and headed toward the mighty Santanoni. It's about a mile to the summit and not too strenuous until the final climb to the top. The herd path rides the ridgeline connecting Panther and Santanoni.

The sun was shining on this fantastic summer day, and everything was going smoothly. Even the bog went well. I climbed up and landed on the wooded summit of Santanoni at 11:53 a.m., 4,607' elevation. Done! The 14th-highest peak and High Peak number 40! The big 4-0. I was closing in on the finish line! Just before the wooded summit, there's a great opening with fantastic views, so I walked back and ate a sandwich before my descent. Another hike summiting all the day's peaks before noon.

While I ate my sandwich, a man and his son passed me and went to the summit before coming back to the same spot to eat a snack. Their snack? Cans of tuna fish. Woof. Now I'm not here to judge, but nothing could sound less appetizing to me on a summit than that. But hey, to each their own. I chatted with them and learned that they had camped at the Bradley Pond lean-to the night before and climbed Panther and Couchsachraga the day before and Santanoni today. That's a great weekend itinerary if you're looking to camp. I asked them how steep the express trail was and if they thought it would be tough going down. "It's nothing to worry about," the man said. Well, that's a slightly different opinion than my new teenage friend from Lake Placid offered earlier.

Time to carry on. I packed up my gear and headed down the mountain anticipating the steep terrain. About 10 minutes into my descent, I passed a group coming up and asked them their opinion of the trail. "Will it be tough to go down?" I asked. Their eyes said it all as they all nodded their heads in unison, declaring, "Yup!" So, the mixed reviews continue, but as I am wont to do, I said to myself, "I'm sure it's fine." It was fine. The trail is steep and there's plenty of slab climbing, holding roots to get down, and some butt sliding, but overall its standard Adirondack High Peaks hiking. Since it is the "express trail," I got back to the Bradley Pond trail junction quickly. Time to get back to the dirt road.

Now that it was daytime, I could see the Santanoni Brook that the trail runs along. There are many great spots to swim in, little pools of water that would have felt amazing to sit in. It's the kind of Adirondack river I would spend hours swimming in during the summer. Maybe another time, though. I picked up my pace because it was all about getting back to the car now. Once back at the road, I had the long mile-and-a-half dirt road walk back to my car. I was almost finished with the Santanoni Range, a range that I've been nervous about from the start of my journey.

I put an earbud in for this final trek to pass the time, and I made it back to the trailhead at 3:15 p.m., totaling my day at 11 hours 20 minutes. A great day. A little muddy, but overall I found the Santanoni Range to be more enjoyable than I anticipated. Since today was Sunday and I had to work at 6 a.m. tomorrow, it meant I had to drive back to New York City today. Nothing like a long car ride after a long day in the High Peaks, right?

I got in my car and made a quick pit stop at the old MacIntyre Iron Furnace where I walked down to the river and jumped in so I could clean up before the drive back to the city. The post-hike, pre-drive river dunk is a must.

Another very successful solo day in the woods here on the mighty Santanoni Range. Panther, Couchsachraga, and Santanoni for peak numbers 38, 39, and the big 40. I'm in the 40s here on my quest to hike all 46 High Peaks in one summer.

# 16 Allen Mountain

Allen (4,340')
**Mileage:** 17.8 miles
**Elevation Gain:** 3,502'

Starting at the Allen Mountain trailhead on Upper Works Road in North Hudson, just past the MacIntyre Iron Furnace, comes Allen. Oh, Allen, what a misunderstood and underappreciated mountain you are. Allen is a mountain that gets pushed off to the end for most aspiring 46'ers until they can't push it off any longer. It's understandable why people don't get excited for this peak, and it's typically due to the eight-mile approach to the base of the mountain. After those eight miles through spectacular Adirondack country, the ascent involves slabs with slippery red slime, climbing roots along the slabs, and a whole lot of work. It's a character-building mountain.

The rumors about Allen should not get you down, and I will tell you why: the approach is awesome and the summit views off the back of the mountain are amazing. Sure, it's a long approach, but it's on unique trails, in unique woods, crossing suspension bridges and rivers, with a feel all its own. This hike stands alone in the High Peaks. That's what makes it special in my mind. The eight-mile approach is also flat, so you can make great time. It's a fun wilderness adventure, so just embrace it.

Once you get to Skylight Brook and begin climbing Allen, it's over 2,000' of gain in a mile and a half. It's slippery and steep, especially the final 0.5 miles.

This is another trail that cuts across many other trails throughout the approach, so it's important to study that map and all the different junctions you will encounter.

Overall, I love Allen Mountain because it offers a unique Adirondack High Peaks experience. I feel it is underappreciated for what it brings to the table in the scheme of one's journey to 46. I've hiked it on sunny days and rainy days, and they both brought a memorable experience. Allen's Summit Sandwich-ability ranking is a 3/5. Make sure you

# ALLEN MOUNTAIN

walk around the summit because there are great views; you just have to find them.

Okay, time to get into my short night at the Allen Mountain trailhead and a soaking-wet day in the Adirondack backcountry.

The amazing summit view from Allen and the famed tree. *Photo by James Appleton*

## Allen Mountain

*September 1, 2018. Today was the day I put off until the very end, but I couldn't push it off any longer. Allen Mountain was up next for number 45 here on my 15th High Peaks hike of the summer. After finishing work late Friday night, I drove from New York City straight through to the Allen Mountain trailhead. Once again, I stopped in Saratoga Springs at I-87 exit 15 where I stocked up some food and water for the day.*

*Shortly after pulling off the highway and onto the Adirondack country road, a small black bear ran across the road in front of my car causing me to quickly swerve. Well, that certainly woke me up. Classic Adirondack life. I arrived at the Allen trailhead at 1:30 a.m. and parked next to several other hikers sleeping in their cars. I got a few hours of shut eye in the back of my van before waking up at 4:50 a.m. to the sound of hikers arriving for their own adventure. Well, if other people are starting to hike, then I am too. Time to get moving.*

*At 5:20 a.m. I locked my van and began the long walk through the woods to Allen. Oh, and did I mention it was pouring? Because it was . . . really hard. Despite only a 15 percent chance of rain, the water poured from the sky. So, between the rain and the bushes brushing against my body along this narrow trail, it was going to be a wet one. To combat the rain I started the hike wearing both a raincoat and rain pants.*

*My plan for today was simple—summit Allen Mountain. Allen is a remote High Peak deep in the Adirondack wilderness that requires a long, almost eight-mile approach just to the base of the peak followed by 2,000' of gain over the 1.5-mile ascent. The day would total at 18 miles with 3,500' of elevation gain. It was going to be a lot of work for one lone peak.*

*This mountain gets a lot of criticism due to the long approach. Some people even say it doesn't have any views up top (which is false; it has amazing views). If I'm being honest, though, I enjoyed this approach. The trail has a lot of different sections, each with different terrain and feel, which keeps the hike changing and always feeling interesting. This creates a unique hiking experience that the other High Peaks don't offer.*

*Josh warned me to toss my Crocs in my backpack because I'd be taking off my boots to cross some rivers today. Due to some recently built bridges, however, that was not the case, fortunately. I did pack the Crocs, though, in anticipation of some river crossings.*

Speaking of bridges, shortly after the East River trail begins, you'll walk across a steel suspension bridge crossing the Hudson River. This was the first of two suspension bridges on this hike (the second bridge was wiped out due to a storm in 2020). Half a mile into the hike, you'll arrive at Lake Jimmy. I'm told the trail used to have a floating bridge to cross it, but now the trail just goes around the left side of the lake. It was still dark out, so I couldn't see much of the lake at this point. The trail around the lake is narrow, so the morning rain pulled double duty by drenching me from both the sky and the trees and plants along the trail. Shortly after circling Lake Jimmy I made it to the beginning of many old, overgrown dirt roads. If you aren't aware, the Adirondacks have a rich logging history, and the park is filled with old logging roads and tote roads.

Around a mile into the hike I came to an old ranger cabin in the woods. It looked abandoned, and since it was still dark out and the beginning of my day, I decided to check it out later on my way back. It turns out this is the old Mt. Adams watchman's cabin, and the trail junction to go up Mt. Adams is around this point.

It would be easy to accidentally turn onto the wrong trail out here, so it's crucial to know your map and when to expect trail junctions. There are trails and herd paths at different portions of the hike. Using a Garmin GPS or some GPS cell-phone apps (All Trails, OnX, Gaia, etc.) is extra helpful on this mountain. They don't replace having and knowing your map, but they're helpful tools in addition to the map.

After passing the Mt. Adams junction, the trail runs along miles of gravel and dirt roads, so it's easy to follow and oddly enjoyable in my opinion. You will eventually see Allen in the sky poking out in one of the meadows you'll pass through. However, since it was raining today, I couldn't see anything in the sky. The trail traverses its way along different ponds and rivers followed by open meadows before going back into the woods. I found it to have a great vibe all around. This hike doesn't deserve the hate it receives.

Not long into the hike, I passed the group who had signed in just before me. Was I trying to pass both groups that had signed in before me and beat them to the top? Of course. I'd be lying if I said I wasn't. One group down, one to go . . . maybe. After passing this group, I stepped over the large metal gate and continued on the trail.

Just under four miles into the hike I came to a sign pointing me to go right to the Opalescent River crossing. There is another wooden suspension bridge over this river, which used to just be a pure river crossing, so again I didn't have any need for my Crocs, thankfully. After crossing the river, the trail becomes wider once again, walking along flat roads.

I came to a trail junction with a trail heading toward Marcy. There is a sign pointing left to Marcy and a brown wooden sign with a yellow arrow pointing to the right, which is the beginning of the Allen herd path. Go right.

The trail continues its mix of flat dirt trails along old logging roads until it comes out to a larger gravel road out of the woods. This was Opalescent Road. At this point I couldn't tell which direction I was supposed to go. After checking out the area for a minute, I noticed a small cairn. I was just below the gravel pit and the second Allen trail register. When you exit the woods and land on a perpendicular dirt road, just go left.

The gravel pit, as it's affectionately known, is an old gravel parking lot of sorts. At the other end of the lot is the next trail register for Allen. It was now 7:10 a.m., and I had been hiking just under two hours to get to this second registry. I decided to drop my pack for a minute and change my socks since I was a bit damp for the day and the rain had let up. The sun was trying to poke through the clouds. Today was the type of day where you just got used to the rain and eventually it didn't matter anymore. Regardless, I changed into a different pair of socks and carried on after taking a couple bites of my Snickers bar, of course. The summit of High Peak number 45 was a mere 3.5 miles away.

I finished the logging road section and entered back into the woods. Hello again, dirt. The trail still doesn't gain elevation for a while as it winds through the woods for a couple of miles along the southern base of Mt. Redfield. The woods were darker than usual due to how thick the canopy is. I even turned my headlamp back on for various sections. Between the dark woods, the rain, and the general sounds of the forest, it created a spooky little vibe this morning.

The majority of the almost eight-mile approach is mostly flat with various elevation changes throughout, but in general it's flat. This approach crosses over many small brooks, so there are plenty of places to gather *water. Just don't drink out of the thunder box you'll pass. Oh, what's a thunder box, you ask? I'll get to that later.*

*Shortly after crossing over Skylight Brook I came to a little waterfall with a pool at the bottom next to a cairn marking the beginning of the climb up Allen. I finally made it to Allen Brook where the herd path to the top begins. I took in the view and enjoyed a quick swig and a snack. It was no longer raining, and the long approach was behind me. Time to start climbing. Next stop, the Allen Mountain summit!*

*By this point in the hike you will be ready to climb, and that's exactly what you're going to do. The trail just goes up, up, and up. The ascent is 2,000' of gain over 1.5 miles, after all. I was plenty warmed up, though, after that long approach, so I welcomed the steep elevation.*

*It didn't take long for me to experience the infamous "red slime" of Allen Mountain. I always thought people were exaggerating about how slippery it was. I figured they were being overdramatic. I was wrong. This stuff is like ice when you step on it. So very slippery. Thank God I had trekking poles, because climbing this mountain without them would be extra difficult—going up and definitely coming down. The trail involves a lot of slab and slide climbing, so be ready for that. My piece of advice when you see the slime is to tread lightly. Do not immediately commit to your step with all your weight. Audition it by putting a little weight on your leg to see if you're going to slip, and then step. It will add a little time, but to me anything is worth avoiding a fall.*

*With all the slab and slide climbing, you'll be searching for the path of least resistance a lot. Around halfway up the slide I noticed a cairn that had me going across the slide. This was a bit nerve racking due to the wet conditions, but I made it across. I climbed the slide from the left side. You'll know when it's time to choose right or left. I'm sure people climb from both sides, but for me left felt right. See what I did there?*

*There's a lot of grabbing onto roots and holding on for dear life during the climb. So that's always fun, albeit nerve racking. Don't forget to turn around from time to time as well because there are terrific views to be seen. Of course, those views weren't visible today thanks to the rain, but on a clear day they're great.*

*I eventually finished climbing the slide and was back on a dirt trail in the woods taking me up to the summit. I reached the 4,340' fully wooded summit of Allen at 9:50 a.m. A 4.5-hour trek for High Peak number 45!*

*I passed multiple hikers on the slide, so I thought I would be the first person on the summit, but upon arriving I met a French Canadian couple already there. We chatted and they asked me, "What number is this for you?" to which I responded, "45." They were very enthusiastic that I was almost finished. That was the first time someone inquired about what number High Peak it was for me, and I would go on to be asked multiple times throughout the descent from other hikers. In general, the only people hiking Allen are people trying to become a 46'er and usually those who are near 46 on their journey. I felt a unique camaraderie with the other hikers on this mountain today. It's like we are all on the same team, rooting for each other to be successful up the infamous Allen Mountain. We're all trying not to slip and fall and nearing the end of our journeys to 46. Everyone is working toward the same goal, and we all know how difficult that goal is. It was cool. Let the record show I really enjoy Allen Mountain. It's an underrated and underappreciated mountain. There's also an amazing view on the summit; you just have to look around to find it.*

*Since I knew how long the hike out was going to be, I didn't stay long and started on my descent. I was anxious about slipping and falling on the hike down. While climbing I could tell it was going to be a beast to come back down. I was not wrong. I recommend taking your time getting down this mountain. Slow and steady wins the race.*

*I passed a few different groups of hikers on the way down and asked each of them, "Have you slipped yet?" One of them took a hard fall with bruises to show for it. Most of them, however, answered, "Not yet, thank God." Avoiding a painful fall is on most people's minds out here. I prepared my mind for a fall or two on the way down, but thankfully I made it off the mountain unscathed. It was a miracle. I was back at the Allen Brook pool with the cairn. The couple from the summit, who passed me on the descent despite leaving after me, were chatting with more hikers at the waterfall. They told people, "This is number 45 for him!" and they all shared in their excitement for me and wished me good luck on Big Slide this Monday. The High Peaks hiking community is truly one in a million.*

Now that I was off the mountain and back on the flat trail, I started moving quickly. I had a lot of miles to cover. It wasn't long before passing the Allen Mountain "thunder box." If you're not familiar with the "thunder box," it's a wooden toilet completely out in the open. Picture an outhouse or privy but without any walls. Now imagine walking along the trail minding your own business only to round the bend and unexpectedly come face-to-face with someone going number 2 clear out in the open, literally just off the trail. I get it; when nature calls you have to answer. We've all been there. It's okay, though; there's no shame in using the thunder box. When you got to go, you got to go. It's there for a reason, after all.

Anyways, I was moving quickly through the woods as I passed a couple of people hiking in for the day. They asked, "Hey, is the red slime actually slippery?" I stopped dead in my tracks. I slowly and dramatically turned toward them in slow motion, my dead eyes staring deep into theirs, and emphatically said, "Yes. What you've heard is true. Prepare yourself." Then lightning struck followed by a crash of thunder as the couple slowly walked off. Just kidding. There was no lightning or thunder. The red slime is slippery, though. The rumors are true.

I hustled and made it back to the second trail register at the gravel pit. At this checkpoint I felt like I was officially off Allen. Just some flat miles remained. So I had a small moment of celebration for the fact that I had one High Peak to go. Of course, I still had about five miles to my car, but that was okay.

Just after crossing the wooden suspension bridge over the Opalescent River, I met another solo hiker coming in for the day. I felt it was late in the day to be this far away. After a quick chat I asked if he had a headlamp, to which he responded "no." I offered him my spare light, which he did not accept. He assured me he was okay. We said our good-byes and went our separate ways. Allen is not the mountain I'd want to be on at night without a headlamp, that's for sure.

By this point in the day, I was ready for the hike to be over. I wanted to be home since I was basically running on fumes from Friday morning's 5 a.m. wake-up, followed by the 13-hour workday, then a 5-hour drive, 3 hours of sleep, and this 18-mile hike. I was ready to be home with my family. So I started moving as fast as possible once I was back on the gravel logging roads. A jog-walk hybrid. Some may even call it "power walking."

Then I made it back to the Mt. Adams trail junction and the Mt. Adams watchman's cabin. I decided to check it out this time around. So I walked up to it but got a strange "old cabin in the woods" vibe when I noticed the door wide open. I decided today was not the day to die alone at the cabin. Yes, I chickened out and went back to the trail and kept going. I did go into this cabin on future trips to Allen, though. It's what you would expect it to be.

A face that sums up my climb up Allen Mountain in the rain. *Photo by James Appleton*

I was almost finished going back to my car as I began the trip around Lake Jimmy. Then onto the steel suspension bridge over the Hudson River and back to the trailhead. I made it. I actually hiked the infamous Allen Mountain, and solo no less. I signed out at 2:45 p.m., totaling my 18-mile single-mountain day at 9 hours 25 minutes car-to-car. After putting off Allen all summer long, it was finally done. And it was more enjoyable than I anticipated. I got in my car feeling accomplished and drove home to the family in Saranac Lake. One more High Peak to go!

Another successful wet, slippery day in the woods on Allen Mountain for number 45 here on my 15th High Peaks hike this summer. The completion of my quest to become an Adirondack 46'er in one summer was now one mountain away.

# 17  Seward Range (Seward Mountain, Donaldson Mountain, Emmons Mountain, Seymour Mountain)

Seward (4,361'), Donaldson (4,140'), Emmons (4,040'), Seymour (4,120')
**Mileage:** 19.7 miles
**Elevation Gain:** 5,876'

Starting at the Seward trailhead on Corey's Road, located between Saranac Lake and Tupper Lake on Route 3, this hike is what your 46'er journey has been building toward. By this point, your mind, body, and Adirondack soul are in prime hiking shape and you're ready for the big one: the Seward Range with the addition of Seymour. If you followed this guide as written, this will be the biggest day of your 46'er journey. I did this on purpose.

This hike can be accomplished in one giant day, or it can easily be broken up into an overnight with great camping options along the way. The Seward Range is often spread out over two separate days, with Seward, Donaldson, and Emmons one day and Seymour another day. So if you feel that's the better choice for you, then feel free to break this day up into two separate hikes. The Seward Range and Seymour all score very low on the SSA Scale, unfortunately. Extremely low. You've been warned. Another character-building range.

Originally, I was going to break these up into two hikes on my list, but I changed my mind. Hiking in the Adirondacks and becoming an Adirondack 46'er is hard. The journey to 46 is about challenging yourself in the mountains and grinding out those big, hard, blister-ridden days in an embrace of the ADK backcountry. At this point into your High Peaks journey, you're more than ready to push yourself and demand a little extra from your mind and body. Think of this hike as the big climactic championship game scene in your High Peaks movie, and your final hike on Big Slide is the victory lap.

# SEWARD RANGE (SEWARD MOUNTAIN, DONALDSON MOUNTAIN, EMMONS MOUNTAIN, SEYMOUR MOUNTAIN)

Coreys Rd.

Seward

Ward Brook Truck

Blueberry Pond

Blueberry Foot

Blueberry Horse

Blueberry Horse

Calkins Creek Truck

Seward Range

Calkins Brook

Blueberry Lean-to

Blueberry Horse

Ward Brook Lean-to

Number Four
#1 Lean-to

Ward Brook

Seymour Trail

Ouluska Pass

Seymour
Mtn.

Seward
Mtn.

Donaldson
Mtn.

Emmons
Mtn.

Calkin's Lean-to

N

0    0.5    1 km.

0    0.5    1 mi.

If you want to break them up and do some camping, you most certainly can, since there are lots of great options along the trail. You could hike all four in one day and then camp, or you could hike Seward, Donaldson, and Emmons, camp overnight, and then climb Seymour and hike back out. But if you want to push yourself and let this be your big pre-46'er finale, it can be accomplished in one single day. I believe in you.

My recommendation is to take the Calkin's Brook trail up Donaldson first, then out-and-back to Emmons, and finally over to Seward before heading all the way down the mountain back to the Blueberry trail. From here you will turn right and hike further out to Seymour. Seymour is tough, especially at this point in the day because you just climbed all the way down Seward only to go all the way back up Seymour. After Seymour, you'll have that pesky five-mile trek back to the trailhead. Again, it's a big day (or not as big if spread out), but it's doable if you commit to it. See the map for camping options.

For the best ratio of big finale without completely killing yourself, I'd recommend hiking all four mountains in one day (start early), then camp at one of the lean-tos and get a good night's sleep in the great outdoors knowing the hard work has been accomplished. A victory night under the stars. The next morning you can hike back to the trailhead. If you've been following this guide as written, that means you will be at 45 of 46; one more mountain!

Let's get into my spontaneous and massive day in the Seward Range . . .

Seymour—the final summit of a very long day in the Sewards. *Photo by James Appleton*

## Seward Range (Seward Mountain, Donaldson Mountain, Emmons Mountain, Seymour Mountain)

*August 17, 2018. I had no plans of hiking this weekend following a long week grinding away at the Hollywood "movie factory." Then I got a text message around 3:00 p.m. on Friday afternoon from a fellow aspiring 46'er, Eli. He and I met randomly twice on the trail (Colvin and Skylight), and thanks to social media a friendship was formed. He was texting me saying he was thinking of hiking the Seward Range tomorrow. Knowing I still had to hike that range, I thought about it for a minute before responding, "Hey, I'll join you!" Well, it looks like I'm hiking the High Peaks this weekend after all!*

*So, after wrapping my 13-hour workday on Friday in Brooklyn, New York, I got in my car and started driving north back home to the Adirondacks. I often sleep in my van on Friday night at a rest stop along I-87 while driving home after the workweek, but since I didn't get out of work and on the road until around 8:30 p.m., that wasn't an option. I had to drive straight through to make it to the trailhead for our 5:30 a.m. start. There was little room to spare.*

*Fortunately, all my hiking gear was still in my van because the weekend before I had hiked the Santanonis and immediately left from the trailhead for New York. So I had everything I needed—backpack, boots, bladder, trekking poles. Food, however, was not something I had. I stopped at exit 15 in Saratoga Springs to stock up on food for the day at the gas station. I couldn't bring my usual PB&J sandwiches, so I had to improvise, gas station style. The Seward Range would be fueled by hardboiled eggs, beef jerky, and Snickers bars. Oh, and two gallons of water, which I transferred to my bladder and water bottles. Not ideal fuel, but sometimes we must learn the hard way, right? Let's continue . . .*

*The drive had a great vibe that night because I knew adventure awaited, I wasn't hiking solo, and I had no choice but to make it all the way to the trailhead. So I had to stay awake despite being up for close to 24 hours already. Another funny thing about this drive is that I literally passed my house in Saranac Lake as I drove to the Corey's Road trailhead. Sure, I could have gone home to sleep for an hour, but I figured it would be better to sleep in my van at the trailhead instead of scaring my wife. No one likes an unexpected visitor in their home in the middle of the night, you know?*

*I arrived at the trailhead just after 2:00 a.m. I will say, driving the six miles down Corey's Road at that hour had an eerie feel to it. Oh, it gets very remote very quickly back there. Thankfully I made it to the trailhead without needing to pull over to sleep. Eli was meeting me at 5:30 a.m., so I passed out in the back of my van for a couple hours' sleep. Once I turned my van's lights off, I noticed something: it was dark out there. I mean dark, like dark where you couldn't see your hand in front of your face. But enough of that; time to get some shut eye. I have another big Adirondack adventure starting in a few hours.*

*Off went my alarm at 5:15 a.m. and my nap was over. Time to get ready to hike. I ate some more of my gas station food and filled up my water bottles and bladder as headlights lit up the woods and the sound of tires on the dirt filled the air. Moments later a car pulled into the trailhead. It was Eli, right on schedule. So we said our hellos and signed in at 5:50 a.m. Time to hit the trail.*

*Our plan for the day was to start on the Blueberry trail and take the Calkins Brook trail up to Donaldson, then out-and-back Emmons, over to Seward, and down to the Ward Brook trail. At that point Eli and I would go our separate ways since he hiked Seymour last week and lives a couple hours away. I would finish the day solo climbing Seymour and back to the trailhead. It was going to be a big day at roughly 22 miles with more than 5,500' of elevation gain. The Seward Range was officially underway.*

*The Adirondacks welcomed us with another beautiful bluebird summer day. The hike began walking along the Blueberry trail, which gains minimal elevation on a wide gentle path, a perfect start to the day. Since we were hitting Donaldson first, we turned right onto the Calkins Brook truck trail, and after winding through the flat woods for a few miles it was time to climb. The trail runs along the Calkins Brook for most of the ascent, so once you get above the water you're near the summit.*

*Before we began climbing, I quickly ate one of the gas station breakfast sandwiches from the night before. I had planned to eat this in my van before hiking, but I didn't get around to it. It wasn't great, but desperate times call for desperate measures. I had a feeling that my food, aka my fuel, was going to be the big challenge today. Do I have enough? Will it properly fuel my body? We will see. I am a person who likes creating systems, so once I find something that works I stick with it, and food on big* hikes is no different. I'm not particularly fond of trying new things 15 miles back in the woods, but it's what had to be done today.

We started climbing Donaldson. For being mostly unmaintained herd paths, I found the trails in the Seward Range to be some of the best herd path trails, if not the best, in the High Peaks. They felt like maintained trails without the trail markers. Not too worn, decent on the feet, with minimal exposed roots to slip on. It was pleasant. After we got to the top of the brook, we were almost to the summit. Before leaving the brook, it's wise to refill your water bottles because this is the last water source you'll see for the day.

Eli and I enjoyed great conversation and in a flash we walked out on the lookout summit of Donaldson Mountain at 8:45 a.m., just under three hours from signing in, standing at 4,140' elevation for High Peak number 41. This was my favorite summit of the day and has a summit sign with views over the Seward Range. Time for a PB&J sandwich. I wish. Since I didn't have one today, I ate half of my king-size Snickers bar instead. The sun was shining and the temperatures were excellent. We had that going for us. Eli and I stayed on the summit for around 10 minutes before starting the out-and-back trek to Emmons.

The mile trip from Donaldson to Emmons might be the easiest part of the day as the trail moves along the ridge with little elevation change. It's a welcome quality about hiking the Seward Range in my opinion. We carried on along the Seward Range trail and landed on the wooded summit of Emmons 30 minutes after leaving Donaldson for High Peak number 42. Nothing like summiting another mountain with minimal effort. Emmons is named after Ebenezer Emmons, a geologist who named the Adirondacks and who also led the first recorded ascent up Mt. Marcy in 1837. A prominent figure in Adirondack history.

Ready for some more High Peaks trivia? Emmons is the westernmost High Peak, standing at 4,040' elevation and ranking number 40 of the 46 elevation-wise. The summit is wooded with some views over the trees if you're tall enough, so it's not the most spectacular summit, but any summit is better than no summit.

Once we got to Emmons, I ate the other half of my king-size Snickers bar. Eli wanted to stay on the summit for a while and relax. I obliged and we hung out for a good 20 minutes before he could probably tell I was antsy to get moving. After all, I had to summit Seymour as well today, so I still had a long day ahead of me.

We said good-bye to Emmons and headed back to Donaldson. As usual, it felt like we made it back in half the time, and we blew over the Donaldson summit toward Seward. It's only 0.8 miles from Donaldson to Seward. The elevation loss/gain between these two mountains again is minimal, and it goes quickly as you follow the herd path on top of the range.

We got to Seward 90 minutes after leaving Emmons at 11:30 a.m. Seward has an elevation of 4,361', the tallest mountain of the day, marking High Peak number 43 on my quest to 46. A very wooded summit with zero views. There are some lookout views on the way up, but the summit is entirely surrounded by trees. Eventually a family joined us on the summit. A mother, father, and their two teenage sons. They were all close to becoming 46'ers themselves. A family who hikes together. Eli gave them all an "Aspiring Adirondack 46'er" sticker as they left toward Donaldson.

Since Eli and I were going to split after Seward anyway, I decided to keep moving since he wanted to stay longer. So we said good-bye, and I started the solo trek down Seward. This was a challenge. The first half of the Seward descent is all rock slabs, grabbing onto roots, climbing, and praying to God that the traction holds and your feet don't slip. Classic Adirondack High Peaks affairs, right? Since it rained the day prior, the trail was very slippery.

After I finished the steep slabs portion, the bottom half of the trail is a different yet still standard Adirondack affair. A dirt herd path trail with some rocks and a lot of exposed roots. Oh, and don't forget about the mud. It's not as bad as some trails, though.

Climbing down the wet slabs was slow going, but now I could start cruising and make up lost time. Then out of nowhere I hear someone flying down the trail behind me. It was Eli. Despite staying on the summit for 15 minutes longer than I did, he still caught up to me. He is a wild man. I can climb at a nice pace, but descents are always slow for me. I was glad he caught back up, and we chatted while we finished the trail together.

Near the bottom there is a large mud pit that required some careful navigating. It gave me flashbacks to my hellish time at the beginning of Cliff Mountain. We made it down and arrived at the Ward Brook trail.

We were officially off Seward. At this point Eli and I split for good as he headed back to the trailhead, and I went further into the forest a half mile to climb Seymour.

I was feeling pretty good so far, and I ate a bag of peanut M&M's to fuel up for the final peak of the day. Then I came to the cairn marking the beginning of the Seymour herd path. Time to go all the way up and all the way down. Eli told me this trail is a lot like Seward with the slabs, so I wasn't looking forward to that due to my semi-fatigued state, but I started out with a bang. I moved quickly up the trail, through some mud pits, hopping on rocks.

I was moving well and was pleased that I was eating up mileage without seeing any signs of slabs. Eli's description made me feel it was one big rock climb. Thankfully that wasn't the case, but after more stops than usual to catch my breath I came to the beginning of the slabs. My low quality and quantity of food was starting to show as my performance started to dwindle. I was getting tired very quickly. I did what I could do. I ate more beef jerky and started scaling the slabs, grabbing the roots along the side and climbing up the best way possible. Up until this point the trail was a consistent elevation gain without any flat sections to catch my breath.

The trail kept climbing and never let up. I was tired. The slabs didn't help, but I eventually made it up to a more level section and thought to myself, "This looks very peaky," which is something Josh and I say to each other when we think we're at the top. I was positive I was at the summit and was so glad to be there because my body was tired. Then I saw something ahead up in the sky. The summit. Well, I certainly got pump-faked hard by this false summit. It was a real emotional blow this late into the day. So I sucked it and carried on up the trail as fatigue and a few choice words went through my brain.

Not long after this false summit, I made it to the real summit marked by a wooden summit sign reading "Seymour Mountain." I made it. Thank God. I was relieved, ecstatic, and, most of all, exhausted. The 1.4-mile ascent with nearly 2,000' of gain up this relentless trail was complete!

It was 3 o'clock when I summited Seymour. I had summited Seward at 11:30 a.m. Therefore, this one mountain took me many hours to get. That's okay, though, because it shouldn't be easy, and it wasn't. Seymour

Mountain stands at 4,120' elevation for High Peak number 44. I'm so close now I can feel it. The summit is wooded, but there are still plenty of mountain views to enjoy. Knowing I had the 1.5-mile descent followed by the 5-mile walk back to the car, I only stayed for five minutes before heading back down.

The trip down wasn't too eventful. I moved slowly getting off the slabs, but then I was able to pick up my pace and make better time. Just before I got to the mud pit toward the bottom, I passed a group of hikers from earlier in the day who were just starting Seymour. It was such a nice feeling knowing I was done.

Soon I was back at the cairn at the Ward Brook trail. Yes! Filled with a boost of adrenaline, I took a left to start the final stretch of the day, a 5.5-mile flat walk back to my car at the trailhead. Although, if I'm being honest, another 5.5 miles felt like 100 miles.

Despite the long walk back to my car, my spirits were high because I accomplished all four mountains in one day, a hike many people told me needed to be broken into two days. I know people do this in one day all the time, but it was a great feeling being one of those people. I pushed myself today and was able to get it done. It was another confidence-boosting day in the backcountry.

There are multiple lean-tos and campsites along the Ward Brook trail, making this range a good candidate for camping if you want to go that route. Since all my hikes so far were day hikes, I wanted to finish all 46 as day hikes.

Around two miles into the walk back I started jogging to eat up mileage faster. That didn't last long, though. I put in an earbud and enjoyed some victory music to pass the time. I arrived back at the trailhead and signed out at 6:10 p.m., completing this 22-mile, 5,500' elevation gain, four High Peak adventure in 12 hours and 20 minutes car-to-car. A monster of a day was in the books, and only two mountains remained to become a 46'er!

Another successful day in the woods here in the Seward Range. Donaldson, Emmons, Seward, and Seymour in one day for High Peaks numbers 41, 42, 43, and 44 on my 14th hike. All that's left are Allen and Big Slide here on my quest to summit all 46 High Peaks of the Adirondacks in one summer.

# 18 Big Slide Mountain

Big Slide (4,240')
**Mileage:** 7.6 miles
**Elevation Gain:** 3,126'

Starting at the Garden trailhead in Keene Valley comes the day you've been working toward, the day you earn the title of Adirondack 46'er, something nobody can ever take away from you. By now you are likely a different person from when you first hiked Cascade and Porter for numbers 1 and 2. The reason I chose Big Slide to be the final mountain on your 46'er journey (as I did on my own journey) is because I believe your final mountain should be more of a "victory lap" than another long, hard day in the Adirondacks. Big Slide is the perfect mountain to finish on thanks to its constant views, short mileage, and amazing summit. It's also a hike you can take family up with you to join you for the finish. Big Slide is a mountain that allows you to reflect on your journey and enjoy every second of the day start to finish. It also scores a perfect 5/5 on the SSA Scale. Your 46'er finish deserves a 5/5 SSA score.

Since this hike is shorter than most, it can certainly be climbed early on in your journey, but I found it to be a great choice to save for the end. The victory lap mountain. Hike some other smaller ADK mountains instead if you're trying to find your trail legs early on.

I recommend climbing this mountain via The Brothers Trail. These are three small peaks, or humps if you will, with lots of views to enjoy throughout, making the hike extra scenic. Once you climb over the third brother, it's time for you to finish this journey and see the culmination of your hard days in the High Peaks as you earn the title "Adirondack 46'er."

When you're climbing mountains, nobody can do the work for you. As I stated earlier in this book, these mountains have a lot to teach you, and at this point they've taught you two things:

# BIG SLIDE MOUNTAIN

1. You can do anything you choose to do when you have a plan and put in the effort.
2. Nobody else will do the work for you; it's up to you to take each step.

These are great lessons to learn. The mountains never disappoint in teaching us things we need to learn.

Well, the miles have been hiked and it's time to complete this incredible, life-changing journey. The journey will never truly end, though, because these mountains are a part of you now. They have a lot more to teach you. Your Adirondack adventure is only just beginning.

If you've been reading this book throughout your journey and you followed my 18-hike route to 46, I have one more word for you—congratulations!

## Big Slide Mountain

*September 3, 2018. Labor Day. Today was the day. After growing up in Lake Placid and never imagining I'd become an Adirondack 46'er, it was actually about to happen. What started on May 18 with Porter and Cascade was culminating just a few months later here on my 16th hike. Big Slide Mountain for number 46 of 46. This mountain had sentimental value to me because about five years earlier I had tried hiking this with some friends and I turned around because I just couldn't handle it. It was too hard. I was too fat and out of shape. Now I was back to conquer those demons and finish my quest to summit all 46 High Peaks in one summer. It was go time!*

*Josh came with me on this final hike. He picked me up in Saranac Lake at 4:00 a.m. and we began our drive to the Garden. Like a child on Christmas Eve, I barely slept the night before out of pure excitement. I also was nervous about whether we would get a parking spot. The whole way down I was trying to come up with a game plan if there weren't any parking spots left. It was Monday of Labor Day weekend, so I assumed the lot would be full of people camping. I had to hit the trail today no matter what because today was the day. If I had to walk a different trailhead, so be it. Nothing could stop me from getting to that summit.*

*As we approached the turn in Keene Valley, I was taking mental notes of how long the walk would be if we parked down there. It would be a long walk, to say the least. We passed the metal sign before the parking lot, and it was flipped down reading "Parking Lot Full." Oh no. My heart sank. But we kept driving to see for ourselves. Maybe a spot was available. Then as we pulled up the dirt road into the trailhead, we saw something miraculous. Something no one in the High Peaks has seen in decades. A near empty parking lot. Hallelujah! There were only five cars spread out in the entire Garden parking lot. It was amazing, and I knew right then it was going to be a great day!*

*So we parked right at the front of the lot, grabbed our gear, and signed in at 4:50 a.m. On the trail registry I wrote my name and "#46 of 46" because I saw a man do that on Haystack, and I thought, "I can't wait until I can write that." So I did, and it felt great. Hello again, Big Slide Mountain. I'm back, and I will not be turning around this time. Next stop—the summit!*

*Just as Josh and I started walking toward The Brothers Trail, we heard a very loud whooping sound in the woods that stopped us dead in our tracks. We gave each other a look . . . and then kept walking. About 10 steps later we heard two more in the distance, again stopping us cold. Had I been hiking solo, I likely would have sat in my car until the sun came up. Since there were two of us, however, we shrugged it off and kept going. I'll tell you, there's something about the early hours in that Garden parking lot.*

*Our plan for the day was to ascend and descend via The Brothers Trail. Short, sweet, and straight to the point. Given all the long day hikes I did throughout my 46'er journey, I wanted today to be as quick as possible. With this being one of the shortest High Peaks hikes, I purposely left it until the end. I wanted my final hike to feel like a victory lap instead of another long, tough day. Weighing in at eight miles and just over 3,100' of elevation gain, it would be exactly that. The perfect peak to finish on.*

*It's no wonder I turned around years ago, because after a short windy trip through the woods the trail begins climbing and doesn't let up. It's a bit relentless toward the beginning, climbing up to the first brother at 1,400' of gain over 1.4 miles. This mountain is a fan favorite because it* offers so much in a small package. Lots of classic Adirondack terrain, from dirt trails, to scrambles, to slab climbs, to views throughout; it has it all.

We made it up the first brother well before the sun began to rise, so we had great nighttime views looking down on Keene/Keene Valley, along with silhouettes of the mountains. It was great. All the different lookouts and views throughout the hike make this mountain one of the best. Plus you get to enjoy them going up and down.

We were fortunate and got to enjoy the sunrise from the top of the second brother. It was excellent and a welcome bonus since we didn't intend to be at the summit for sunrise, but we still got to enjoy it like we did. Climbing the three brothers involves lots of open scrambles at various points, making this a fun hike.

After hiking over the third brother, the trail drops down into a little col. The trail gains a lot of elevation over the first couple miles before leveling out for a while as you travel up the ridge.

Due to the joy of seeing a goal realized and the fact that I, James Appleton, a non-hiker who grew up here in the High Peaks region was about to become an Adirondack 46'er, my spirits were high. In what felt like minutes since we signed in, we came to the trail sign marking 0.3 miles to the summit. I was less than half a mile from becoming a 46'er, an accomplishment nobody can ever take away from me. An accomplishment I truly worked my butt off all summer to achieve. On some days I didn't feel like waking up at 3 a.m. Days in the rain. Days by myself. Nights sleeping in my van at the trailhead following a 70-hour workweek. This accomplishment meant the world to me (and still does), and I was less than half a mile from the finish line. Let's do this!

This final 0.3-mile stretch of trail is steep, but I was so excited to get to the top that I just flew right up it. Up some wooden ladders, up some slabs and boulders, and then I was there. Josh ran up in front of me to film my summit moment, and then I climbed the final rock to make it to the summit at 7:12 a.m. Big Slide, standing 4,240', for High Peak number 46 of 46! I did it. I actually became an Adirondack 46'er. I had set a goal of hiking all 46 High Peaks in one summer. Mission complete. Goal accomplished. Little by little, hike by hike, mountain by mountain, I plugged along and made it a reality. I was on cloud nine. The summit of Big Slide is a boulder lookout, and a great place to hang out, with spectacular views of the Great Range.

To add to the magic of the day, the clouds were moving fast, so we had excellent views during our summit stay. For a guy to go from "never really hiked before" back in May to now being an Adirondack 46'er here on September 3, that says a lot about what can be done when you choose to do it, when you set a goal and make a plan with the steps needed to accomplish it. I was so proud of myself for seeing this through from start to finish. A life-changing journey.

My wife, daughter, and parents were planning to meet up for some celebratory pie at Noon Mark Diner, so Josh and I started hiking back down. The weather was great. We had lots of views throughout the descent on each of The Brothers. We made it down Big Slide, down The Brothers, and back out to the trailhead in a little over two hours. We even passed several hikers going up the mountain who saw my sign-in and congratulated me. It felt great. We were back at the trailhead to officially sign out at 9:45 a.m., totaling the day at just under five hours car-to-car. Aspiring no more! I was an Adirondack 46'er. The perfect victory lap peak to end my 46'er journey on.

We had some time before meeting my family in Keene Valley, so we drove to Chapel Pond and took a dip in the water. It was glorious. Then we drove over to Noon Mark Diner where my parents greeted me with a gift, the 46'er book Heaven Up-h'isted-ness! The History of the Adirondack Forty-Sixers and the High Peaks of the Adirondacks. A great historical book I highly recommend to anyone hiking the High Peaks. We all enjoyed a couple of slices of pie, and then we drove home. This time, however, I was driving home an Adirondack 46'er.

Another successful day in the woods on Big Slide for number 46 of 46 and a very successful summer adventure in the woods where I summited all 46 High Peaks of the Adirondacks to become a 46'er. I set a goal and did everything I could to accomplish it. It was an adventure I will never forget. It's also only the beginning to this adventure!

Thank you to everyone who has taken time out of their own lives to read my 46'er story. It was an amazing ride and one I would encourage anybody to take. There's something about those mountains that changes people for the better. Thanks to Josh and Eli for hiking with me and to everyone else I met out on the trail. Thanks to my wife, Kinnon, for dealing with my 3 a.m. (and earlier) alarm clocks, and thanks to the 46'ers organization, the DEC, trail crews, Verplanck Colvin, and everyone who keeps the Adirondack Mountains forever wild. Remember to always leave no trace, do the rock walk, and if you carry it in, carry it out. See you on the trails, and thank you all for reading my story!

James Appleton
Adirondack 46'er #11,287

The moment I became an Adirondack 46'er—a moment I'll remember forever. *Photo by James Appleton*

# A TRANSFORMATIVE ADVENTURE

Well, there you have it. My Adirondack 46'er journey from start to finish. A transformative experience that changed the entire trajectory of my life. If you had told me upon stepping on the summit of Porter Mountain for High Peak 1/46, "You're going to write a book about climbing these mountains," I would have said you were crazy. Life is a wild adventure.

When I began the 46 High Peaks, they were just a list of mountains. A list of mountains I saw in the background all my life growing up in Lake Placid. Never in a million years did I think I'd ever earn the title "Adirondack 46'er." It is an accomplishment and experience I will cherish forever.

By the end of the journey, these mountains were no longer just "a list of mountains." Rather, they were 46 individual characters in one epic adventure tale. Every mountain and trail plays an important role in the story. Some mountains bring unexplainable joy as you step onto their majestic summits; others build grit into your life as you persevere through tough terrain all for a summit that could be described as lackluster. Every mountain belongs in this story and brings something unique to the journey. I hope you go on this adventure remembering these words, especially on the hard days. I want you to look for the good qualities of each mountain and what they offer your life and your 46'er story. Sure, Blake and Couchsachraga might be hard, but they help you build mental toughness like nothing else. That's a win. A sunny day on Marcy or the Lower Great Range will help you remember how beautiful the world is on those days when the world has bogged you down.

All 46 mountains on this list belong, and they all have something great to offer your story. Even on the wet days in the clouds. In fact, you'll probably find yourself telling more stories about the hard days than the bluebird days. So enjoy every step of this journey because you will think back to it for the rest of your life. I guarantee it.

## Back to the Trailhead...

Now that you know what gear to have in your backpack, what your pre-hike homework entails, where the trailheads are located, what your 18-hike route looks like, and what to expect on every mountain, it's time to talk about the "other stuff." Next, I'll dive into other topics to set you up for success, from weather, to camping regulations, to getting in shape to climb mountains, and more.

So lace up your boots with a double knot and let's get into it.

Looking up at Marcy near Lake Tear of the Clouds. *Photo by James Appleton*

# WEATHERING THE ADIRONDACK WEATHER

There's something about Giant and Rocky Peak Ridge. One summer morning, Josh and I decided to climb Giant and Rocky Peak Ridge from a trail neither of us had climbed—the Roaring Brook trail. The weather forecast called for a beautiful bluebird sunny day. It was a great time to revisit some mountains I had only climbed once in the rain. A day filled with extremely wet boots and zero views. We summited Giant first where we were greeted with magnificent views. A blue sky, a handful of clouds, and a view that takes you to the end of the earth. The last time I was on this mountain, I was socked in and completely drenched. After enjoying a summit sandwich, it was time to head over to Rocky Peak Ridge. That's when everything changed.

As we made our way down to the col and back up Rocky Peak Ridge, the clouds rolled in at an alarming rate and the floodgates opened. Our hike went from a classic sunny day in the High Peaks to a classic wet, rainy day in the High Peaks within 10 minutes. With no warning, the rain pummeled us. Between the time the rain started and the time we got our raincoats on, we were already drenched. Yes, it happened that quickly. We put our jackets on anyway and continued up to Rocky Peak Ridge where a wet, windy, socked-in summit awaited us. We didn't stay long before heading back to Giant. After all, Rocky Peak is above the tree line, and with the stormy weather it wasn't a safe place to be.

Upon climbing back up Giant, we were greeted by something special and unexpected, sunshine. Yup. Suddenly the sky was sunny and blue once again. In the time it took us to out-and-back RPR, we experienced sunshine, pouring rain, and back to sunshine. It was time to take off the rain jackets and dry out.

In this chapter I'll dive into all things weather to help you prepare for the unexpected so your Adirondack backcountry adventure can be as dry as possible. Like my day on Giant, the weather can turn in a flash, so it's important to be prepared for that. I will go over what to do in case you get caught in a storm—turn around—and I'll offer my suggestions on mountains to climb on rainy days and ones to save for those beautiful bluebird days.

Let's talk weather . . .

## The Mountains Don't Care about Your Forecasts

First and foremost, *the Adirondack Mountains do not abide by weather forecasts.* The mountains make the rules. That is why it's important to always be overprepared and ready for anything when you're out there. I've been on the mountains in the summer when it hailed, and I've been on them in the winter when it rained. They make the rules. That's why the mountains must be respected because remember, *the mountains don't care about you.* The forecast may call for a sunny day, but the mountains may have other plans. Having rain gear to keep your body dry is always essential, in every season, regardless of forecasts. A wet core can lead to big problems.

Like the Pacific Northwest, the ADK is lush, green, and beautiful because we get so much rain. That's why you must always be prepared for these elements regardless of the weather forecast. It's also important to remember that the temperature on a summit is usually 20+ degrees cooler than the trailhead, so always keeping a mid-layer in your pack—even in the summer—is a good habit.

Should you get caught in that unexpected rainstorm, you'll want to stay as dry as possible because hypothermia can set in even in the summer months. Remember, the temperatures at the peaks drop significantly at night, and being wet will make matters much worse. So do yourself a favor and always keep a raincoat in your backpack.

## Orphaning a Peak: Live to Hike Another Day

The unpredictability of weather in the High Peaks creates a very real possibility of having to orphan peaks and turn around. To "orphan" a peak means you simply turn around without summiting the mountain. This can be frustrating in the moment, but turning around and coming back another day will be far less frustrating than an injury, an unexpected overnight, or worse.

Never risk safety to get to a summit. Throughout your 46'er journey, you may have to do this once or twice. It's a common occurrence for hikers, and the longer you hike the more at peace you will become with the idea. Do yourself, your loved ones, and anyone who may have to rescue you a favor by turning around when dangerous conditions arise; the mountains aren't going anywhere.

## Thunder and Lightning

If you're suddenly caught in a thunderstorm, you need to descend from the summits and ridges as quickly and safely as possible, especially if you're on an exposed peak. One thing to keep in mind is that thunderstorms often develop in the mid-afternoon (yet another good reason to start before the sun rises), so the earlier you start the earlier you can finish. Thunderstorms develop quickly out there even on a sunny bluebird day.

Ideally, it's best to skip your High Peaks hike altogether if there is a storm in the forecast. The ADK has hundreds of fantastic smaller, quick hikes perfect for when the weather isn't ideal. You can also hike a trail that doesn't involve summiting a mountain on those days.

Like my hike on Giant and Rocky Peak Ridge, sometimes storms show up unexpectedly, and they move in quickly.

Remember what your mother always told you—make good decisions.

## What to Do If You're Caught in a Thunder and Lightning Storm

The following are some tips to stay safe if you get caught in a storm:

- Don't panic and don't run.
- If you hear thunder, prepare for lightning. Head back down the mountain.
- Get out of any open areas (i.e., summits) and get back into the tree line for cover.
- Avoid standing near any water sources.
- Avoid standing under the area's tallest tree or any isolated trees.

- Let go of your trekking poles (metals attract lightning).
- If in a group, spread out at least 15 feet.
- Do not settle in a small cave or under large rocks since these places can attract lighting and rocks can fall if struck.

## Spring/Fall at the Trailhead, Winter at the Summit

When you live in the Adirondacks, you become accustomed to long winters. Come April, even the biggest winter enthusiasts tend to be ready for spring. Once the snow begins melting at the lower elevations, that feeling of the upcoming spring and summer truly fills the soul. Every season I excitedly head out for a spring hike, enjoying the green woods at the trailhead only to get higher in elevation and find winter once again. These hikes always force me to change from "summer hiking" mode back into "winter hiking" mode mid-hike.

During the spring and fall seasons, the trailhead may be green and brown, but the summit will still be covered in snow. Shoulder season hikes require preparing for both seasons of hiking. It's not uncommon to climb a High Peak in May or October wearing a T-shirt at the trailhead only to need snowshoes near the summit. Be prepared for the conditions, and don't forget that the top of the mountain is a different place than the bottom.

## Sunshine versus Rain

With all the weather talk, I want to offer my top picks for sunny- and rainy-day hikes. Throughout your 46'er journey, it's likely you will be hiking in the rain at some point, since it's nearly impossible to avoid. All the mountains are better served on a sunny, bluebird ADK day, but wet days in the High Peaks have their own magical quality too. There's still magic in the misery. However, I'd rather see you save certain hikes for a sunny day to experience the mountains in all their glory. The following are my top picks:

**Sunny Day Picks**

>Marcy, Skylight, and Gray
>Upper Great Range
>Lower Great Range
>MacIntyre Range
>Giant and Rocky Peak Ridge

**Rainy Day Picks**

>Street and Nye
>Cliff and Redfield
>Santanoni Range
>Seward Range
>Marshall

## Snow and the Six-Month Adirondack Winters

It's important to be overprepared in the mountains, and here in the Adirondacks that means being ready for snow. Every ADK local knows that a string of sunny days with melted snow in April is just the season of "false spring," and a few more snowstorms are still to come. Since "winter" often begins in November, sometimes as early as October, the mountains, summits, and trails experience snow much sooner. The High Peaks typically start to experience snow at higher elevations beginning as early as mid-September, and it often sticks around until June. You will want to keep those layers and microspikes in your hiking pack more than not.

Hiking in the winter is a truly amazing experience as you traverse the mountains in waist-deep snow with snowshoes on your feet while the trees are covered in fluffy, Dr. Seuss–type snow. The peaks offer a picturesque winter wonderland as far as the eye can see. Winter hiking, however, is an entirely different beast than "regular" hiking and requires entirely different skills, gear, mind-sets, and preparation. I'm not going to dive too deeply into winter hiking in this book because it could realistically have its own book dedicated to its intricacies.

I will say this—winter hiking is not for everyone. I repeat, winter hiking is *not* for everyone. It's only for those who will invest in the proper gear and will put in the work to learn how to do it because things can turn bad quickly in the winter. If you're not properly prepared, a winter hike can have fatal consequences in minutes. The snow-covered mountains must be given the highest degree of respect and attention to ensure your safety.

Even if you only plan to hike in the spring/summer/fall, you may encounter some snow and will at least need extra traction to get through some slippery, icy, snowy sections. So let's talk briefly about traction and layers so you can be ready if the snow starts to fly, or the ice hasn't melted.

## Traction, Traction, Traction

I recommend keeping a set of microspikes in your pack from October to June. Yes, that means there are only three months without spikes. You

A late-winter day in the High Peaks. *Photo by Kinnon Appleton*

may even need them in September. Climbing mountains is dangerous enough, but adding ice and snow to the mix without real traction on your boots can become deadly. There have been many times in the High Peaks when I thought to myself, "There's no safe way down this ledge without spikes on." There are many different brands of microspikes to choose from; just make sure the spikes you're purchasing are made for mountains. There's a big difference between traction for walking your dog on a sidewalk and that for climbing icy ledges in the backcountry. There are times when you may need crampons (typically used for ice climbing), but in my winter hiking experience, I've found microspikes and snowshoes to usually be sufficient.

## Layers, Layers, Layers

Now that I've talked about traction, let's talk layers. The summits are typically around 20 degrees colder than the trailhead. That cool, brisk 50-degree fall morning at the trailhead will likely be below freezing at the summit. Therefore, it's important to bring that mid-layer fleece, or even that "puffy coat" for the summit. I recommend a puffy in the 800-fill ballpark.

It may still be summer-like temperatures in April/May or September/October where you live, but I can assure you it will not be that way in the High Peaks. Please plan accordingly because this specific subject of preparedness could be the difference between life and death in the mountains. Read this next statement out loud: *The mountains don't care about you.* So it's your job to be prepared with the proper gear and to respect the mountains so you can enjoy all they have to offer.

Weather in the Adirondack Mountains can change fast and without warning, so it's up to you to be prepared for it. Now you know to keep a raincoat in your pack all year, microspikes and a mid-layer in your pack most of the year, and what to do in case you get caught in a storm. Next, I'll dive into how to properly prepare your body to climb the High Peaks. Yup, I'm talking about your physical fitness.

Climbing mountains is much more enjoyable when you're in the proper shape to do it. Let's get you into "mountain shape."

# PHYSICAL PREPARATION FOR THE MOUNTAINS

## Training to Climb High Peaks

One summer afternoon as I was coming down McKenzie Mountain with my brother and sister-in-law, I experienced an alarming sensation—my body stopped working. Mid-stride, my out-of-shape, overweight, on the verge of death-by-hiking body literally stopped working. My brain was telling my foot to move, but my legs wouldn't move. I couldn't take another step. It was as if I was suddenly paralyzed on the trail. This, my friends, is called "bonking," and it was a result of severe dehydration and being way too out of shape for the hike I agreed upon doing.

After a lot of Gatorade and eating everyone else's food and water, I eventually regained movement and by the grace of God made it out of the woods. What an unfortunate day. Honestly, any day I ever spent on the trail prior to 2018 I would call an "unfortunate" day on the trail. Why? Because every time I ever hiked, I was in terrible shape, which resulted in a terrible experience. I never enjoyed hiking for this exact reason. Hiking mountains when you're not in the proper shape to hike mountains is awful, plain and simple.

Fast-forward to the spring of 2018—down over 65 pounds and four years into my own fitness transformation, I decided to finish the Saranac Lake 6'er. I had three mountains left to climb. It was a spontaneous decision, but suddenly, five years after starting the Saranac Lake 6, I aspired to finish it. So I embarked on a solo trip up Ampersand Mountain, and low and behold, it wasn't nearly as difficult as I remembered. I summited the mountain with ease. Suddenly hiking was significantly more enjoyable because I was in the proper shape to do it. The following day I climbed Scarface, and the day after that I finished my Saranac Lake 6 on St. Regis. A few days later I began climbing the 46 High Peaks with the very story you've read in this book.

I'll say it again for good measure—hiking mountains when you're not in the proper shape to hike mountains is awful. I can attest to this for almost every mountain I ever climbed growing up. I have also seen people who can run a half marathon but are destroyed after hiking in the High Peaks because it's a different kind of physical exertion. There's being "in shape," and there's being in "mountain shape." One isn't better than the other; they're just different.

In this section I'll help you prepare your body and mind for climbing mountains so that you can climb with confidence knowing you'll make it to the summit and back feeling strong and capable. No more feeling weak and broken when you get back to the trailhead. There's enough to worry about in the backcountry, like routes, weather, trail conditions, river crossings, Sasquatch, and more, so if we can eliminate the physical fitness portion of the equation, you will have a significantly better experience. Climbing mountains is more fun when you're in the proper shape to do so.

Let's get your body and mind prepped, primed, and ready to climb some High Peaks . . .

A fall afternoon on Mt. Van Hoevenberg, one of many sub-4000' mountains that offers a big High Peaks view in a short hike. *Photo by James Appleton*

## Mental > Physical

Climbing mountains is as much a mental game as it is physical. In my opinion, people who have already hiked Adirondack mountains have the mental edge over physically fit people who haven't because they know what to expect, how hiking affects their body, and how to pace themselves. When it comes to hiking in the Adirondacks, I will always put my money on someone slightly out of shape but who has climbed ADK mountains before over someone who is in great shape but has never climbed a single mountain before. That mental edge is real, so if you have mountain-hiking experience but you're a little out of shape, rest assured that you'll probably do fine because you know what to expect on the trail. The mental edge is a big component to successfully climbing mountains.

## The Best Way to Get in Shape to Climb Mountains is by ... Climbing Mountains

I'll say it again to be dramatic ... the best way to get in shape to climb mountains is by climbing mountains. So don't feel like you have to stay away from the trail. You're better off getting on the trail and going for a hike. Just pick something small and work your way up in a linear fashion. Climb smaller mountains first and gradually climb bigger ones over time. That is the best way to get in shape for hiking. There's a reason people talk about finding your "trail legs." Climbing smaller mountains allows you to gain an understanding of the trails, gear, how your body holds up while hiking, what foods work for you, etc. This same approach should be taken when you try winter hiking for the first time too.

Fortunately, the Adirondacks are filled with amazing mountains of all sizes perfect to get you ready for the High Peaks. For example, the nine mountains that make up the Lake Placid 9'er hiking challenge are a great list of peaks to take you from the couch to a High Peak. They build off one another, and by the end of the Lake Placid 9'er challenge, you will be ready to hike the High Peaks with confidence.

Don't sleep on visiting these smaller mountains first before you begin your 46'er journey. The smaller mountains offer an experience all their own and are just as enjoyable as the High Peaks.

## James's Favorite Sub-4000' ADK Mountains

The mountains listed below are peaks I hike frequently and enjoy very much. They're significantly shorter than a High Peak and require smaller time commitments but have incredible payoff at the summit.

Another reason I enjoy these mountains is because they're big enough to get the legs and lungs working but small enough to hike spontaneously. Mountains like these are the perfect ones to climb to get into High Peaks shape, mentally and physically. They offer an obtainable challenge for anyone who chooses to climb to the top.

| | |
|---|---|
| Mt. Jo | Blue Mountain |
| Mt. Van Hoevenberg | Mt. Arab |
| Hurricane Mountain | Coney Mountain |
| Jay Mountain | Ampersand Mountain |
| Baxter Mountain | Scarface Mountain |
| Catamount Mountain | Baker Mountain |
| Silver Lake Mountain | Bald Mountain |

Targeted training in the gym to get into High Peaks hiking shape courtesy of Great Range Athlete training programs. *Photo by Jonathan Zaharek*

## How to Get in Mountain Shape When You Don't Have Mountains to Climb

It's not lost on me that most people's homes are not surrounded by beautiful mountains in every direction like mine is here in the Adirondacks. That is why I am including this section to offer guidance on becoming mountain-ready from your local gym or your home. As someone who trains people professionally, has lost almost 100 pounds, and made strength training a foundation of his life for the last decade, I've learned a thing or two about getting strong and in shape.

Trap bar deadlifts are, in my opinion, the ultimate exercise to get in mountain shape. *Photo by Jonathan Zaharek*

When you implement a training regimen that mimics the strength and conditioning needs of the trail, you set yourself up for success in the mountains. In this section I'm going to offer some exercises that I have found to be most effective for attaining and maintaining the proper strength and conditioning to climb mountains. I will also give you a training template you can follow based on my popular Great Range Athlete training programs—which are training programs strategically designed to get people in mountain shape from their gym or home.

It's time to become unstoppable in the mountains . . .

### Key Muscles to Strengthen

**Upper Body 1: Back**—It's easier to carry a loaded pack for 15 miles with a strong back.

*Key exercises:* Trap bar deadlift, squats, rows, lat pull-downs, farmers carries, rucking.

**Upper Body 2: Shoulders, traps, and triceps**—Needed to hold the backpack, propel the trekking poles, and pull yourself up those ledges.

Great Range Athlete training programs are strategically designed to transfer gym efforts to peak trail readiness. Available at www.46outdoors.com.
Design by Teddy Reiser

*Key exercises:* Military press, dumbbell overhead press, lateral raises, shrugs, tricep extensions, skull crushers, farmers carries, rucking.

**Lower Body: Glutes, quads, and hamstrings**—Your legs do most of the work. Not all, but most. Make them strong.

*Key exercises:* Trap bar deadlift, squats, lunges, RDLs, leg curls, leg extensions, running.

**Abs/core**—A stronger core makes life easier, especially when life involves a heavy backpack.

*Key exercises:* Planks, squats, farmers carries, rucking.

**Calves**—Overlooked and underappreciated, your calves do an enormous amount of work on the trail.

*Key exercises:* Calf raises. Lots of them.

**Heart**—Your heart is a muscle and needs to become strong like the others.

*Key exercises:* Circuit training, HIIT, steady-state cardio, heavy lifting, running.

## A Mountain-Ready Training Guide

Thanks to a decade of relentless strength-training pursuits, coaching others, and my own mountain endeavors, I have found that building strength via compound movements along with slow-and-steady circuit training translates perfectly to the trail.

Your training doesn't need to be complex to be effective, either; you just need to target the key muscle groups essential for hiking—legs, glutes, back, shoulders, and arms—and make them strong.

## A Trail-Ready Training Structure
Monday: Strength Training
Tuesday: Bodyweight Circuit
Wednesday: Off/Walk
Thursday: Strength Training
Friday: Steady-state Cardio
Saturday: Go hiking or rucking
Sunday: Off/walk

*Two Strength Days*: Begin each day with a compound movement using weight that challenges you for the desired rep range. Follow this with a three-exercise circuit using dumbbells and/or bodyweight exercises—we call these "grind" circuits. Next, complete a hiking-specific conditioning movement, and end with a core-strengthening finisher.

NOTE FOR "GRIND" CIRCUITS: Move from exercise to exercise at a steady, comfortable pace. You do not need to sprint to each new exercise. Simply move at a constant yet casual pace because this movement mimics the cardiovascular demands of the trail. Not too fast, not too slow.

*Bodyweight Circuit Day:* Zero equipment needed. Engage in high-intensity, heart-pumping exercises designed to build cardiovascular health and muscular endurance. Pick three to four bodyweight movements, do 10 to 15 reps of each movement, set a timer for 30 minutes, and do as many rounds as possible in 30 minutes. Then try to complete more circuits next training session.

*Cardio Day:* A 45-minute steady-state session tailored to your preferred method—run, bike, hike, swim, row, you name it. I recommend doing something you find enjoyable.

*Rucking Day:* Strap on your pack and hit local trails or neighborhood hills. This is about building functional strength and replicating the hiking experience. Load your pack as heavy as you can handle.

## Sample Week of Mountain-Ready Training

| Monday | Tuesday | Wednesday | Thursday | Friday | Saturday | Sunday |
|--------|---------|-----------|----------|--------|----------|--------|
| Strength 1 | Circuit | Rest/walk | Strength 2 | Cardio | Hike/ruck | Rest/walk |

### Example Strength Day 1

| Compound Movement | Grind Circuit (5 rounds) | Hiking Conditioning | Core Finisher |
|-------------------|--------------------------|---------------------|---------------|
| Trap bar deadlift 3 × 10 | Dumbbell push-press × 10 Goblet squat × 15 10 burpees | 50 step-ups onto a bench wearing loaded hiking backpack | Planks 3 × 1 minute |

### Example Bodyweight Circuits

| Warm-Up | Warm-Up | Warm-Up B | Warm-Up |
|---------|---------|-----------|---------|
| 3 minutes of jumping jacks 5 rounds of 20 push-ups 20 squats 20 four-count flutter kicks 20 lunges (10 each leg)<br><br>Rest 1-2 minutes between sets if needed | 5 burpees 50 jumping jacks 5 burpees<br><br>As many pounds as possible (AMRAP) in 20 minutes:<br><br>10 burpees 20 squats 40 mountain climbers | 5 burpees, 50 jumping jacks, 5 burpees<br><br>4 rounds of: 12 regular push-ups 12 diamond push-ups 12 wide push-ups<br><br>4 rounds of: 12 jump squats 6 forward lunges per leg 6 reverse lunges per leg 25 calf raises | 3 minutes of jumping jacks 100 burpees<br><br>Rest as needed |

### Example Strength Day 2

| Compound Movement | Grind Circuit (5 rounds) | Hiking Conditioning | Core Finisher |
|-------------------|--------------------------|---------------------|---------------|
| Barbell squat or leg-press machine 3 × 10 | Push-ups × 10 DB Lunges × 10/leg Mountain climbers × 50 | 50 burpees | Side planks 3 × 45 seconds/ side |

### Example Cardio Days

| 30–60 minutes of steady-state cardio of choice. Find a good pace and maintain it. | Run/bike/hike/ paddle | Elliptical/rower/stair climber | Brisk walk |
|---|---|---|---|

**Example Rucking Days**

| Wear Loaded Hiking Pack | Add Weight to Hiking Pack | Wear Loaded Hiking Pack | Add Weight to Hiking Pack |
|---|---|---|---|
| Walk for 60 minutes at a medium pace. | Walk for 60 minutes at a medium pace. | Walk for 60 minutes at a fast pace. | Walk for 60 minutes at a fast pace. |

Barbell squats in various rep range strengthen your legs, glutes, upper back, and core—all the muscles needed to be a strong hiker. *Photo by Jonathan Zaharek*

## Train Smart and Hike with Confidence

The best way to prepare your body and mind to climb mountains is by getting on the trail and climbing mountains. By starting small and building up with each hike, you set yourself up for high-quality hiking experiences. If you're like most people and need to prepare for the mountains via the gym, this training method has you covered.

Being physically prepared for the mountains before you arrive at the trailhead will remove a lot of anxiety that comes with hiking. Starting your adventure knowing you will not struggle to make it to the summit is an empowering feeling and adds immeasurable joy to the overall hiking experience. With these training guidelines, you can now create your own program to become mountain-ready so you arrive at the trailhead with confidence. Train hard so the mountains become easy.

Speaking of training hard and being physically fit for the High Peaks, next I'm going to talk about what happens when someone is not prepared and the people who will have to rescue them . . .

# SEARCH AND RESCUES

I would be remiss to not include a quick section regarding forest rangers and search and rescues in the High Peaks. According to a *Times Union* report, from 2012 to 2022 there were over 5,400 ranger search and rescues throughout New York State. Of those numbers, no area had a higher count than the Adirondacks' High Peaks Wilderness.

I am confident the information and instruction in this book will help you become an informed, safe, and prepared hiker in the Adirondack High Peaks who, barring any unforeseen injury or circumstances, will not need a rescue. When you see Rangers in the woods, give them a big thank-you for what they do. They are the unsung heroes of the High Peaks.

Far too many unprepared hikers venture into the backcountry to climb mountains that can eat them alive. If you take the information in this guidebook to heart and apply the information I've laid out, I am confident you will have a safe and successful High Peaks adventure.

# LET'S TALK CAMPING!

Camping in the Adirondacks is a surreal experience. Sleeping miles deep in the woods, no sounds from cars, no lights from society, waking to the smell of pine and the sound of a loon's cry. It's just you and nature—the way it used to be. True perfection. Camping adds to the hiking adventure, so if you want to camp during your 46'er journey, I highly recommend it. Regarding this book, I made your route purely day hikes, but feel free to camp as much as you want. The Adirondack High Peaks has no shortage of campsites and lean-tos.

In this section I'll go over some rules and regulations regarding campfires and camping in the High Peaks so you're prepared and aware. Remember what I said earlier in the book: If you start a forest fire in the ADK, I'll be the one leading the army to come find you. So let's avoid that. These rules and regulations are designed specifically to protect the Adirondack Park. The Adirondack Park is bigger than all of us, and protecting it is more important than any individual's camping trip. These rules are put in place to protect the very place we all love.

So grab a log and gather around the campfire. Let's talk camping . . .

A quick rest stop to check the map while hiking the North-ville-Lake Placid Trail. *Photo by James Appleton*

# Campfires and Camping: Adirondack Camping Rules and Regulations

Who is ready for the hard facts straight from the source? The following information is taken directly from the New York State DEC website (dec.ny.gov) as of writing this book, so there is no guessing regarding camping and campfire regulations. These regulations are important to know before you head into the Adirondack backcountry. You can be ticketed by a Forest Ranger if you're caught camping illegally or breaking rules, but more importantly the rules and regulations exist to protect the Adirondack Park.

Remember what Smokey the Bear taught us:
"Only *you* can prevent forest fires!"

## Adirondack Camping Rules and Regulations

- Camping is prohibited within 150' of any road, trail, spring, stream, pond, or other body of water except at areas designated by a "camp here" disk.

- Groups of 10 or more campers or stays of more than three days in one place require a permit from the DEC Forest Ranger responsible for the area. Call 518-897-1300 to get the name and contact information for the local ranger.

- Lean-tos are available in many areas on a first-come, first-served basis. Lean-tos cannot be used exclusively and must be shared with other campers.

- Use pit privies (outhouses) provided near popular camping areas and trailheads. If none are available, dispose of human waste by digging a cat hole six to eight inches deep at least 150' from water or campsites. Cover with leaves and soil.

- Do not use soap to wash yourself, clothing, or dishes within 150 feet of water.

- Except in an emergency or between December 15 and April 30, camping is prohibited above an elevation of 4,000' in the Adirondack Park.

- Camping above 3,500' is prohibited in the High Peaks except for designated campsites.

- Camping on summits is prohibited.

- Black bears are present throughout the Adirondacks. Campers must store all food, garbage, and toiletries in a bear-resistant canister or food hang.

- Bear-resistant canisters are required in the Eastern and Central High Peaks Wilderness.

### Fires and Cooking in the ADK Park

- Fires are prohibited in the Eastern and Central Zones of the High Peaks Wilderness and above 4,000' throughout the Adirondacks.

- Fires should only be built in existing fire pits or fireplaces if provided.

- Use only dead and down wood for fires. Cutting standing trees is prohibited.

- Campfires must be less than three feet in height and four feet in diameter.

- Extinguish all fires with water and stir ashes until they are cold to the touch.

- Do not build fires in areas marked by a "No Fires" disk.

- Only charcoal or untreated wood can be used as fuel.

- Build campfires away from overhanging branches, steep slopes, dry leaves and grass, and rotten stumps or logs.

- Scrape away litter, duff, and any burnable material within a 10-foot-diameter circle.

- Carry out what you carry in.

## Where to Set Up Camp

The best place to camp is at designated tent sites. These sites are typically flat areas with deeper, harder soils more resistant to heavy use and erosion. These sites minimize the impacts of camping. Many sites have nearby pit privies and rock fire rings. Campers are encouraged to use designated tent sites whenever possible. They are often close to trails and provide views of ponds, lakes, streams, or rivers, too.

All designated primitive tent sites have yellow and black Camp Here markers. Many sites on lakes and ponds are identified by a yellow number against a dark brown wooden plaque typically attached to a tree near the water's edge.

Camping is allowed outside of designated campsites so long as you're set up at least 150' from any trail, road, or body of water. Avoid building any fires at your campsite unless in a designated campsite with a preexisting fire pit.

Look at your High Peaks map to learn where the campsites and lean-tos are located along your hike.

## Lean-to Use

Lean-tos are abundant throughout the High Peaks region and around the Adirondacks. In fact, there are roughly 200 of them, and they serve as a great camping option. Personally, I prefer lean-to camping due to the ease of setting up and tearing down camp and not having to carry a tent. Here are a few rules, regulations, and lean-to etiquette facts to be aware of before camping:

- Tents are *not* allowed inside lean-tos and must be at least 150' from the lean-to.

- Lean-tos are available on a first-come, first-served basis and cannot be reserved.

- It is proper etiquette to share your tent site for one night if a second camper or group of campers arrives after dark, especially when it is raining, cold, or windy. In the morning, the second group should pack up and leave to look for another location.

- Lean-tos should be shared by multiple parties until filled (normally eight people). These situations are rare but can happen in heavily used areas, such as the Eastern High Peaks Wilderness.

A campfire in a designated campfire pit on Long Lake after a long day of hiking. *Photo by James Appleton*

## Time to Go Camping!

Now you're ready for an overnight adventure in the Adirondack woods. You know when and where campfires are permitted, where you can set up your tent, proper lean-to etiquette, and more. All that's left now is to strap that camping pad to your pack, pick a site on the map, and start walking. The quiet nights and early-morning echoes of a loon await you. Enjoy the fresh mountain morning air. There's something magical about waking up deep in the woods of the Adirondack Mountains.

You're almost ready to set out on your Adirondack High Peaks adventure. Before you do, however, let's get you even more fired up with some testimonials from 46'ers who were transformed by these mountains.

# ADIRONDACK 46'ER TESTIMONIALS

I was completely blindsided by the overwhelming amount of emotions when I climbed my first High Peak. I became addicted after that. Now there's nothing I crave more than to disconnect from regular life to go out in the woods. I can't explain it. Maybe it's spiritual, and maybe I haven't visited enough places, but I don't think there's anything like the Adirondack Mountains. They have recreated who I am and changed my life forever.

—John Lafarnara #12,138

I climbed my first High Peak in 2014, Phelps and Tabletop, while at a work conference in Lake Placid. Prior to that trip, I would play golf in the conference tournament. One year a vendor, Tom, asked me to climb a High Peak. I didn't know what a High Peak was and really had not hiked since Boy Scouts. I have been hooked on the outdoors ever since. The journey to become a 46er has changed me physically, training to always be ready for a big-time adventure. It has made me mentally stronger, especially on some of the longer hikes with death marches out in the dark. This has also snowballed into deciding to change my lifestyle. This led me to FIRE and semiretirement to spend more time with my family in the outdoors. It also led to my becoming a rafting guide and creating the WNY Hiking Challenge to help protect the outdoors and give people the same experience outdoors that I had climbing that first High Peak.

—Mike Radomski #12,326

I was going through my second divorce and was completely depressed. Earlier in the year I contemplated suicide, only to be saved by a text message from a random friend that I barely knew. As we got to know each other, she talked about the 46. Over the next couple of months, I met new people who ALL were hikers in the ADKs, and that's when I knew the mountains were calling. I had just summited Armstrong (HP #12) when I came across the first humans I had seen all day and came to realize I had spent almost seven hours by myself in the woods. I knew at that exact moment—I was going to continue to enjoy my life, and I put my past behind me. I had a new life to live. I became a 46'er in exactly 365 days. The Adirondacks saved me.

—Joshua Amodio #10,261

Climbing all these mountains showed me what I am capable of. I consider finishing them in a couple of years to be one of my favorite accomplishments.

—Sharee Patterson #9,387

The Adirondacks is the place I come to when I'm no longer capable of carrying myself onward from my mental and physical burdens. It absorbs all my discomfort and ache without wanting anything in return. It challenges me, gives me time to reflect, grow, weep, to contemplate, to resolve, and most importantly it helps me gain a renewed and healthy perspective of the world and life. The Adirondacks bring forth challenges to leave me feeling whole again, stronger, and at peace once more. These mountains saved my life through showing me how to overcome life's hardships without another, that I can overcome and persevere. The Adirondacks is my home, my peace, my comfort, and the teacher who brought forth the light of my true self.

—Sara Williams #15,359

As a recovering alcoholic, I found peace and serenity on my journey of becoming a 46'er. I shared my recovery story as much as I could. Then I created a group called Just Go Outside where I ask people to do just that; go outside and enjoy the outdoors!

—Patrick Bourcy #12,852

Climbing the 46 High Peaks gave me a reason to be outdoors. A way to be task oriented and accomplish goals while still connecting with nature and the land. Learning and understanding how humans can interact with and read land has been a major factor in shaping my personal philosophies. Having a set of places to take my body safely into the backcountry and learning how to do so efficiently has been one of my greatest tools to not only understand the world better, but to understand myself. Without hiking challenges like the 46 High Peaks, humans would be missing out on beautiful opportunities to connect with community and themselves.

—Camran Hartman #12,268

The High Peaks/Adirondacks have been a part of my life since I was a small child, and when I finally completed my 46er journey in 2019, I knew I still wasn't done with these mountains. There is something special about hiking and especially about this wilderness—it bonds people together, builds character, and makes you stronger both mentally and physically. The Adirondacks will always be home; these mountains will always bring me peace, and this wilderness will continue to teach me lessons and sharpen my skills.

—Shaine Kaschak #11,886

Crossing one of many suspension bridges in the Adirondacks. *Photo by Josh Bliss*

# TIME TO HIT THE TRAILS

But first, a quick recap . . .

There's a lot of information laid out in this book. I tried keeping it as concise and impactful as possible to set hikers on the right path (how 'bout that pun?). Now I will quickly recap some particularly important information that I want you to remember before heading into the backcountry.

In the spirit of adventure, allow me to hammer home a few pertinent points one more time:

- Learn and apply the 7 Leave No Trace Principles.
- Know your route, study the map, check forecasts, and always do your pre-hike homework before you hit the trail.
- If you carry it in, carry it out. Everything. Every time. Banana peels and all. The ADK is a beautiful place and should remain that way. Don't be afraid to pick up any trash you stumble upon along the trail—the park deserves heroes like that.
- Camping is prohibited above 3,500' in the High Peaks and must be at least 150' from a trail, road, or water source, unless at designated campsites. Camping on summits is prohibited.
- Campfires are prohibited in the Eastern and Central High Peaks. Again, campfires are prohibited in the Eastern and Central High Peaks. No fires.
- Bring more food and water than you think you will need.
- Make sure you have the proper footwear that can withstand climbing mountains, getting wet, and getting muddy.
- Don't wear cotton clothing. Choose moisture-wicking material.
- You will need to make a reservation to park at the St. Hubert's/AMR/Ausable Club trailhead if hiking between May 1 and October 31 (as of writing this book).
- Park only in designated, legal parking spots. Do not try to create your own parking spot if the trailhead is full upon your arrival.

- Always have your raincoat and an additional warm layer in your backpack.
- If you hear thunder, turn around and take cover into the tree line. Avoid open areas. Don't panic. Avoid standing near water, under lone trees, or under the tallest tree in the area.
- Most Adirondack 46'ers had to turn around and come back another day for one or all of the peaks planned that day. There's no shame and it's part of the journey. Never risk your safety to summit a mountain. These mountains will still be here long after we're gone.

I have one more recommendation for you throughout this journey. Journal. Write down what happened on every hike, what you saw, who you met, how the bog was, the weather, the summit sandwiches. Trust me when I say this; you'll be glad you can always relive your Adirondack 46'er journey.

Okay, enough writing, James . . . get these people to the trailhead. Their adventure awaits!

# GO ENJOY THE MOUNTAINS

Well, there it is. You made it through this book unscathed, and you're ready to head into the Adirondack backcountry more prepared than ever. By finishing this book you've put yourself on the path to a transformative Adirondack High Peaks adventure, one that you will tell stories about for the rest of your life.

Remember that a 46'er is a person, not a mountain. The title of 46'er comes with great responsibility to the land both inside the "Blue Line" of the ADK and beyond. Give back to the mountains as much as you can because they are going to give you more than you ever imagined.

I have full confidence that anybody who steps foot in this park and climbs these mountains will be transformed by the end. The journey is an evolution of oneself physically, mentally, and spiritually. These mountains were here long before any of us and will be here long after we're gone. What an honor it is to have the opportunity to experience them, climb to their summits, and learn about ourselves in the process.

Throughout your journey you will evolve as a person. The way you think about life will change. How you viewed the mountains during your first hike will be quite different as you approach your last. This is an evolution you'll feel within yourself. I will not lie and say it's going to be a "simple" walk in the park. Some days you'll be ready to quit hiking forever, as you're soaking wet, 10 miles from your car, covered in mud, out of breath, and wondering, "Why am I out here?" Those are the moments that produce growth because growth comes from overcoming hard times. Keep going. Keep climbing. You will look back on those "hard" moments with awe of what you were able to accomplish. You will remember how you persevered. Those moments will become the war stories you'll love to tell. Don't worry, though, because there will be more days where you'll experience unexplainable joy, gratitude, and awe thanks to these mountains. The lessons you learn in the Adirondack Mountains will stay with you forever.

Now you know where the trailheads are, what mountains to hike together, what gear to have, and what to watch out for so you can climb the High Peaks with confidence. You no longer must worry about the unexpected and unknown because you have done your homework by reading this book. You're now prepared to step into the great outdoors with certainty and transform into the strong, resilient, Adirondack hiker you aspire to be. You are ready to embark on the journey because you deserve an outdoors adventure worth remembering for the rest of your life. The 46 High Peaks are now characters in your story, each unique with their own personality and their lesson to teach you. With the help of this book, and a little grit and determination, those mountains are about to give you the adventure of a lifetime.

Thanks for reading, be safe out there, and enjoy the journey because it's going to be one hell of a ride.

James Appleton #11,287
46'er

Celebrating a successful winter sunrise on Mt. Marcy with a swig of water and a well-deserved summit sandwich. Cheers to you for reading this book and good luck on your Adirondack 46'er journey. These mountains are going to change your life forever. Guaranteed. *Photo by Jonathan Zaharek*

# ACKNOWLEDGMENTS

Thank you to J. E. Appleton for her contributions during the editing process.